PEOPLE'S PARTICIPATION IN SUSTAINABLE HUMAN DEVELOPMENT
(A Unified Search')

About the Author

Dr. Kamal Taori belongs to the UP cadre of the 1968 batch of the I.A.S. He had a short stint in the Army and has doctorate in Rural entrepreneurship.

Kamal Taori was born, brought up and educated in Wardha. An idealist, with bubbling energy and enthusiasm, right from the beginning, whose exposure to the harsh realities of life and society, and encounter with corresponding hurdles and hardships, has in no way dempened his spirits. Quite the contrary, it has reinforced his resolve to awaken about a positive change in society through scientific, rational, analytical explorations.

There are times when he does feel pained and anguished with the insensitivity of some of those around him, and more often than not, is quite vocal in expressing the same. This has led him into a number of love-hate relationships. Most people either instantly fall in love with him or detest him. Some even feel envious and jealous of him.

He has been with the Khadi and Village Industries Sector for nearly 12 years. This was his opportunity for a deeper understanding of Gandhi, Vinoba, Lohia and Kumarappa and to sublimate his ambition into a mission with holistic action.

A short assignment with the UNDP, and subsequent study of the United Nations system were helpful in the convergence of his life-long studies, experience and understanding into a world-view and a global vision. He is always concerned about what could have been done, as against what has been done.

He is very intolerant of the gap between human word and action, and is consistently working at ways and means of ushering people out of the web of hypocrisy, without which, he seems convinced, its unique potential cannot actualize into a living reality. He finds no reason as to why it cannot emerge amongst the richest and most powerful nations in the world, and is fully alive to the need for the right policies.

He has a very sharp intellect and extraordinary capacity for instant macro-analysis of any situation, and to probe into its micro linkages. He is very prompt in conducting a SWOT analysis, both subjective as well as objective and insists on learning lessons from past experiences on perpetual basis.

He is leading a crusade for bringing about transparency and accountability and viability in public life.

A Social Science Scientific researcher and author of a number of books and research papers, he has organized and led many a seminar and workshop on a whole range of socio-economic issues and topics.

Sensitised qualities and potential constructive creative, humane, compassionate, goes out of the way to help the genuinely needy and a strong optimistic believer in frank, fearless, sustainable human development potentials.

PEOPLE'S PARTICIPATION IN SUSTAINABLE HUMAN DEVELOPMENT

(A Unified Search)

KAMAL TAORI *I.A.S.* (VIDYARTHI)

CONCEPT PUBLISHING COMPANY, NEW DELHI-110059

ISBN 81-7022-734-8

First Published 1998

Published and Printed by
Ashok Kumar Mittal
Concept Publishing Company
A/15-16, Commercial Block, Mohan Garden,
NEW DELHI - 110059 (India)

Phones : 5648039, 5649024
Fax No. : 91-11-5648053

FOREWORD

I had the opportunity of going through analysis and the recommendations of short term assignment of Dr. Kamal Taori as Honorary consultant of UNDP. He was born in Wardha. He joined army and subsequently became an officer of Indian Administrative Service of U.P. Cadre. He has wide experience of serving Uttar Pradesh in different capacity. He has analysed the process of charity to creativity, capacity and confidence building alongwith the experience of international bodies of United Nations like UNDP, UNICEF, UNESCO, APTCO including World Bank, Asian Development Bank etc. The book is very elaborate and interesting in clarifying issues of development.

Many of the suggestions may not be easily digestible to the international bodies who are used to function in a different atmosphere, culture and work norms but the experience of grass-root ethos need to integrate and converge, understanding clearly process of change and urge of masses to become entrepeneur needs to be appreciated. The compulsion of convergence and golden opportunity to link up UN System, resources with Member of Parliament Local Area Development Scheme is superb confluence. Any scheme in isolation is bound to fail. The lessons of history and UN systems brings this fact. When the resources scarcity is all around and aspiration of the masses knowing no limits, this is the right time to selectively take area based social, socio-economic, economic and technological enterprises inducting programme which can usher in a bright scenario for all those interested in sustainable human development.

India has unique place in the community of nations. It is not only a country but much more than a sub-continent. With its diverse dispersed seemingly heterogeneous nature and systems no single solution of any dimension can be provided. What is best possible is only enunciation of these principles which would help in developing plan of action which will suit local conditions.

There may be very few people who will understand reasoning

behind recommendations and the plan of action. It is here Gandhi, Vinoba and Kumarrapa coupled with spiritual, economic, behavioural and attitudinal composition for synergisation development needs to be examined. Recommendations are to justify need far multi-disciplinary planning, action, research, codification extension model building.

I wish recommendations are further adopted, widely disseminated and shared for sustainable human development requirements.

Laxmi Das
Ex-chairman
KVIC
Chairman, Federation of Constructive Societies

PREFACE

I have tried to bring out various aspects of development as I have experienced, felt and understood. There can be no dispute that we can always be wrong. I with my limited experience has tried to evaluate, analyse things from my angle. It is a different matter that I had made consistent effort to understand issues from various angles. In this process of learning there have been moments of despair, frustration and also rising hope from all quarters. Whether it is literature of West or East or ancient practices available through our grand-mother, it has been quite satisfying to take philosophical, practical, holistic view of things. In this process the experience of UNDP has been quite enthusiastic and battery charger. What they have been saying precisely needs to be appreciated, re-defined, re-adjusted to the local situation and implemented ruthlessly.

We had enough analysis of the problem at local, national and inter-national levels. What is required is clear understanding of very limited options where we have to *go back to nature* to be self reliant by reducing our needs, re-define definitions, quality of life and continuously keep searching for holistically sustainable, spiritually and humanly guided ways of life. By neglecting mother earth we can never be happy in the longer run. It is only by learning to working together and with clear appreciation of the humanistic compulsions we can be happy in the longer run. This pre-supposes, broadening of mind by sensitising ourselves to the feelings not only of vocal human beings but also the non-vocals and other silent creations of nature. This is not a simple proposition but all other so called tried options are bound to fail in the longer run.

This book is not an end. However, I am convinced that many people are making sincere efforts in this direction and hence by convergence, open mind, transparency and willingness to genuinely search for happiness we can definitely come out with better solutions. Before I close let me remind that *Anonymus* has said.

For every ailment under the Sun
There is a remedy or there is none
If there is one try to find it
and if there is none never mind it.

KAMAL TAORI (VIDYARTHI)

CONTENTS

PART-IV: CORRESPONDENCE, LETTERS AND READING MATERIALS

LOOKING BEYOND

I had a very interesting and satisfying life all these years. There has been fascinating challenges, opportunities, difficult days, frustration, humiliation, gains, moment of joy and utter displeasure. But this is not new. This happens with everybody. Only the insensitised can have ill feeling in this path of human life.

My knowledge for the improvement of situation is duty bound leading me as optimistic. In this process I have developed various models which I think holistically, rationally, transparently and collectively need implementation and examination. It is here the challenges lie but experience must be shared. Churned knowledge or experience must be codified, widely discussed and cross-checked to see whether the pattern can be a model. This multi-disciplinary, multi-dimensional, multi-focussed and multi-shared perception may help in the development of these process and systems which we call sustainable human development. As opposed to domestic product concept, the human development index concept is a much more refined indicator to human development. India has filtered systematic, traditional, scientific knowledge for its well meaning children. This book is to record those grievances, areas of concerns and essential areas for immediate action which would pave the way for a new era, based upon equity, justice, transparency, viability, rationality, humanity and all those qualities which make a nation great. In this situation the aim of this book is also to bring out element of Hidden Investible Potential Power of Organisation (HIPPOO), Known Investible Potential Power of organisation (KIPPOO) and Threatening Investible Potential Power of Organisation (TIPPOO) which is another form of strength, weaknesses, opportunities and threats (SWOT) analysis but the more focused emphasis is on hidden and known elements.

This book is also intended for sharing those experience, learning process and lessons through which I had the fortune to pass. It may help to realise the need to open up, liberate yourself from ignorance and understand how policies are framed, how they are implemented, their monitoring systems, indicator of success and how the masses of target group remains isolated and new laws get flouted unintendedly because of impractical implementation.

This book also aims to look those hope generating landmarks, signals, turning points, indicators which if rationally and systematically arranged in a coherent manner may help in clearly analyzing the pattern. I rationally think that I am one of those very lucky few persons who have undergone diverse experience and hence can claim to be a modest analyser of diverse developments around us. This I would like to share.

Invitation of UN in India to join them for exploring the convergence issues between UN systems and Member of Parliament Local Area Development (MPLAD) scheme was an golden opportunity to re-look at my own mind set. This time also it is essential that those experiences are shared. The highest to lowest i.e. from the field to Member of Parliament with UN Systems, I thought that it was a right opportunity. The report which I have submitted is a part of this book.

What may be new for me may not be new for all. However, I feel that the following may be something different from other literature which talks of sustainable human development, convergence etc.

(1) I have not just tried to bring out various policies, marketing, monitoring, organisation building, funding, implementation antinomy and dichotomy but had tried for convergence of seemingly confliciting.

(2) It is based upon a tour. May be a short one to three different MPs thrust areas with different linkages, background, culture, practices. There was much difference in financial level, commercial level and even different age level of Member of Parliament.

(3) The role of Non-Governmental Organisations (NGOs) has to become more and more progressive. It aims at not only charity associated awakening type of programme but also developmental, commercial, educational. This aims mind opening and capacity building of Non-Governmental Organisations to face challenges of rising expectation of the masses.

(4) The greatest hope of our time is the growing emphasis on human led improvement through UNDP. In the field of human development pioneering work have been done by Shri Maqbool Haq. This has to be rational analysis through GDP versus HDI analysis and their implications on State, people, funding institutions, policy makers i.e. Member of Parliament, behaviour pattern of the masses and over all impact of sustainable convergence, containment and happiness.

There are no ready solution for any four problem but definitely there are models, small examples which may if examined with multi-dimension may help in clearing many issues. These small hope models are everywhere around and beyond. It is high time to codify, modify, adopt and spread them wherever and whenever possible. As rightly said, "It is better to light lamp than criticizing darkness." This is to be done invariably by all of us.

UN System, i.e. UNDP, ILO, WHO, UNICEF, UNESCO, UNIDO, UNCHS etc. have carried out various projects to be called experiments. To what extent they have really become replicable, cost effective, hope generating, transparent, viable and on the whole widely acceptable? With the stringent resource scarcity UN Organisation is passing through these days, it is appropriate to see if low cost and high impact at moderate cost model for poor country and poor people can be developed. Many such models are available in India for copy by UN systems which may help in better propagation of their objectives.

During this process of experience the UN Systems have developed models over a period of time. What they have prescribed 30 years, 20 years and 10 years before may not be relevant today. Those who have worked for the long time in these organisations would surely bear me out when I say that they are not the same principle-wise when they were there. Here I would like to give one example for their overall shift from Chemical to natural and eco-friendly which is an indicator that the practices, projects, systems, funds which they offered were not conducive to the objective. The question of adequacy of resources needs to be holistically probed. We have enough literatures which bring out the lessons of UN funds and total results.

The question of liberalisation, privatisation, capacity building, industrialisation, exports, eco-friendly, unemployment, balanced developments have to be examined and redefined. This book attempts to develop those factors which may help in appropriate redefining process.

In the process of shift from charity to creativity, capacity and confidence building (C to CCCB) many forces have to be analysed. This process has various dimensions and pitfalls. While reducing dependency on State is advocated by many the capacity creativity and confidence building (C to CCCB) process has hardly been holistically prioritized to develop harmonious and friction-less model.

The time in which we are living is a very fascinating. Those who are above 60 or so would bear me out when I say that those who have worked and lived in this age group in India and Indian sub-continent were belonging to the systems of 4000 years to 5000 years filtered practices, while they will be dying in a time when the clock has turned back. It is pity that those who are less than 20 years would be missing that heritage and the wonder is that all this has happened in just 50 or 60 years period. Further mind boggling wonder is that many of us are direct contributors through our own doings and practices to this process. This book tries to analyze, share some of these unbelievable policy, implementation, monitoring issues which made this happen.

Time or *yug* is a great factor. The convergence issues are part of this *yug* process. Time is the only greatest factor. The time in which we are living offers us rational, scientific opportunity to try and implement some of these experiences and feel joy of living with eternal natural laws. The fallacious prescription offered so far may be good for few but harmful for long term welfare of the masses. This churning process may lead to crux of the matter.

Some issues of our time need holistic analysis include the following.

(1) Massive aspiration to do something. It is here each individual feels committed to do something of his own.
(2) Easy availability of focussed communication through Radio, Television, Fax, Computer with comparatively much better infrastructure.
(3) Cost structure is an important force both for services, recruitment and practical weight.
(4) 30% women are essential for Panchayati Raj bodies.
(5) All round resource scarcity.
(6) Over dependence on State.
(7) Deteriorating Working standards.
(8) Lack of transparency and replicability.
(9) World movement towards eco-friendly.
(10) Reemergence and reengineering of issues relating to development.
(11) Ills of organised industries becoming clear.
(12) Need to develop replicable model.
(13) Failure of earlier acclaimed successful models.
(14) Realising need to restructure marketing.
(15) Growing international interest in Gandhi, and concern of Globalisation and Self-Reliance.
(16) On-going restructuring of financial, legal and administrative institutions.
(17) Dwindling of industrial resources.
(18) Ever increasing population

The above are some of the issues concerning our time which

make it compulsory to look into holistically.

In this connection the following question needs detailed examination.

(1) How the programme run by UN Systems, World Bank and people themselves benefited larger target group?
(2) How do the lessons meet time test for success?
(3) Are they replicable? How, when, where?
(4) Are they sustainable? How?
(5) Are they cost effective? How?
(6) Are they eco-friendly? How?
(7) Do they help shift people from charity to creativity, capacity and confidence building (C to CCCB).
(8) Do they help in self development?
(9) Do they help in repaying capacity building of the institution?
(10) Do they help in developing brotherhood, feeling of unity and broaden vision in the masses for overall happiness.

The World Bank policies of money associated with control and finance, taxation, incentives lead to decide and dictate. When the whole systems are managed by funds and loaning, we have a number of cases where investment assisted development programme have created havoc. Easy and ample foreign money leads to expensive technology and systems building. The question of low cost and high impact will cause zero impact and low cost negative impact have hardly been studied in totality. It is here the lessons of various components could have been codified, shared, examined, churned and better principled prescription evolved if the programme is linked up with MPLAD Scheme on initiatives of UN Systems.

This calls for the following action.

(1) Re-defining multi-dimensionally various definitions.
(2) Demystifying various concepts.
(3) Developing suitable models to suit vision of tomorrow.
(4) Relying more on rationality, scientific analysis, analytical approach, rather than borrowed implanted concepts.
(5) Decentralised Government and involvement of all with Panchayati Raj System.

A very important change which has taken place with reference to India is constitutional positioning of village Panchayat as Local Government. This important change in policy would make things better for future. But there are many obstacles. They need to be removed and better and effective communication is required with MPLAD Scheme, UN Experience and Panchayati Raj convergence would definitely be opening new vistas for happiness/development. Immediate need is to clarify issues, develop models, think universally but act locally. Here the policy issues whether of funding, technology, marketing, competition etc. need to be cleared. And in this process MPLAD scheme with UN umbrella and peoples initiative can surely develop models. The bottlenecks, the pitfalls, gaps would surely be identified for better humane governance and sensitised development process. This is a challenge of our time.

It is in the light of above that the assignment offered by UNDP to the author helped in clarifying action part of the planning. Visits to Kotawakalna in West Bengal, Jabalpore in Madhya Pradesh and Coimbatore in Tamilnadu did help in developing a convergable plan of action for future replication. The golden opportunity must not be lost of. The MPLAD Scheme, initiative and self urge of local people coupled with expertise and experience of world UN System invariably could lead to better competitive, people oriented sustainable process of development.

My effort, sincerity would be highly rewarded if I am not misunderstood. There are missing factors at every level. The insensitivity, overdependence on state, loss of confidence, regional variations etc. do call for a flexible but integrative, cohesive and accommodative, convergible model for replication and this is happening all around. What is missing is adequate appreciation of peoples capacity to solve their own problems. My effort are precisely dedicated in this direction.

I am grateful to all in UNDP, outside UNDP and people of India and the Hon. MP's who enabled me to look beyond. Error, if any, at any stage is regretted.

I am also obliged to people of UP in particular and India in general who helped me in understanding seemingly conflicting issues in development

Wardha KAMAL TAORI (VIDYARTHI)

26 January 1998

PART-I

BACKGROUND

1

DECLARATION BY PARLIAMENTARIANS' FORUM

The declaration opens up new challenging opportunities for working together for a sustainable future. These become important at this point of time because of the various challenges of poor work culture, lack of transparency overdependence on state, poverty, unemployment, resource scarcity, insecurity and poor mind sets.

New Economic Policy and Need to Work Together with Transparency and Viability

With the passing of 73rd and 74th amendment to the Constitution of India it becomes imperative that many Economic and Social Development Programmes including Human Development are implemented through Panchayati Raj institutions. While liberalisation, opening up of the economy make it compulsory for the unorganised, decentralised entrepreneurs and institutions to be more competitive, it is also essential that the Policy Planning and delays in implementation processes are studied, better communicated and delays in implementation is minimised.

It is well expected that Parliamentarians' Forum and UN Systems convergence through Panchayati Raj institutions could be very effective for developing models of sustainable market led development on cost effective, replicable basis.

Challenges of Common Problems

The problems connected with the poor work culture and related issues of delay, deficiencies, cost over-runs and poor success of programmes are well known to even a remote observer of Indian scene. As resources become scare, need to optimally utilise them becomes paramount. The problem is confounded further by over staffing and perverted mind-sets, especially at the critical stages. Hence there is need to take holistic look at the whole gamut of problems to develop replicable, self-supporting and transparent models.

Limitations of Producing a Blue Print in Short Time

In the area of six constituencies of Parliamentarians in a diverse field it has not been an easy and a simple job to try and converge resources availability with UN Systems on the one hand and trying to identify felt need of diverse target group as a part of a sustainable, practical, time-bound document, proposing step-wise action plan. Despite serious limitations effort has been made to collect, compile, collate and codify as much information as possible to achieve the objectives of the short-term consultancy. The Consultant feels the preparation of the document would not have been possible without direct, active and personalised interventions by Shri Bhaskar Bhattacharji and his Secretary, Ms. Nishu Narula. Lack of codified resource availability from UN Systems remains a critical area for consideration and it is here their cooperation was very useful.

General Issues

1. India is such a vast, diverse, culturally rich but ridden with multiple and multifarious, conflicting and at times synergetic sub-continent that unless a holistic view even when relating to constituency of Parliamentarians is taken, any suggestion is bound to fail. The lessons of developmental planning action whether in social, economic or related field makes it imperative that systems must be made to perform not by personalized approach but by principles. *Apart from transparency and viability effort must be made to involve as much stake holders and role players as possible to make self sustaining plan.* The biggest difficult areas of coordination, cooperation and coexistence can be effectively tackled only when holistic view is taken. To develop this the Consultant would strongly like to recommend a visit to Rale Gaon Siddhi near Pune to have a look at a model of sustainable human development. This model would need critical examination by multi-disciplinary team and approach to locate areas for further improvement/corrections to make it more useful. Over a period of time new technologies have emerged which make the job of replication easier, cost effective and also less time consuming.

With proper policy prescriptions and by adherence to the principles of modern management as applicable to rural setting, it is possible to achieve impossible today.

It is also strongly recommended that alongwith additionality of funds and resources a better mind setting programmes for stake holders and opinion makers would also be concurrently launched. Here the *conviction, openness and capacity of the brain stormer itself would be a critical factor.* While discussing with the stake holders, UN systems representatives and honourable Parliamentarians' this factor emerged as one of the important criticality.

About U.N. Systems and Agencies

During the period of consultancy, I had the opportunity to interact with various officials and beneficiaries of UN agencies. Various literature, reports, documents, studies were also gathered and some commonalities have been identified. Despite the fact that Resident Coordinator of United Nations Mr. Hans-C von Sponeck was very kind to issue a D.D. on 5.9.95 to all heads of UN Agencies with copy to World Bank, ADB, IFC, IMF, with a request to nominate the coordinating officer for accessibility and support to the consultant, the fact remains that this could not be done.

1. During discussions it emerged that various institutions have their own funding, monitoring systems which operates through Government of India organisations or selected non-governmental organisations. There has been no coordination within UN systems.
2. There has been realisation that India has potential to become self supporting in many fields but something is missing.
3. The lessons of the financing of the past made it essential that future funding is converged with the contribution of the beneficiaries. This will make the project viable, sustainable, replicable and also transparent.
4. By paying special attention to intangible factors of success better results would come.
5. Member of Parliament Local Area Development Scheme under which Rs. 1.00 crore is available to each Member of Parliament is ideal for learning to working together because of the implementation of the (a) policy, (b) transparency and (c) viability and need to involve all because on Indian political scene, programmes, projects and their cost structure meant for rural unorganised sector have not been very successful.

6. By implementing this programme ourselves, learning with past lessons would definitely multiply enthusiasm.

As mentioned above by jointly working with Parliamentarians' Forum with multi-disciplinary, multi-dimensional and seemingly heterogeneous plan of activity through planning, action, research, codification, extension and loanable systems, it is possible to have better policy prescription for sustainable human development especially for rural areas. As findings of various studies have brought out in a vast country like India, there is need to have enough flexibility through transparency, peoples' initiatives and viability. This is *possible only through initiatives precisely of this nature.* The apprehensions of political implication perceived and shared with consultant by some system managers seem to be largely unfounded and unwarranted. If programme could be developed as model, through inter-disciplinary nature with clear output expected with convergence of social, economic and socio-economic with monitoring management and mind setting issues--this opportunity should be taken as a very timely intervention in doing away with delays, inefficiencies and all those factors which make programme success doubtful. It is here the consultant would like to thank profoundly Mr. Michael W. Ellis, Country Director, WFP and Mr. Christopher Ronald, Director, Regional Office, UNDCP who took major initiatives in going beyond their immediate charter. WFP has a very important role in Jabalpur constituency and were very keen to introduce some policy and system changes which would make programmes more effective and investments cost effective, transparent and catalytic. I wish at some or other point of time other major funding institutions could not only share their experiences but also become active partners in this task of bringing various systems both of village, block, district, state, and UN system together.

Enthusiasm, Optimism and Apologies

There is need to develop as mentioned in the declaration and also in terms of reference a synergistic inputs. The people targeted had to pay special attention to lead activities, cost of experimental institutions with the active involvement of all important role players including Hon'ble Member of Parliament. This factor has made the job interesting, challenging and also very difficult. My enthusiasm, optimism has doubled with discussions. It seems that there is lot of confusion due to lack of clarity and proper appreciation of Indian situation. There are many problems because of hypocrisy, communication gap and effective target setting. But it is here that the proposed Action Plan must be implemented by learning to working together.

Policy Issues

Keeping in mind the role of Member of Parliament in policy making system, it was found appropriate that material should be developed by integrating schemes available with funds at his discretion with felt priority needs perceived by people and the Member of Parliament. This is not simple job. It is only with transparency, viability, plan of action that a model which can meet the test of replicability can be developed.

Needless to say, priority would differ from place to place and people to people depending upon their organisational and constitutional analysis. Multifarious system of World Bodies cannot be expected to be sensitised to the SWOT of the local people when it comes in organisational sector. There is no simple solution. In this connection if we take the experience of earlier efforts of working in unorganised sector we come to some basic point of difference. Style of functioning or system of monitoring or involvements of local people or developing entrepreneurship if examined from various programmes and as projected by international bodies we find some basic missing elements. No wonder, these programmes have not become replicable because of common problem of the following nature :

(a) High Cost low impact;
(b) Lack of involvement of actual beneficiaries by contributing labour resources--long term risks;
(c) Initiative from selected group or vested interest;
(d) Lack of marketing culture, including entrepreneurship development;
(e) Basic policy weakness in developing micro enterprises;
(f) Lack of desire to learn from earlier experience;
(g) Missing link of urgency for replicability, transparency and availability.

2

NEED FOR CONVERGENCE

I felt that in the 3 constituency areas which I visited like in any programme affecting different programme priorities, schemes, it is important that uniform and divergent factors are identified. In uniform factors we can list the following.

1. Various Schemes of Government of Indian Uniform pattern.
2. More or less uniformity of Panchayati Raj priority.
3. Coverage by TV, Radio and Political compulsions.
4. Rising aspirations of the masses, especially women, socially disabled, educated unemployed etc.
5. Indifference of insensitized bureaucracy including bankers, market force.
6. Poor experiences of the past in doing justice to unorganised.
7. Lack of linkages and communication barriers.

While the above are some of the uniform factors, the following can be taken as divergent factors which call for separate prioritisation of any programme to be taken on area basis:

1. Different absorbing capacity of various groups are of different level.
2. Potential contribution of people is of different degree
3. Transparency and viability, though essential, is already at different level.
4. People's representatives and institutions are functioning with different ethos and magnitude.
5. Education level of the masses and their priorities for further programmes is of different level.
6. Dependence on state is already at different levels.
7. NGO's are at different level of functioning and acceptability.

Some of these factors make it imperative that any programme which is suggested should have components of following nature:

1. *Social Component:* These are those components which are basic, essential for any civilized society. They include primary education, drinking water, equality, health, family planning, general sensitization, sanitation, housing etc. These cannot be compromised. But in a situation like Jabalpur they would be of much higher priority than, say, Kotawa Kalna where basic essentialities have already been made available to a considerable degree. At this level the role, experience, patterns of assistance, inputs to the local people etc. by these organizations have been found to be of very practical, people oriented and appropriately developed and suitably financed. There has been gradual improvement in programme content, types of funding and involvement of local institutions, both as NGO's and Panchayati Raj. This is the first stage. Only the priority would differ as per the prevailing condition in the area. In these areas dependence on grants may have to be comparatively more.
2. *Socio-economic Category:* This is that stage where many programmes/activities can become economically viable and with proper policy prescription it should be possible to make them self-supportive. They are not all the time necessarily a social component programme. They have potential to become income generating, viable, replicable and market led sustainable development programme models. Because of various other factor like wrong policies, wrong funding, wrong planning, vested interest emphasis etc. these programmes may not be as viable and acceptable as they should be. To give some example we may include following programmes in this category:

1. Bio-gas,
2. Sulabh type latrines,
3. Nurseries,
4. Minor irrigation,
5. Vocational education,
6. Infrastructure creation,
7. Many self-employment type of programmes which may include indoor, rural and cottage industry, service and business of micro enterprises sector.

In achieving successes of the above category the role of ILO,

APCTT, micro enterprises sections etc. become very important. Because of wrong policy prescriptions in terms of financing, taxing, market expertise distribution systems, pricing structures, etc. many of these programmes in this category remained only in social category which in turn heavily depend on Government grants and subsidies. The point to note here is that with better marketing planning and funding system it should be possible to do the following:

1. Reduce cost of investment with better synergy.
2. Developing better marketing structures
3. Device policies for competitive analysis and long term eco-friendly contents of the programme.

This programme also has all potential to develop local entrepreneurship of the masses which would ultimately turn into a mass self-employment type of programme. But the biggest bottleneck is wrong policy and duplication of schemes. By adopting an integrated approach with MPLAD programme and UN system it is possible to come out with a better model.

3. *Economic Programmes:* Keeping in mind the local SWOT analysis and hidden investable potential power of the people's resources, infrastructure to the NGO's and other known investable potential power it should be possible to dovetail it with economic activities which would ensure minimum essential meeting of demands. Since greed has no limit, it is important to have effective technology, checks and balances through humanized led development programmes, marketing with adequate surplus resource generation and overall elements of sustainable human development. The economic programmes have to be linked up with self-reliance and quality upgradation programmes. Over dependence on urban type of capital intensive, production process has to be done away with. *It is here the self-employment and charity to creativity, capacity and confidence building needs to be analyzed both as planning action research project and financialty viable programme.* These are the critical areas where integration and linking with other ongoing programmes of UN systems, principled contribution of various resources etc could be very very useful in developing well controlled replicable models to be developed over a short period. Needless to say, they must be cost effective, transparent to be replicable.

Thus package of programme becomes most difficult and challenging, but the massive aspiration of people to do something on their own because of the collapse of capital intensive *industries is much easier now to implement.* It must be very different in the past because the whole trend was towards urbanization and factory type of manufacturing process. It is only now that policy again makes it easier to think on these lines. Micro enterprises becomes reality provided other issues in policies, funding, marketing, licencing etc. are immediately and properly sorted out. It is here convergence of the MPLAD experience and UN system expertise becomes essential. Selected models could ensure simultaneous planning action research, codification, extension, loaning through developing selected simultaneously developable, replicable models.

4. *Monitoring Organizational Effects:* This is the fourth group in the priority which is inbuilt in all above three. When it comes to unorganized sector our experience brings out the fact that monitoring of organizorship or managerial factors have no place in rural programmes. I may venture to add that even in the organized public sector enterprises this factor has been most missing. However, in unorganized sector it has catastrophic impact. Just to give an example one can take two UNDP funded programmes known as: (1) Handmade paper project, (2) National rural leather project.

   If we go into various components of these two programmes where the consultant was national project director and national project coordinator, one would immediately come across various components which make programme replicable or short-lived. Whether it is in policy, transparency, organization of the beneficiaries or product development or research and studies or technology development or codification or any other factor the cost effectiveness, long term impact, ignition of entrepreneurship led desire for self-development becomes crucial. Same way, various issues were taken up with UNDP for looking into lessons of other programmes. It is sorry fact that hardly any work is available in these economic type of activities which must be cost effective. It is here need for different categorized, felt needed programme/activity has to be simultaneously planned and implemented, monitored and codified, marketed and financed to genuinely draw conclusions for replication. Computers facts, drive for eco-friendly natural products, etc. make our job challenging and also simple. The various literature both coming from West and East countries make it easier for us to grasp this point. For the convenience of everybody a list of selected material for reading and its importance in solving the problem of poverty versus imbalanced prosperity is required. Those who are interested must read some of these literature because they will make the picture clear which is otherwise cloudy, polluted and devoid of hope signals. One may also add that the hope signals are very clear, transparent and developing in a pattern so swiftly and uniformly.

5. *Liberalization, Self-reliance-dichotomy:* With the liberalization of economy various changes have taken place, monopolies have been broken. Resource scarcity has been felt. Subsidies are under criticism and close examination. Calculating of resources by higher echelons like IITs, IIMs, universities, public sector undertaking, organized sectors etc have come under close scrutiny. Whether it is press, airlines services all are under severe stress to perform. Alternatives are emerging. Monopolies have shattered. A competitive, compatible strength building and examination is under process. Memorandum of understandings for better performance are being inspired. Hidden investable potential powers are being made known by taking long term threatening aspect of hidden powers. Liberalization has opened up new avenues to fully tap once untapped strengths. Liberalization also compels the uncompelled to become competitive or disappear or realign. It is here words like self-reliance may seem redundant and unworkable. Self-reliance have its own compulsions and hidden strengths. As liberalization opens up minds it also provides opportunities by *restructuring policy systems, organizations and institutions.* This becomes a challenge. Those who have inherent capacity to develop own models to suit their aspirations have nothing to fear from the onslaught of liberalization. They have to become competitive. It is here potentials have to be re-examined by tapping multi-disciplinary and multidimensional models and plan of action. How do we begin? It is here a present opportunity is a golden one where MPLAD scheme in convergence with UN system opens up on a very selected basis, opportunities for carrying out multi-disciplinary-multi-dimensional but area focussed, short duration planning action research models.

3

LESSONS FROM CHINA

Starting from 1986, the SPARK programme aimed at speeding up economic advancement of its vast rural areas. The key of the programme lays stress on the development of rural and township agro industries by relying on application of science and technology achievements to ensure quick return. The SPARK programme entered into the second phase from 1991-95 and focusses on the following key sub-sectors:

-- agricultural production and processing
-- animal husbandry and processing
-- light industrial products
-- textile products
-- composite fertilizer
-- building material
-- non-metallic mineral products and fine processing
-- products to support key industries
-- new types of equipment needed in rural areas
-- planting and associated processes

India and China share many similarities in their economic and social development. Policy reforms undergoing in India also make it imperative that the lessons of China are properly utilized. This would mean exchange of information and experience, promotion of enterprises cooperation and organizing technology fairs and mutual visits.

Mr. Vivek Rae of UNDP had been to China recently and it will be worthwhile if he could share his experience by addressing the officers working in the village industry sectors.

The SPARK programme in China is receiving the support of the World Bank. This programme has the following major methods of implementation:

- -- development advanced and market-oriented technology that suits local conditions, requires less investment and gives quick return
- -- collects funds mainly through enterprises and bank loans. The State offers only a small part which is non-gratuitous
- -- in the light of local conditions to gradually develop regional mainstay industries by providing guidance to different industrial sectors setting up demonstration :ojects.

The SPARK programme has given new prospects for surplus manpower in rural area, modernized rural areas by transforming through vitality activities, the traditional family size activities have been developed into village type of activities and comprehensively utilized agriculture, forestry and technical development by on-site processing, storage, transportation and preservation. This has resulted in comprehensive regional development by promoting overall economy.

Parliamentarians Forum, Local Area Development Priorities and Spreading the Spirit of SPARK in the Rural Areas

The SPARK programme has galvanized township and village enterprises and fuelled income and employment growth throughout the country. While nobody can dispute the need to have convergence and right application to suit Indian ethos and culture, there is a need to usher in a minimum critical mass through suitable infrastructure, training, technology and marketing emphasis.

In a country like India where multiplicity of organizations duplicating various common programmes with poor systems of communication and insensitivity of extension machinery, it is high time that the nearness of the Forum to the rural entrepreneurs, artisans and opinion-makers is fully utilized. The following may be the immediate plan of action:

Short term

1. Mr. Vivek Rae may be requested to share his experience with a group of 6 MPs and selected programme incharges so that an implementable strategy could be developed
2. A brief note may be circulated in advance so that the local blocks, chambers of commerce and associations of training centres could be briefed for making suggestions.
3. Based on the local raw material available, demands of products and goods in the area, a cost effective policy package with planning action research component could be developed.

The above could be completed in a period of maximum two months. Simultaneously, the State Governments may be requested through Parliamentarians' Forum if they would be willing to share the experiement of SPARK programme. For the next two years, this programme could be implemented with cooperation of experts in the field.

Neem Foundation and Parliamentarians' Forum

There are very few foundations in India with an urge to revive the traditional scientific, medicinal and economic value of important rural resource like *"Neem"*. The value of neem from environmental, health, economic, technical and sustainability aspects was very well known in the ancient India. It is only in the last few years that USA has taken initiative in demistifying the hidden economic value of this important plant. Neem Foundation was registered as a charitable organization in the year 1994 at Bombay to highlight, propagate, codify and disseminate the scientific importance of this plant. As is well known, this plant is available in abundance in major parts of rural India and has potential to generate millions of jobs in rural areas through various activities around this industry.

4

RURAL INDUSTRIALIZATION POTENTIALS AND UNIDO

UNIDO as a specialized agency of the United Nations has been working in the field of promotion and acceleration of industrial development. As a part of industrial development in the various projects/programmes implemented since 1968, the emphasis has been on human resource development, technology transfer, equitable development and on the whole international cooperation in investment and technology.

India is a very vast country with diverse felt needs in the field of rural industrialization. Keeping in mind the fact that still about 70% of its people live in rural areas and the fact that they do possess various skills, resources and infrastructure to industrialize the rural areas, industrialization through effective technology, communication, infrastructure and suitable policy prescriptions would be able to give a big thrust. Even the success of various on-going programmes of rural development, anti-poverty and overall sustainable development would succeed only with proper thrust on rural industrialization programme.

It is in this connection the question of exploring the potential of rural industrialization with UNIDO and its expertise becomes very important in the days to come.

UNIDO has reoriented and restructured itself emerging as a major service organization providing technical assistance support through 12 major groups of services for the achievement of development objectives. They include the following:

-- Industrial policies and private sector development
-- Operational support for sectoral development
-- Investment promotion
-- Technology for competitiveness
-- Environment and energy
-- Human resource development
-- Women in industrial development

-- Enterprise restructuring and privatization
-- Small and medium scale industry and rural industrial development
-- Quality standardization
-- Industrial information and statistics
-- Africa and least developed countries

In case of India, UNIDO had an impressive track record in institution building, appropriate technology transfer and has organized feasibility studies, industry specific development, etc., from time to time.

Priority Themes of UNIDO with reference to Industrial Information, Investment and Technology Promotion Level

Based upon the past experience, UNIDO offers a system of integrated support to developing countries at the following three levels:

-- at policy level,
-- at institutional level, and
-- at enterprise level.

As a part of support programmes, UNIDO has the expertise through its industrial and technological information bank (INTIB) which provides expertise in collecting, storing, retrieving and disseminating information. It also has technological investment experience and keeping in mind that its focus in 1996-97 would be Africa, Asia-Pacific, Latin America. The entire project planning exercise would have to keep in mind the specific requirements through capacity building and technology transfer, negotiations and turnkey facilities. This will help in cross organizational cooperation. With private sector actively playing a role in all walks of life, specific areas of policy, technology and financing will have to be identified for better programme making.

Projects with Impact

UNIDO has brought out in 1995 a brochure which includes the following which may be of interest to the *Indian rural industry sector:*

-- Handicraft innovation through image building and entrepreneurship-cum-production development strategies which resulted in prototype display in major exhibitions, products attracted high level media attention, groups invited to participate in future fairs, export orders and awards for products.

-- Build Operate Transfer (BOT) to help governments of developing countries to finance improvements in basic infrastructure. This project may be of interest to India for rural industries infrastructure with private initiatives where common facility centres for quality, brand image building, demonstration, godowns, banks, telecommunication, etc., could be available.
-- The art of negotiation through UNIDO's capacity building programme on technology transfer negotiation.
-- Women in informal sectors--needle women to business women
-- Women entrepreneurs in food processing industry
-- Improvement in technology and management in the Brazilian textile industry, etc. etc.

Changing Vision for Rural Industrialization in India

The father of the nation, Mahatma Gandhi had organized All India Spinners Association in 1920 and All India Village Industries' Association in 1924 to lay focus on various aspects of *artisan based rural artisan activities.* They were not taken till recently as a part of industrial sector. With the growing realization that the industrial and technological requirements do have many commonalities whether in the rural or urban sectors or in organized or unorganized sectors and after about four decades of experience of industrialization through small, medium and heavy industries, it is abundantly becoming clear that in the days to come India will have to focus on its *competitive and compatible advantage areas* with the agriculture and milk revolution, it is high time that a focussed attention is diverted to the areas of value addition of the rural raw material with better effective technologies for not only industrializing the rural areas but also to *suitably induct packages for self-supported growth model developments.* It is clear that agriculture including animal husbandry etc. have been a way of life for Indians and with the growing realization and opening up of the economy, it is being increasingly felt that the local raw material whether from agriculture, horticulture, forest, fisheries or in terms of spices, minerals, herbs, food and food processing, etc. could be some of the promising industries which could be set up in the rural areas provided suitable technology and policy package are made available.

India had a very rich heritage of artisans where skills were passed on from generation to generation. These artisans are in various fields like leather, pottery, handmade paper, herbs, stone carving, construction and water management fields. With the passage of time, even services sector has been included in the list of rural industries. The traditional village industries concept has undergone radical change with the restructuring and reorganization of the premier institution that is Khadi Village Industries Commission which has been working in this field. Recently, the KVIC has been given about one thousand crores of rupees as a consortium fund to give greater thrust to rural industries programmes with insistence on *viability and transparency.* This becomes more important since tranditionally KVI sector has been operating through non-governmental organizations (NGOs) and cooperatives but now artisan entrepreneurs could also be included in their target group. This is over and above the State organizations and decentralized local bodies which have always been eligible to avail finances from KVI sector.

In the field of rural industries, KVIC has identified the following groups of traditional industries which are basically artisan based and have the capacity to emerge as a major rural industries with better technology, market orientation, computerization and overall exposure to realization of competitive strength building requirements. Some of the most important industries selected for technology upgradation include the following:

- Handmade paper industry
- Rural leather industry
- Food processing industry
- Rural pottery industry
- Herbal industry
- Training, technology and servicing industry
- Bee-keeping industry
- Non-edible oil, health soaps and *Neem collection/processing industry.*

All the above industries are proposed to be established through *cluster approach* with total support system. It may be mentioned here that UNDP has been implementing the handmade paper industry programme with KVIC since 1991 and now Government of India and KVIC have taken a policy decision to have a national programme. It will be in the fitness of things that the experience of handmade paper and leather project at Ambala is suitably improved upon to be useful in all the above programmes of national stature. KVIC also has a very ambitious programme for export and marketing of the products from rural industries. They have about 14,000 outlets all over India manned by NGOs. With better training, human resource development, exposure to foreign markets and research and development in the field of *health food and eco-friendly manufacturing processes,* it would be possible to integrate with market compulsions, the financial viability and self-supportive systems build up. Experience of UNIDO in other fields of computer designing, product adaptation and upgrading of quality, management assistance to Ahmedabad Textile Research Association, agro industrial development and assisting for project of pilot test house for export quality controls, faculty development of KVI sector and transfer of technology to African countries, turn-key project marketing and export capacity development could be immediate areas of cooperation.

Apart from KVIC, there are federations, non-governmental organizations and organizations of institutions which could be utilized for developing and acting as the agents for technology transfer. Based upon the lessons of the past, the non-traditional and traditional industries would have to be provided with suitable technological packages in the following fields:

- -- Production and manufacturing technologies
- -- Storage and shelf-like improvement including quality standards and other specifications laying down
- -- Technologies in the field of communication and organizing the unorganized through better human resource development and training and skill upgradation packages
- -- Communication and market-led development and financing systems with special thrust on optimum utilization of existing infrastructure for cost effectiveness

Another area of special importance for the success of rural industrialization programme would be in the field of sharing of experiences with countries of India's size and dimensions. Here, the lessons of China may be of great use. Even the experience of Gramin Bank of Bangladesh in cost effective financing could be tried through some of the reputed institutions available in the KVI sector. There are pockets of artisans all over India which can be *nurtured as export villages.* All these will need a very effective technological back-up both for coordination, follow up, monitoring and mid-term corrections.

There are some other programmes which could also be linked up to give a greater impetus to the proposed rural industries programme. With technology missions operating in various fields, it is high time that the technology mission for rural industries specially in the traditional sector is constituted.

Parliamentarians Initiative on Sustainable Human Development and UNIDO

The Members of Parliament programme of local area development (MPLAD) is a very challenging opportunity to try on experimental basis innovative sustainable models with viability and transparency. UNIDO has a wide experience of supporting rural area based programmes for technology upgradation in the field of jute, leather, spices, handmade paper, pulp, industrial training, entrepreneurial development, agro industries and export oriented units. Recently, there has been a mission to develop a programme for women entrepreneurs training specially through food processing and other small scale type of industries.

UNIDO could be involved in the selected 6 parliamentarian constituencies in the following ways:

1. In Jabalpur--some of the industries include leather, herbal, tourism, essential oils, entrepreneurship development, export oriented units.
2. Coimbatore (Tamilnadu)--Handmade paper cluster, leather, food processing and tourism linked industrial activities.
3. Katwa (West Bengal)--Effective technologies in the field of jute, paddy processing, handmade paper, leather, tourism and export oriented units on cluster basis.

There are some industrial activities which are common to all the 6 constituencies. Programmes on *"Neem"*, organic manure, entrepreneurship development, export-led clusters, exposure to foreign investment and study tour of selected manufacturers of products could be some of the common areas. The technical support services both at programme and project level may be considered for establishing of marketing production training centres with peoples and non-governmental organizations. In Coimbatore, there are NGOs which can take up these programmes, while in Katwa (West Bengal), the block and Panchayat institutions are transparent, viable and willing to share these responsibilities.

Since KVIC also has been restructuring and reorienting its policies towards provision of suitable technologies with package of market oriented facilities and training, it will be with fitness of things if a Memorandum of Understanding between KVIC, the beneficiaries in the constituencies and UNIDO could be considered with the following objective:

Depending upon the local resources and specific needs

(a) marketing production training clusters could be commissioned.
(b) services of volunteers and technical experts could be made available to study the type of improvements required in the existing technological levels.
(c) sharing the experiences of lessons of other programmes with special emphasis on technology, marketing and training including entrepreneurship development lessons.
(d) special thrust could be on programmes which have been implemented successfully whether in India or outside.

Since Members of Parliament have a very important role in the policy making and correcting process, the first-hand experience of working with decentralized local institutions of governance with UN system would be very relevant. The experience till now has been the neglect of technology upgradation of unorganized sector and because of compulsions of transparency, viability and bankability compounded with all-round resource scarcity on one hand and need to develop replicable models with peoples' active participation on the other hand, leave us with very little choice. The programmes with planning action research, components could help in developing realistic implementable cost effective models by utilizing various resources and technologies available within systems by linking up the hierarchy of the needs of the people with income generating priorities and rural industrialization necessities. It should be possible to develop replicable programmes of rural industrialization in a short period.

Poverty Alleviation and Rural Industries Importance

It has been clearly accepted by the UN system that 5 main groups of activities can be distinguished that address poverty directly:

(a) activities to facilitate economic development
(b) targeted anti-poverty programme
(c) provision of special services
(d) productive employment
(e) activities that address the cause of poverty from a long-term perspective

Based upon the above overview of policies and activities to be undertaken by the UN system, the development strategy, identification of income generating activities particpation through intensive activity generation and providing basic service as a part of social safety net, it is important that monitoring is done on a very effective manner.

Rural Industrialization-Neem Foundation and MPs LAD Programme

In a country like India, rural industrialization has to be based upon the availability of rural raw materials, the skills for using the right technology for value addition, including storage, packaging and marketing along with in-built systems for developing support systems. *Neem* is one of those plants which have not received any attention in the industrial promotion programmes. While it is true that in the most backward, tribal, hilly and desert areas, it is available in abundance. By developing a proper policy package, this plant has potential to generate sustainable jobs through following activities:

- nursery and plantation
- security of plantations
- collection of various products including *Neem* seeds, leaves and barks
- storage of *Neem* seeds and value addition related activities. This includes processing of *Neem* seeds and converting it into various value added products including soaps, pesticides, weedicides, insecticides, etc.
- carrying out further research in the areas of scientific cultivation and propagation of *Neem* related activities through marketing led development.

Neem Foundation has been interacting with some NGOs and State Governments but the attention which this important industry should receive has not been bestowed. Even funding institutions have not taken seriously the viability aspect of this industry so far. The ecological and environmental factors also need to be well publicised and propagated. With the involvement of MPs Parliamentarians' Forum it is expected that the *Neem* industry could benefit in the following ways:

- the rural area would receive benefits of various schemes available to *Neem* programme. For example, Ministry of Agriculture and Cooperation, Government of India gives two rupees a kg. as additional incentive to seed collector through non-edible oil Board (NOVOD) but except Rajasthan no other State has been able to make this facility available to seed collectors in the rural areas.

-- There are various infrastructural facilities required for the growth of *Neem* related industries. Apart from science and technology and continuous research and development for better and continuous product developments, standardization and inter-mixing with other eco-friendly product range, it is essential that this receives focussed attention. Despite the best efforts of Neem Foundation, not much could be done.

-- Through better policy package and integration with ongoing schemes of poverty alleviation, an entrepreneurship development in the rural areas, this could be one of the cent per cent women oriented programme. For example, for collection to intermediate level of value addition, all activities including storage, funding, etc. could be earmarked for women and their organizations. This will provide additional income and enhance the entrepreneurial capacity development through better availability of incomes.

-- The role of financing institutions would be properly appreciated once Neem Foundation, UNDP and Parliamentarians' Forum could develop a long term memorandum of understanding as a part of income generation programme for rural institutions.

Neem Foundation and Future Vision

As a part of its commitment to total sustainable human development with greater thrust on empowerment of women and youth, Neem Foundation is committed to work jointly and collectively with all important forums, both in short term and long term. In the longer run, it is the economic value of the *Neem* which will give impetus and sustainability to the efforts. With growing emphasis on friendly environment and emphasis on life-styles, it is imperative that effective coordination with various institutions is established. The role of Panchayati Raj institutions as the change agents for development and social and economic well-being of the local people, it is essential that they are given suitable representation in the strategy to be developed. There are also areas relating to making available degraded, desert and other barren lands to the local population, NGOs and other entrepreneurs for cultivation. With drip irrigation and watershed management programmes, it is quite possible to develop viable, bankable and transparent programmes for *Neem* based rural industrialization. The following are other areas for the attention of UNDP/UNIDO and Parliamentarians' Forum with special reference to Neem based linkage for future:

- -- target groups
- -- funding mechanisms
- -- marketing systems
- -- enterprise development
- -- policy issues
- -- support services
- -- coordinating issues
- -- infrastructural issues

It is also proposed that a workshop be organized to highlight some of these activities for better policy prescription and linkage development.

5

SCIENCE AND NEWNESS

Keeping in mind the need to pay adequate attention to the requirements of all segments of society it is essential to have a wide spectrum of social, economic, socio-economic and management related issues in mind. This approach would have the following advantage:

1. We can develop better model of funding, monitoring and expectations for self-employment as a part of long term success of the project and also be cost-effective.
2. The training capsule will have to be different for different target groups depending upon their capacity to bear the cost and adaptiveness. This is essential to cater to the differentials in the overall varying capacity of the beneficiaries.
3. The overall need to make the programmes viable and transparent and also widely acceptable it is essential that the question of replicability is properly understood in its wider dimensions. The issues in human behaviour, greed, technology levels and marketing implications have to be holistically understood to draw suitable lessons for future. This will be possible only when this differential approach is understood in totality.

What is New in the Blueprint?

Though this document does not claim to be very innovative, bold and new in approach there are some factors which have been kept in mind to make it useful from replicating issues. This aspect makes it imperative that it does combine newness based upon lessons of the past experiences of this nature. Actually the consultant feels that probably for the first time this type of exercise is being done to pool various expertise and resources of UN systems and agencies to work with grass-root level institutions in different parts of India with active involvement of the Honourable Members of Parliament with different background and political affiliations. Hence it is important to know some of the newness in this blueprint for working together with transparency and viability for sustainability.

It tries to take a holistic look at the issues involved

It visualises long term implications of pooling expectations, tries to integrate synergetic inputs and looks at the matching outcome in a time bound and stepwise approach.

It is cost-effective to make it replicable and integrative.

It has Human Resource Development aspect in mind from the very beginning and lays down suitable Management Information and control mechanisms for monitoring purposes. It is based upon the fact that this bold innovative experiment must not fail at any cost and the best of information and coordinating mechanism be utilised.

It advocates *Parcel Approach based upon Planning, Action, Research, Codification, Extension Loaning* approach so that at no point important link is found missing in the success of the programme.

It emphasises need to pause intermittently and have a holistic look at the distance travelled and to look again at the future course of action. This is essential to ensure success and not to repeat the well known mistakes occurring frequently in these types of decentralised programmes.

In a big country like India, need for *Transparent Flexibility* needs no emphasis. This is easily achieved by following practices prevalent in village level institutions of West Bengal where each Panchayat displays prominently on boards the receipt and expenditure statements.

Efforts have been made to identify 'Mental block pockets' which normally hinder success of decentralised types of programmes of social, economic dimensions.

The importance of Gender related issues become more important as we march towards 21st century. Hence following is proposed as uniqueness in *gender related programmes:*

1. It makes a sincere effort to combine self-employment, Effective Technology, Bankability and openness and integrates with Panchayati Raj Institutions.
2. Direct contact with the beneficiaries through organising entrepreneur (O.E.)
3. Depending upon raw material supply, skills and demand level of entrepreneurs, it identifies emerging fields for confidence building activities.

4. It tends to ultimately converse as holistic self-supporting model for replication.

As a plan of action a discussion was held with Department of Science and Technology and others, they expressed willingness to fund a survey for identifying those criticalities in technology which would make this a reality. In selected areas with the active collaboration of local bodies it would be better to do this in a short time of about 3-4 months.

Science has a role in this aspect of technology identification for women and how they could be involved. The better course would be to give 3-3 constituencies to each of these organisation of UN and Government of India. Madam Chandani Joshi was inclined to this approach and was prepared to be associated with this initiative from the beginning if this would mean taking some innovative initiatives as a follow-up of China conference.

6

UN SYSTEM PROFILES AND LESSONS FOR POSSIBLE INTERACTION

"Each of the four priority areas for UNDP activity-eliminating poverty, creating employment and sustainable livelihoods, promoting the advancement of women and regenerating the environment--has important gender dimensions. While it is necessary to separate these priority areas for analytic purposes, in the real world, their gender dimensions and complex interlinkages cannot be ignored if development policy and programming are to be effective. UNDP is therefore, committed to working with our partners in the international community, governments and non-governmental organizations to reinforce these interconnections and to enhance the participation and leadership roles of women in political, economic, social and cultural life and in development."

-- James Gustave Speth, Administrator, UNDP

Interaction--Lessons within UNDP

UNDP has also other programmes which may be considered for linkage building. These include:

- -- Area planning
- -- Institutional development
- -- Employment
- -- Rural industries
- -- Experience sharing of important projects
- -- Technology transfer etc.

Gender Issues

In UNDP it would be proper to develop some association with Planning

Commission and others like DST-APTCC wherein better policy presentations could emerge. Help of various 'foundations' like Neem Foundation of Bombay could be taken to focus women, technology, finance, policies marketing-R&D-Exports etc. in 'Neem & Women' type of programmes.

The purpose of all this is to identify those issues and areas which would help in developing 'models' with thrust on replicability and sustainability.

Some Programmes within UNDP for Replication

Linkages with small farmers Agri business consortium/MS Swaminathan Research Foundation

The Planning Commission and UNDP enabled the identification of pilot projects to 12 districts that have the potential to maximise employment to assist less poor especially women, taking advantage of advances in bio-technology and economic reforms. These projects have been vetted by NABARD and are due to be implemented through appropriate mechanisms under the ages of SFAC which is to provide venture capital assistance.

The methodology and approach used by the MSSRF in identifying this project would be valuable for LAD scheme. Identification and establishment of feasibility of such projects in these areas should be followed up with and approach to SFADS to source capital required to commence the enterprises. The linkage will be built on knowledge and experience already gathered through implementation of UNDP project.

The identification phase should take no more than two months. The feasibility and the market studies could take a few more weeks. Thereafter, the SFAC should be moved to provide the capital assistance needed to launch the enterprises. The critical role for the MPs and UN agencies would be in establishing an implementation mechanism which is participatory and which can ensure that the economic gains from such enterprises go to those most in need.

Alongwith the above there is scheme for establishing bio-villages where ecology, equity and economic gains are consciously integrated in activities to provide livelihood in rural areas.

Outside UNDP Systems

(1) World Food Programme, Mr. Ellis, Country Director has been extremely frank cooperative and visionary in his approach. They have

even volunteered to work as a coordinating agency in Jabalpur. Mr. J. Fleuren, Adviser has also been nominated as coordinating officer for Jabalpur.

World Food Programme--has forestry, women and child development, irrigation, fishery and settlement with MIS, information and training as their areas. In Jabalpur constituency the following appear to be the main field of activity.

UNDCP Discussion with Mr. Christopher Ronald, Regional Director on 15 September 1995 has been very encouraging. Both long term and short-term, quantity and quality success ratios with reference to performance indices before and after were discussed. The need for multi-disciplinary programme approach with emphasis on model development by raising basic questions were considered. The challenges which this project offers in the selected constituencies could be broken in the following categories:

(1) Social Programmes
(2) Economic Programmes
(3) Capacity building programmes
(4) Technology programmes

Indirectly, the various activities around which the sustainable development will include the following:

(1) Agriculture and animal husbandry led activities.
(2) Rural Development activities.
(3) Rural industrialization activities.
(4) Sustainable human development oriented activities.

The purpose of dividing the various activities is to highlight the level of development and need to provide suitable policy packages with demonstration model to achieve overall objective of the whole exercise. Ultimately the objective is to develop replicable models.

From the above analysis angle the Raghuvir Nagar slum area project which was visited by Mr. Ronald may be examined. Since both long and short term funding, monitoring, cost effectiveness and people's perceptions would need to be examined, these observations could be very useful.

UNICEF

When it comes to planning, education, child development, community development, health, water and environmental sanitation, UNICEF has a very important role. They have not only well manned-field offices but also very good rapport both in the district and the states. They also have carried out policy changes as per field situation and aspiration of the people. Many of the programmes are replicable, principled and have lot to be shared by others. UNICEF can immediately share the policy, funding, monitoring and transparency related changes which they have carried out in the recent past alongwith the results and the critical areas for further planning from all respects.

In Coimbatore and Katwa areas they could be the lead agency if they could nominate suitable officer. Now, that FAO has agreed to be the nodal agency for Coimbatore, it will be better if Katwa/Kalna area could be taken over by UNICEF. However, since they are the only UN agency having a very wide network and a good public contact, it would be in the fitness of things if some senior most officers in UNICEF could be nominated to be the coordinator.

The consultant had the opportunity of interacting with UNICEF field officials at Coimbatore and Kalna and must compliment them for many innovations in the field of their activities. In the year 1996 they will be completing 50 years and it is high time a lasting, integrating transparent relationship with MPs Forum and decentralised Panchayati Raj institutions through UN system is developed to be a real trend setter.

The India and its population book, by UNICEF mentions on page 4 the following:

"UNICEF is an organisation of peaceful revolutionaries, like most revolutionaries, it is clear and single minded in its mission to safeguard children's rights to survival, development and protection in a world which still tolerates crimes of violence and neglect against them.

"India since independence in 1947 has seen the unfolding of a peaceful revolution--The Transformation of conditions for its children. UNICEF, which has been working here since 1949 is proud to be playing a part. Yet, despite the very significant achievements for children in this country, the revolution of child survival development and protection remains unfinished.

"One of the most pressing challenges facing India today is how to extend the benefits of development to its poorest, who comprise one-third of a rising population and particularly to women and girls, the most disadvantaged and vulnerable of all it is in this context that UNICEF's thesis investing in children pays off has greatest relevance.

"UNICEF does not have its own programmes, preferring to build up national capacity by channelling assistance through governments and non-governmental organisations. The approach favoured by UNICEF lays emphasis on cost-effective ways of providing services which are universal in coverage and aimed at redressing inequality due to gender, ethnic group or income communities should not only participate in the design and management of projects, but feel that they actually own them. Thus ensuring the likelihood that projects will be self-sustaining.

"Discussion with various interested groups both within UN systems and outside gave me the impression that UNICEF has been one of those organisations who have been continuously trying to involve maximum role players in their formulation and implementation. They have also had innovative programmes in various fields including gender and development. The factors of empowerment like income, culture and developing systemic barriers have been some of the important innovations. They are also fully aware of the unique opportunity the Panchayati Raj amendment offers. It is here their long term association with Parliamentarians' Forum could help developing suitable model for replication through cost effective programme management and developing communication channels. Despite all this there will be some areas for consideration like:

"1. To what extent have the community based convergent services been successful? Based upon the need for CBCS have the objectives been reached?

"2. Have programmes of bio-gas, health food, traditional items of nutrition relevance both from health and economic aspects?

"3. Can hand made paper which is eco-friendly, having stencil and folding-tearing strength much more than bamboo and eucalyptus paper, be utilised for generating more jobs on hand and printing durable literature on the other?

"4. Can more cost effective like low cost practical consultancy areas and systems be developed by training the local ruralites to take up more and more activities for effective programme implementation?

"5. What are the critical areas both in funding, monitoring and replicating the good work done by UNICEF? Ultimately, despite all this efforts if the problems are still of enormous size, obviously there is a need to look for still better systems of delivery. This will call for more action based research and experience sharing so that the whole of the target group could be covered more effectively through better systems.

"6. There are many programmes being taken up by World Bank and other agencies affecting children, women, education and overall health aspects--to what extent have efforts been made to share experiences with them. For example in water and sanitation and gender and development aspects various agencies of UN are doing similar work.

"7. With a clear focus approach for education, health, nutrition, water and sanitation, child labour, health, it should be possible to have better integration.

UNICEF is also likely to be the lead agency for Kalna area where they have comparatively many other facilities. With emphasis on income generating activities and greater thrust on empowerment and awareness issues it should be possible to develop transparent viable and replicable models."

KVIC-UNDP, UNICEF, APCTT, and Parliamentarians' Forum

KVIC has a mandate of Government of India to generate jobs on a massive scale through better transparency and viability. This process has already started and the experience of national eco-friendly programmes with UNDP have brought out some interesting issues in viability and replicability of traditional industry sector. KVIC has been one of those NGO sector autonomous body of the Government which had not opened up to take challenges of our times. With the growing awareness to tie-up with national and international bodies for generating sustainable jobs through cottage and tiny industries and artisan based activities it is high time that an effort is made to develop some working linkages for better model development through the joint efforts. The outline of this synergistic approach could be the following:

(1) KVIC has various programmes, technological expertise in the fields of bio-gas, food processing, khadi, leather, handmade paper, herbal, marketing, exports, funding, training, low cost practical consultancies etc. All these could be on a selective basis.

(2) By working in the selected constituencies all would stand to benefit by working together. The aspect of system development with integration of social, economic, educational training, marketing technology etc. aspects could be looked into holistically.

(3) The close interaction with these organisations could be possible through cluster approach on viable and transparent basis.

Bombay could be the base centre for MIS since KVIC HQs. selected models like Lijjat (Women's organisation), Raile Gaon Sidhi of watershed management and various activities of income generating nature are taking place around.

(4) It would be proper that a meeting may be held in UNDP once the suggestion is agreed in principle. KVIC, UNDP, NGOs, APCTT etc. would all stand to benefit in the longer run with these integrative exercise. It would be better to form a small committee to implement this programme. Incidentally, it may be mentioned that KVIC has about 1000 crore rupees consortium funding available with them for viable marketing oriented rural industries programme.

(5) Another area of joint collaboration will be joint monitoring, training, and developing internal and external control mechanisms. The units may be organised into federation so as to ensure proper implementation.

(6) KVIC also has a number of equipment manufacturers under its fold. With their cooperation, it should be possible to launch jointly a rural technology mission for improving the quality and productivity. Initial discussion with Mr. Bajpai of APCTT have been very encouraging.

(7) The success of economic programmes for employment generation will depend upon the capacity to produce production services of quality and capacity to market in a competitive world. KVIC has recently appointed a committee to study marketing aspect of rural industries product. The recommendations of the committee can be shared by the entrepreneurs. Policy issues if any, can also be taken up with the Parliamentarians Forum.

It is expected that by forming an MOU with the above organisation it will be very useful in the longer run to tackle the problem of sustainable employment generation in the selected pockets.

1. FAO

I had the opportunity of very good discussion with Mr. Rosenger on 22 September 1995 alongwith Mr. O.P. Dewan. Initially due to misconceptions they had lot of reservations about the utility but when explained properly he was kind enough to nominate Mr. Dewan to be the coordinator and they voluntarily preferred Coimbatore as their lead district for synergistic experiment. It was also decided that Mr. Panda,

Secretary, Agriculture, Tamil Nadu, would be involved by FAO to further develop plan of action with Dr. Aram by involving Shanti Ashram and others working with them in forestry programme.

I could collect lot of materials and had the opportunity of going to various activities in which FAO could carry out holistic planning action research codification and experiments based upon their past experiences and present compulsive need to integrate social, economic, socio-economic and managerial controls related programmes on both short and long term basis. Even though they are working with joint forest management activities, there is always scope for learning even within UN system.

The learning from their "Experience and technical cooperation among developing countries" booklet is a very good document and it would be meeting a greatly felt need if the organisation of farmers could be involved in sharing these experiences. The data base and the various activities relating to trade, nutrition, human resource institutions, policy analysis, animal production and health division, land and water division, plant protection and production division, fisheries department, forestry department etc. could really train the people in the felt need areas. The booklet on attacking rural poverty, women in agriculture development, FAO's plan of action 1945-1993 and forestry statistics today and tomorrow are very important documents. The other areas of interest are the main task of the organisation which are following

-- It carries out a major programme of technical advice and assistance for the agricultural community on behalf of governments and development funding agencies;
-- It collects, analyses and disseminates information;
-- It advises governments on policy and planning;
-- it provides opportunities for governments to meet and discuss food and agricultural problems.

While thanking Mr. P. Rosenegger for voluntarily and enthusiastically adopting Coimbatore for innovative experiement I am sure the linkage with Dr. Aram the Hon. M.P. Rajya Sabha and also a well-known dedicated Gandhian who has also been Vice Chancellor of a Gandhian University and FAO would be very useful for days to come because the priority and direction of FAO is to eliminate hunger and poverty as they mentioned in their booklet titled "FAO what it is what it does--The connection between hunger and poverty is recognised in the goal of World Food Security. . . . finding answers to the problems of the smallest and the poorest farmers is stressed through policies and programmes that promotes integrated rural development--through the cultivation of food and fodder crop, animal husbandry, small scale fisheries and forest industries, either individually or together for greater food production and self reliance."

Some of the areas in which FAO could contribute through this synergistic approach may also include the following:

1. Linkages missing as per the experiences mentioned in learning from experience, booklet by FAO.
2. Cost of developing low cost consultancies for self managed institution of farmers and its linkages with other programmes like bee-keeping, value addition activities of agriculture, increasing the overall viability so that agriculture and forestry along with fisheries and other activities could offer package for long term sustainability.
3. The effectiveness of training in all fields of activities may be examined with the experience of UNICEF which the consultant has, found to be of great assistance.
4. The potentially high growing areas of organic manure, need based fertilizers, pesticides, weedicides and insecticides etc. need priority. Somehow, in the literature made available to the consultant these areas are not reflected because probably they are not worth looking into!

   Another area requiring serious consideration is the barren, uncultivated land in India. These vast pieces of land show how poor attention has been paid to them in the past. May be the time was not right and other things being equal organisation like Neem Foundation are mobilising people to take up plantation on a massive scale in these otherwise most degraded uncultivable land on commercial basis. The induction of drip technology with water conservation measures prescribed by Shri Anna Hazre may open up entirely new chapter in the field of sustainable holistic food and agriculture related activities. From FAO's policies and actions and the policy framework charter both at national and international level they have been dealing with these issues but suitable plan of action may have to be integrated in the days to come.
5. Keeping in mind the priorities of our time and the declaration of Parliamentarian Forum it is high time that a suitable planning action research extension and loanable package of programme is developed with NGO and others in the field of four activities, identified by the consultant.

UNESCO

It was with very great difficulty that the consultant could get an appointment with Director. However, the meeting was very pleasant but it seems there are areas of communication gap as felt by consultant. Incidentally, during the discussion Mr. Nag, PRO of Tata Steel from West Bengal who was instrumental in forming Chamber of Commerce with multi party composition also happened to be present. The Hon. Member of Parliament of Kalna has invited UNRR to visit Kalna--a historical, spiritual family tourism and a growing economic activity place on 28 September 1995 for addressing a workshop on the theme of sustainable human development and issues in people's participation in the development process. Mr. Nag briefed about the potential of developing income generating activities through UNESCO with self help, environmental friendly activities alongwith cultural tourism and suitable livelihood generating package of activities in that otherwise not so well known area. Despite the fact that lot of infrastructural development activities like hotel, guest houses, electrification of rail lines corporate sector entry in the industrial area and overall mode of economic activities are developing, it would be worth if UN systems could also contribute in popularising and jointly publicising these hitherto neglected historical place. However, the director promised to send somebody to have a look at the place and attend workshop.

The offer of *Chairman, Central Board of Secondary Education* to consider permitting on experimental basis starting of CBSE schools with new sustainable holistic training oriented syllabus based institutions was also shared by consultant. Since many fundamental type of changes are taking place, making traditional type of degree education irrelevant, this issue warrants serious consideration. The problem of vocational education not being popular could also be examined holistically in these new types of education institutions to be started in the selected MPs constituencies. These institutions could also be started by NGOs or Panchayati Raj institutions or even corporate sector and private initiatives. The aim is to *learn from our experiences and to develop replicable models based upon our felt need by integrating with best of the whole world.* It would be impossible to experiment on these lines through any other forum. Hence, through this synergistic effort UNESCO, CBSE, MPs forum and local entrepreneurs could take a lead to suitably revise syllabus to start educational institutions which could prepare students for tomorrow based requirements and considerations of sustainable holistic development.

Even though UNESCO has no funds of its own it has capacity to generate resources from various sources including UNDP. As consultant I was informed, many of the funding agencies are looking for new type of projects. Hence, with better cooperation there should be no problem for minimum fund required.

World Bank

Though the consultant had two rounds of discussions with officials of World Bank nothing concrete could emerge except literature on some policy issues and environment departments papers on various subjects including those on participation poverty assessments. It was also seen that they had two important community based projects i.e.:

(1) 1992 to 1998--India West Bengal Forestry projects with total cost of \$39m (IDA-\$34m)--the objective and strategy of this project has been basically to enhance forest productivity, conserve bio-diversity by transferring responsibilities for forest and plantation management, protection and utilisation to local communities. The micro plans are being developed through discussions with representatives of different classes so that plan could reflect their perceptions and needs.

(2) Same way in 1989, with the cost of \$32 m India, Tamil Nadu integrated nutrition project had certain indicators of success. The following have been mentioned as the reforms/support for learning process:

"The project was confined to one administrative block for the first year, during which the implementation strategy was tested and refined.

A Project Management Fund was created to fund studies and research at the discretion of the project coordinator. The Fund financed 63 studies which identified issues/problems confronted during implementation.

At the micro level, women's groups, created approximately 20 women with a particular interest in health and nutrition, were instrumental in explaining the project to the community.

CNW was accountable to the community Public display of CNW's performance in achieving targets allowed for peer/group monitoring.

Nutrition and health statistics were monitored for each block monthly. Block performance was compared to norms and lagging blocks were singled out for corrective measures."

What remains to be examined from both the above projects as to *whether the concerned UN systems like WFP in the case of forestry project and UNICEF in the case of integrated nutrition projects have been involved? From the perusal of both these projects it seems that if area approach was adopted a better transparent cost effective and replicable model could have emerged.* In the community based plan of action it is very essential that the replicability and transparency with sustainability are invariably included.

Some of the documents about working with NGOs by World Bank definitely give very good appreciation of what should be a sort of synergistic requirements for the experiments with Parliamentarians' Forum and UN systems.

Some of the other documents which the consultant has the opportunity to refer include following:

(1) Participatory evaluation--Tools for managing change in water and sanitation;
(2) Working with NGOs;
(3) Participation in Water and Sanitation;
(4) Participation in Country Economic and Sector Work;
(5) Participation in Education;
(6) Participation and Indigenous Peoples;
(7) Designing Community Based Development;
(8) Participation in Irrigation;
(9) The World Bank and Gender in India;
(10) Toward Gender Equality; (The Role of Public Policy)

After going through some of these documents the consultant has got a feeling that *for a poor country like India which so much diversity it would be a golden opportunity to utilise the apex organisations for developing low cost high impact projects which could become replicable. It would also be a great learning process to examine how far the massive investments are justified by results, through these two projects which were probably completed or are being completed without the direct cooperation with other important UN agencies.*

The social aspect and the need to integrate with grass-root level institutions through MPs contacts if World Bank could join in this programme in the following areas makes a lot of sense:

(1) Providing concessional finance to the innovative experiments
(2) Taking up joint project formulation with MPs forum and UNDP with economic and social aspects of viability.

(3) Involving selected institutions to develop planning action research codification and extension type of model through multi-disciplinary and multi-dimensional approaches.
(4) Sharing some of the concerned areas and plan of action with MPs for identifying potential action points.

In the process of preparing blueprints the consultant made various efforts to try and locate those areas of concern to all. The idea was to codify them for future. Some impressions gathered during these discussions may be summarised below for future use:

(a) Limitations of Bank--There has to be profiled then only funding is possible.
(b) From I.D.F. fund small grants of 10 to 20 thousand dollars may be given depending upon results.
(c) If suitable requests come to Bank, they may consider making projects on poverty, Panchayati Raj, issues of governance etc. for this concept paper has to go.

While reading some of the written speeches and forwards in the World Bank documents with reference to India interesting pieces of information have come to the notice of the consultant. May be they are of some interest and hence some extracts.

Extract from the World Bank and India--Forward by D. Joseph Wood, Vice President, South Asia Region, World Bank:

> "The World Bank and India have shared a cost partnership since the inception of the Bank. This has been for a very good reason in *the area of development,* both India and the Bank share the fundamental goal of achieving poverty reduction on the basis of sustainable growth.
>
> "The history of the Bank's assistance to India has been a dynamic and adaptive one. In the early years, the Bank emphasized infrastructure. During the *seventies and eighties* Bank assistance was broadened to include agriculture and the social sectors. And in the early nineties, support for India's far reaching economic policy reforms and for expanded social and environmental programs have been the focus of our assistance. Throughout this period, the Bank's lending assistance has been complemented by a fruitful dialogue on emerging policy issues. The Bank has also helped to coordinate the Aid India Consortium since 1958. More recently, the Bank's recognition of project implementation as an area in

need of renewed attention saw India as one of the first countries to undertake a comprehensive review.

"In all these areas, the relationship between the Bank and India has shown remarkable resilience, and despite some occasional differences of perspective, has grown in strength and depth.

"The Indian economy is currently undergoing a fundamental reorientation aimed at providing the basis for a recovery of growth with poverty reduction in the nineties. The Bank is proud to have assisted this effort so far. A successful transformation of the Indian economy, continuing along the path of the last two years, could realistically lead to sustainable growth at a pace sufficient to double per capita income in a single generation and to reduce substantially the proportion of absolute poor".

Report of 1993

On page 5 it says "In the early years there was some doubt whether India was creditworthy enough to borrow from the IBRD and the beginnings of the Bank's lending relationship with India were tentative. Although the first development loans (as distinct from loans for Europe's post-war reconstruction) were made early in 1948, it was not until late in 1949 that the first loan to India was approved, marking the start of the long-lasting relationship that was to follow. The rapid increase in lending to India occurred only in the succeeding decades."

On page 9 it says "The World Bank Group consists of the International Bank for Reconstruction and Development (IBRD) and its three affiliates: the International Development Association (IDA), the International Finance Corporation (IFC), and the Multilateral Investment Guarantee Agency (MIGA).

The IBRD accounts for about three-fourths of all Bank lending IDA provides highly concessional "Credits" to the world's poorest countries.

IFC lends directly to the private sector without government guarantees. It also takes up equity positions in companies to foster development of capital markets in developing countries. MIGA promotes private investment in developing countries by providing guarantees on project investments."

On page 36 it says "A dialogue on projects and on sectors is difficult enough for the Bank and for the borrower. But what is even more difficult for the Bank and borrower is dialogue on the general economic, financial and development policies of the borrowing country. Such a dialogue has often been desirable in the past and has taken place. It is, in my opinion, usually going to the essential in the future that the Bank conduct this kind of dialogue with low-income countries which need a large flow of resources from abroad for a long period"-- *by Escott Reid, 1965.*

On page 38 it says "India, moreover, has never been a tabula rasa patiently awaiting advice on development priorities or strategy before deciding on a course of action. Since obtaining its independence in 1947, India has had a Government able and willing to assign a high priority to economic development and has been a repository of strongly held ideas on what needs to be done"--*by Mason and Asher, 1973.*

On page 40, it says "There is no doubt that in both the rich as well as the poor countries, there has been of late considerable disenchantment with the giving or receiving of assistance across national borders. There is no reason why we should object to an assessment of our plans and policies by the aid-giving countries and institutions and much less reason why we should suspect something sinister in every honest advice rendered to us. As long as we ourselves are clear about where we stand and what we wish to achieve, there is no reason why we should fear a dialogue with other people". --*by I.G. Patel 1971.*

On Page 42, it says "The fact of the matter is that the Bank cannot force any Government to do anything. We are only an outside agency that has money to lend but even the amount of money that we can contribute to any one country is a small fraction of the country's own resources. We can only support what Governments and people themselves are prepared to do. We can help in the process. We have a worldwide experiences, we have some idea of what works and what doesn't work . . . In India or eleswhere if these reform programs are not indigenous, they would not survive. The reform programs are fundamentally political; they are economic reform programs but they are essentially part of the political process. No foreign agency can involve itself in such a process. The Bank will not even try".--*by Ernest Stern, 1993.*

On page 44, it says "If the World Bank's influence gets beyond a certain point, *if it begins to look like pressure, even if it is something desirable in itself or something desired by the country itself, pressure by the Bank* to achieve it can be a very deadly political weapon. The World Bank is a source of external finance to India, and it is very easy, when an unpopular measure is taken, for its critics to argue that the country has either been bribed or blackmailed into a policy measure. Unless there is a degree of political sensitivity, one may get a situation where the whole relationship between the World Bank and the recipient country can get awkward . . . The thing to guard against is the role of the World Bank as an agent for pressurizing rather than learning at the infant open door; Whether the World Bank comes in then as a gentle supporter of a door about to open and gives a push, or whether the Government says 'No' because this is something coming from outside in the form of pressure or leverage, that is something which has an extremely significant and rather delicate balance"--by *L.K. Jha, 1971.*

7

GANDHI AND POLICIES FOR SUSTAINABLE HUMAN DEVELOPMENT

> "It will give you talisman. Whenever you are in doubt or when the self becomes too much with you try the following experiment "Recall the face of the poorest and the most helpless man whom you may have seen and ask yourself, if the step you contemplate is going to be of any use to him, will he be to gain anything by it? Will it restore him to control over his own life and destiny? In other words, will it lead to Swaraj or self-rule for the hungry and also spiritually starved millions of our country? Then you will find your doubts and self-melting away". -- *M.K. Gandhi*

Many feel that the policies pursued in the field of holistic rural development have not been very successful. One of the reasons has been lack of accountability and non-involvement of stake holders. It seems that at times of the policy prescribed for improvement had the negative impact. Instead of empowernment it made them further dependent. Policies and technologies have definitely not improved the capacity and capability to be competitive. There is nothing wrong with the masses as far as desire, urge, motivation to improve their total lot is concerned. The real problem is policies and implementation. One can expect that this joint effort would definitely help in correcting those weaknesses. He also said that various civilisation have come and gone but Indian civilization has continued to flow mainly because of "inherent capacity of purging themselves of error."

In this process of purging, cleaning, opening up, reexamining and reprioritization the lessons of positioning of decentralised sector will have to be reassessed. Many social, economic, cultural activities which were not attended to have suddenly become relevant and timely.

While looking at the challenges separately the consultant has tried to codify some of his experiences based upon Wardha childhood experiences, then Army experiences, and subsequently, working in state like U.P. and followed by Khadi and village industry days. It was here real opening of activities measuring problems, lessons, hopes, aspirations and 'despondency reasons' were identified and studied. As a part of study some of the VRAT or VOWS of the Father of the Nation which I understood include the following :

"*Satya* (Truth): Truth is God. Truth in a much wider sense means *Truth in thought, Truth in speech and Truth in action.* Where there is Truth, there is true knowledge, and where there is true knowledge, there is always *bliss (Ananda).*

"*Ahimsa* (Non-Violence): We may not give up the quest for truth, which along is, being God Himself, *Ahimsa* is the means, truth is the end. Without *Ahimsa* it is not possible to seek and find truth.

"Patience, sacrifice, humour: these are the time tested parameters for learning to live with satisfaction and tolerance while enjoying.

"*Aswad* (Control of the palate): Control of the palate is very closely connected with the observance of *Brahmacharya.* What we eat should only be to sustain the body and not for self-indulgence.

"*Asteya* (Not-stealing): It is theft to take anything belonging to another without his permission. However, to take or collect something from others for which we have no real need, also amounts to theft.

"*Aparigrah* (Non-possession): Civilisation, in the real sense of the term, consists not in the multiplication of wants but in their deliberate and voluntary reduction. This along promotes real happiness and contentment and increases the capacity for service.

"*Abhaya* (Fearlessness): Fearlessness is indispensable to attain ineffable peace and connotes freedom from all external fears or fear of disease, bodily injury and death, of dispossession, of losing one's nearest and dearest, of losing reputation or giving offence and so on.

"*Manavata*--Radical humanism--This is a part of spiritual--religious effort to open the mind of individual and societies and understand the unity of all creations by the Creater--It is essentially developing consciousness to awaken conscience for sustainable holisitic development.

"*Sharir-Sharam* (Bread Labour): Everyone, whether rich or poor, must perform his daily work, which should assume the productive form i.e. Bread Labour. How can a man, who does not do physical labour, have the right to eat?

"*Sarva Dharma Samabhav* (Tolerance for other Religions): Tolerance for other faiths imparts to us a truer understanding of our own. True knowledge of religion breaks down the barriers between faith and faith. Reverence for other faiths need not bind us to their faults. We must be keenly alive to the defects of our own faith also, and try to overcome these defects.

"*Swadeshi* (Service of the immediate neighbour): A votary of *swadeshi* dedicates himself to the service of his immediate neighbours. One who allows himself to be lured by the 'distant scene' but falls in his duty towards his neighbours, violates the principle of *swadeshi.*"

Based upon the above gist the consultant tried to link up the economic focus issues along with the cardinal principles of Gandhian approach to rural sustainable development. In this connection, Shri Y.A. Pandit Rao, has mentioned the following *cardinal principles* to Gandhian approach. "(i) Total and integrated development of an area from the view point of self sufficiency in basic need namely, food, clothing, shelter, education, medical care etc. by using local resources, local man-power and local consumption to the maximum extent. Area could be a village or group of villages or a block or a district, depending upon situation, (ii) total development of man, (iii) voluntary effort and voluntary action, (iv) self help and minimum dependence on government, (v) primary, secondary and tertiary sectors of the economy working in close cooperation, (vi) maximum use of small machine, (vii) first concern for the poorest among the poor, (viii) moral considerations in selecting economic activities, (ix) non-political work i.e. above party politics. It would be clear that although Gandhiji believed in simplicity of life but all the same he believed in improving the quality of life."

It seems that because of the various reasons of *our time and neglect* of the *local wisdom, well documented lessons and practiced traditional practices by the family systems have somehow been missed in the speed of development.* Time has come to be clear about the lessons of the developmental processes pursued so far all over the world. In this connection, any development process must have some integrative and sustainable inseparable so that the question of empowerment of self employment, organisership could all be examined with reference to various Gandhian institutions which were started for social, economic, cultural upliftment etc. activities before the independence. The 50th year of independence in 1997 could be the culmination of these studies for ensuring sustainability not *only of values of our time but also the lessons learnt and not learnt* despite their known availability. The fact is that the documentation, picturisation and computerisation coupled with fax and TV has made our job much easier and convenient. May be by dovetailing of Parliamentarians' Forum and UN Systems efforts, the next two years may see a radical sustainable shift in the planning action process. *Anyway, Time alone would be the best Judge.*

Gandhiji--Trusteeship--Corporate Sector and Rural India

It is normally understood that Corporate sector and rural India have hardly any areas of mutuality. May be this view is perpetuated by exploiters and propagators of *status quo.* Traditionally, Corporate sector using big machines and capital intensive nature of manufacturing and aggressive marketing through their lobbying and influencing, manipulative powers managed to escape from their responsibilities of helping the unorganised. Efforts by few have resulted in better publicity, image building, tax concessions and overall unreplicable development models. This point was discussed on several occasions with Shri K.C. Sharoff, Chairman of Excel Industries and also Shri M.L. Dantwala. The gist is that a time has come when through transparency, viability and understanding through cost effective systems development led by economic compulsions, it is possible to work better for *win win win situation for all.*

Maybe the Parliamentarians' Forum and UN systems convergence alongwith World Bank's policy and funding prescriptions could help us in developing replicable sustainable those models which would without destroying environment, people's will to work and need to be self-sufficient and self-dependent with dignity and self-respect would be emerging. Whether we like it or not there are clear indications and patterns in the horizons which compel us to examine whether innovations of technology, enterprise development need to attend to mass aspirations and to develop transparent models based upon cost effectiveness and redefined viabilities. There are forces both of time and experience which make it essential to happen.

8

PEOPLE'S PARTICIPATION

Recently I had the opportunity of getting some literature from 'peoples' centered sustainable development'--a farm programme of UNDP, FAO, UNIDO project from Philippines. Their findings of case studies on the dynamics of people's participation in China, India, Indonesia, Nepal, Philippines, Sri Lanka, Thailand etc. gave them the following conceptual framework.

(1) Development must be
   (a) Socially just
   (b) Ecological sustainable
   (c) Economically viable
   (d) The politically participatory
   (e) Culturally vibrant
(2) The output of this process must be able to :
   (a) Meet basic needs
   (b) Increased potential and productivity
   (c) Reduce drudgery
   (d) Ensure choices
   (e) Improve health and well-being
(3) What is people's participation:
   It is nothing but effective implemented micro level planning.

DYNAMICS OF PEOPLE'S PARTICIPATION

Approach	Methodology	Actor
Initiation	Process of the people, by the people and for the people.	People's organization (POs) Community Based Organisation (CBOs)
Facilitation	Intervention by outside agent. A capacity building process.	NGOs, UN agencies, Funding agencies

Approach	Methodology	Actor
Cooperation	Intervention by outside agent. A process of manipulation for programme/project success.	NGOs, Funding agencies, UN agencies, etc.
Induction	Process where people are coerced to participate through propaganda and sanctions--social, economic and political	Employers, Governments, & Religious organizations

What are the Principles of People's Participation?

	Principles	Elements Involved
1.	Interaction	Social, inter-personal and communication skills;
2.	Socio-political process	On-going, constant change over time.
3.	Individual Need	The more the need the greater the drive for participation
4.	Collective and Demo-cratic Action	Social responsibility and acting with consensus;
5.	Mutual Benefit	Stake and share in the benefit.

Benefits from Participation

Internal Level	Action Level	External Level
Cross consultation	Better informed	Strength in critical mass
Confidence Building	Better planned	Greater-recognition
Cross fertilization	More resources	Greater confidence
Increase in commitments	Better monitoring	Strength in negotiation
Support base	Greater account-ability	Better access to resources

What are the Principles of Relationship Involved in People's Participation

	Principles of Relationship	Elements Involved
1.	Mutual Respect	Respect and mutual trust
2.	Active Involvement	Active involvement is prerequisite to participation

	Principles of Relationship	Elements Involved
3.	Agree to Disagree	Socio-economic process of interaction
4.	Building Consensus	Collective responsibility for decisions made
5.	Commitment to Action	Development means taking action

What are the Operating Principles Involved in Facilitating People's Participation?

- -- All arrangements must be based on partnership mode.
- -- The approach must be participatory, consultative and with consensus.
- -- It must be inclusive, open and transparent.
- -- It must be built on existing successful practices, structures and approaches.
- -- And it must have leverage to bring about structural and policy changes.

What are the Costs Involved in People's Participation?

FARM has suggested that the following five important aspects must be kept in mind while ensuring people's participation and the totality of developmental planning action:

1. Firstly, to recognize and understand the dynamics of people's participation and the critical differences and nuances involved. FARM will have to avoid at all costs "incentives" to gain people's participation. Whatever monetary contribution or work contract given to local groups will be to build their capacity to serve their community.
2. Secondly, participation will be "need driven" and not "project/ programme driven."
   The project/programme can only organize the community and create awareness among them for such a need. The people will decide the extent and the form of the project or programme based on their own need. Who knows, they may not need it at all.
3. Thirdly, anticipate conflicts among the groups involved.
   This is because people's participation means different things to

different people. Among the different meanings given to it are:

(i) conceding to an initiative or plan designed by others to help the beneficiaries (often by means of coercion);

(ii) compliance to a blueprint development design done for the benefit of the beneficiaries (often by means of cooperation);

(iii) cooperation to an initiative of others who work in consultation with the beneficiaries for their benefit (often facilitating people's participation);

(iv) Collective action through an interactive, consultative and consensus building process for the common benefit by the beneficiaries (an initiative of the people by the people and for the people);

(v) the empowerment process which means developing their socio-political skills, providing tools and process for analysis, management and entrepreneurial initiatives to build their capacity to interact with the outside world on a more equal basis.

4. Fourthly, promote common understanding and consensus on the issue of people's participation.

   The FARM approach to people's participation particularly through NGOs may be in conflict with the government's understanding and interpretation of people's participation to convince the parties involved about the efficacy of facilitating people's participation as a prerequisite to development that is socially just and ecologically sustainable.

   Fifthly, FARM must endeavour at all times to ensure the participation in the sub-programmes will be a bottom-up approach.

   The farmers will truly be central to this process. They must be involved in the consultation, consensus building and decision making. In a community all other relevant sectors must be involved and be informed to enable them to respond to the needs and aspirations of farmers. This is one part of the process.

   The other process is also similar. The farmers must plan, implement, monitor and evaluate their development plans. Again a community there are other sectors which are linked with the farmers. It is important that they are also involved and informed to enable them to assist and support the farmers in their development initiatives.

This process is aimed at reducing as much conflict as possible and at the same time responding to the farmers' needs and aspirations in a more focused and coordinated way.

"Differences of opinion should never mean hostility. If they did, my wife and I should be sworn enemies of one another. I do not know two persons in the world who had no difference of opinion, and as I am a follower of the *Gita,* I have always attempted to regard those who differ from me with the same affection as I have for my nearest and dearest".

-- *Mahatma Gandhi*

9

PANCHAYATI RAJ AND SELF EMPLOYMENT PROGRAMME

Panchayati Raj have traditionally been used as a word of politics and power. Whatever meagre authority they have is frittered away in political game. The priority was contracting and implementing this tendency left panchayat in many states with a bad reputation.

The time has come when Panchayati Raj institutions have to be involved actively and purposefully in economic activities including self employment priorities. Due to neglect of Panchayati Raj Institutions in overall development initiatives of their area a huge gap has been created between expectations and fulfilment. It is here that the issues of self-employment policies--programmes lending to reduction of dependence on States becomes important. There are Panchayats which have offered banks security of advances and loan provided they are involved. This means transparency and viability. These are the key words when it comes to economic programmes on decentralised basis getting success in the rural areas. Panchayati Raj has to understand the mind set of bureaucracy and thus prepare itself to facing challenges. It is not an easy transformation. There are areas required in entrepreneurship, policy, clarification, coordination, transparency and overall viability. Glamourisation of self-employment with better policy packages is possible.

Panchayati Raj has to understand the challenges of time specially in states like Uttar Pradesh, Bihar Madhya Pradesh, Orissa, Tamil Nadu where they have hardly ventured into these new areas.

Plan of Action

1. Any Plan of Action has to be area based say a village or a community.
2. The felt needs of the people specially from demand angle needs

proper appreciation. Hence whatever is going out from the village must be stored, value added and marketed at the best prices fetching at that time. On the other hand whatever comes from outside in terms of industrial service or business initiative should be locally developed where possible.

3. There is need to involve all local leaders and initiatives in the action projections. Hence they are leased and the contribution they can make needs codification.
4. SWOT analysis and Hidden Investible Potential Power of Organizations (HIPPOO), Known Investible Potential Power of Organisation (KIPPOO) and Threatening Investible Potential Power of Organizations (TIPPOO) of the area would make the job much easier for analysis and action.
5. Planning, action research codification, extension, loaning has to be the base. Hence cooperation and coordination become crucial with critical areas for monitoring.
6. Training has to be on practical basis. Organisership and entrepreneurship will require two different states of attitudes funding, monitoring and training capsule. Philosophy, Organisership management, Marketing, Production, Training & Technology, Extension & Codification (POMPTEC) would have to be the centre of training for Organisership. While for self employment marketing led production should be the essential of training.
7. Monitoring system with regular interaction with multi-disciplinary team including banks, NGOs for Panchayati Raj is must.
8. Emerging areas of investment in Tourism, Trekking, Health, Food, Sanitation, Nurseries, Transport, Servicing, Education, Computers, Guides, Packaging etc. must be regularly watched.
9. Cost effective systems development need periodical identification of cost escalative activities with better local raw material use and increasing intake should make costs lesser and lesser.
10. Comparative SWOT analysis should be carefully done periodically. The aim should be to develop model so that replicability could be ensured. Before the above is done there is need to exchange notes and experiences with all the role players for avoiding repetition of mistakes. A re-visiting success type of activity would definitely help in identifying reasons for poor performance of earlier initiatives. This would help in better project formulation and implementation.

11. In the world of materialistic greed led growth there is need to plan fruit eating versus root eating. In the plan of action systems for income with honesty, transparency must be in-built. The programmes must have lesser gestation period within in-built possibility and propensity to grow. Traditionally herbs, plants, pilgrim centres, heritage and tourism will be other areas of stable income provided better marketing systems could be developed.

10

WORLD BANK AND NON-GOVERNMENTAL ORGANISATIONS

The World Bank has been laying greater stress on need of developing linkages with non-governmental organisations for various programmes. The discussion paper prepared by World Bank brings out various areas given below, of interest and action in original from their documents.

Potential Areas of Agreement between the World Bank and NGOs

Notes drawn from the NGO "Position Paper", the Banks Response and Elsewhere

In the past many of the papers prepared for the Committee have emphasised the differences between the development philosophy of NGOs and the Bank. While not wanting to gloss over these differences, this paper was requested by the Committee as an exercise in assessing where there may be substantial areas of agreement.

> "No task should command a higher priority for the World's Policy makers than that of reducing *global poverty*"--World Development Report (WDR) 1990.

This statement by the World Bank is one with which NGOs would readily agree and is, therefore, a good starting point for World Bank-NGO Committee discussions. What needs to be considered is how far NGOs and the World Bank are in agreement on what these policy makers should be doing and on what role both the Bank staff and NGOs can play in order to help so that the policy makers live up to their obligations.

Areas in which the Bank and the NGOs are likely to agree are as follows:

> The need for new development priorities to stress poverty alleviation and environmental protection. These priorities should include an emphasis on developing a new human and environment-centred framework of development economics; more open, responsive and accountable governance; the prioritizing of principles of equity (including gender equity and equity between nations); movement away from a dependence on a limited range of primary commodities; a less dogmatic, more flexible policy dialogue to reflect the shared responsibility Northern and Southern governments have in tackling the crisis of poverty.
>
> The need for adjustment in the North--in particular changes in policies with respect to debt, international economics, trade, aid planning and military expenditure.
>
> The need for poverty alleviation to be the paramount objective of aid. This must embrace popular participation, consultation with NGOs and communities affected by aid funded schemes.
>
> The need for a revised approach to adjustment programmes in which social and environmental considerations are brought to the fore.

This is an attempt to describe more fully these possible areas of agreement, with some commentary on where difficulties can be expected.

The Need for New Development Priorities

As crisis deepen around the World-environmental destruction, widening wealth gaps both within countries and between different regions of world, growing populations, and impending food shortages--it is clear that solutions will not be found unless there is a transformation of development as we know it.

In order for this to happen there is a need to rethink economics in order to take into account environmental and human capital. The World Bank itself recognises in its World Development Report 1990 (technical notes to the tables) the inadequacy of GNP per capita as a measure of development growth is not healthy or sustainable unless it is equitable, so it is vital to foster not just any growth, but economic growth that is based on high value-added, as opposed to high inputs of natural resources. Investment in people by making sure they have adequate access to productive assets so that they can use their skills and labour to the full is also good business. Equity is good economics.

NGOs are likely to be pleased to see the World Bank pointing out the important contribution that can be played by land reform, both in poverty alleviation and in fostering growth. However they will be disappointed at the readiness of the Bank to concede its political impracticability. Almost every occasion in WDR where land reform is mentioned, it is pointed out that it might be politically unrealistic, and that investment in human capital (e.g. education) might be a more realistic way of increasing the productivity of the poor. NGOs are likely to see this as a drop out. The juxtaposition of apparently unrelated policy initiatives in the WDR simply affords governments an easy escape route from a politically difficult path. Agrarian reform and investment in human capital should not be presented as alternatives. Both are called for. (After all, are there any predominantly rural countries where poverty has been greatly reduced while land ownership remains highly polarised?)

The Bank, although brave enough to raise the politically sensitive issue of land reform, could be doing the cause a disservice by being faint-hearted about it. At one point it dismisses land reform casually as "reshuffling the stock of existing assets", arguing that because land reform redistributes existing assets rather than creating new ones or improving existing ones it is not developmental in a macro-economic sense. This familiar Bank argument just does not ring true. Access to land can liberate the otherwise strangled productive capacity of the poor and so is one of the most developmentally positive paths one can take. By the same Macro logic one could argue that an irrigation scheme should not be considered developmental since it is merely redistributing water, rather than creating new water.

Democracy is being factored into aid planning. This could be a positive trend, but it depends how democracy is defined. The need is for grassroots democracy, ensuring that governments and their institutions are accountable to the people, that people have the right to free speech, free assembly (e.g. in trade unions, NGOs), access to information about state plans that might affect them, and consultation on those plans (e.g. through the forum of public hearings as happens in the North), and the right to elect local government chiefs, not just national governments (which is probably more important to most people than electing the president). The agreed World Bank-NGO Committee paper on popular participation provides important guidance on how NGOs and the World Bank can strive together towards the democratization of the development process.

The World Bank considers that the more open economies tend to have done better throughout the economic crisis of the 80s than the more closed ones. NGOs would question this, and argue that there is a need to divert from the present emphasis on a limited range of primary commodity exports. Often the human indicators show declines as efforts to safeguard the macro-economy or to maintain imports or debt service displace social needs. What we probably all agree on is that much depends on what is exported. Those countries which remain heavily dependent on a small range of primary commodities have had a very difficult time in recent years as terms of trade decline (in part because efforts to increase export earnings leads to over production—the so called "fallacy of composition" argument), whereas those who export manufactured goods largely have done very well. However, Northern protectionism makes it difficult for more than a handful of countries to pursue this route at present.

Seeking to persuade developing countries to become more like the newly Industrialising Countries and so avoid recession is not very helpful. It is like telling someone who asks for road directions "it's easy to get to your destination without getting snarled up in traffic; the only thing is that you shouldn't start from here". The countries who are in most severe economic crisis are those who are dependent on a small range of commodity exports and Northern protectionalism will not allow that to alter for a long time. The NICs have done well not just because of their attitude to exports but because of what they export (manufactured goods). They have also done well because of the foundation of equity provided by their land reform programme and because of their highly educated workforce.

The Bank cites Africa's difficulties as having much to do with its falling share of the World Market for the goods it produces. But according to WDR statistics the volume of exports has been quite constant (neither increasing nor decreasing)--the problem has largely been the 40% fall in the terms of trade. It is important to note that all other Third World regions increased their export volumes faster than industrialised countries did over the 80s, but they mostly fell behind economically because of deteriorating terms of trade and increasing real interest rates.

The importance of export promotion can be overstated and its statistics can be misleading. Hence the success of Korea is often quoted (exports account for about 35% of the country's GDP) whereas Africa's figure is just 19%. But on that indicator Africa should be seen as more successful than the North. The average for OECD countries is about 14%.

It is increasingly clear that export strategies also need to take careful note of long term, perhaps irreversible, environmental damage which might result from unsustainable "mining" of the natural resource base. An open economic policy without parallel policies of environmental protection and equity leads to results which can be anti-poor and anti-environmental.

However, export promotion does make good sense when (a) exports do not take precedence over the needs of the poor, (b) export earnings are used for the benefit of the poor and (c) there is equity in the world market-place i.e. when producers really have a chance of getting markets they need and decent prices for what they produce.

The Soviet Union and China were both quite successful in turning away from global economy but they had huge internal markets; this is not a realistic option for most Third World countries, and even these are now trying to open their economies. Other experiments with "de-linking" (e.g. Burma, Ghana, Tanzania, and Peru) have largely failed.

So a mixed approach is needed, one that is not totally free market, nor delinked. It is important, therefore, that the World Bank avoids giving the impression that it is dogmatically pro-market or anti-government intervention. Likewise NGOs--in criticising adjustment--must be worried of becoming unwitting allies of privileged groups who benefit from subsidies, cheap imports and protection.

Structural Adjustment in the North

By 1989 average commodity prices were 33% lower than in 1980. With the resultant serious economic crisis which much of the Third World finds itself in, it is surprising that how these countries have managed to survive at all.

Northern NGOs need to pay more attention to development policy issues, devote more effort and analyses to the impact on South of their governments' policies, and press their governments for reforms, for example, clearing up environmental problems at home. The solution to the major global problems depends in part on the emergence of NGO networks that can mobilize public opinion for change.

One such change would be the curbing of the arms trade, with the emphasis on resolving conflicts through diplomacy. A reduction in the Northern defence budgets would enable to be diverted into development and global environmental protection. In fact a 10% cut in NATO spending could finance a doubling of aid.

Because of policies in the North (Mainly the maintenance of high budget deficits) the world suffers the highest real interest rates in 200 years. Protectionism has actually increased in recent years, in spite of the Northern rhetoric of the importance of free markets. Now there is more protectionism than there was in the 1930s. The increase in protectionism throughout the 80s costs the Third World about $100 billion per year (twice what they receive in aid). There is an evident need for measures to ease protectionism, especially in Northern agricultural policies, and generally improve terms of trade with the South. Interest rates should be reduced (in particular by eliminating the US budget deficit), and aid and financial flows to the South should be increased. Apart from this the North needs to evolve truly comprehensive debt reduction strategies.

When Northern Governments make commitments to new initiatives (e.g. new plans for debt relief, new multilateral schemes for environmental protection etc.) they must genuinely be new resources, and not a cynical double counting of aid that was already intended for the Third World (robbing Peter to pay Paul).

Debt

The World Bank is right to say in the World Development Report (1990) that the low income countries are simply unable to "grow out of their debt". Adjustment by itself and maintaining debt service cannot solve the problems for crisis countries, which need external as well as internal changes. Countries which have no hope of recovering credit-worthiness should not be pressurised to meet their debt service obligations. A recent Bank report on adjustment in Africa showed that those countries which adjusted strongly did better (grew faster) than 'weak' reformers but this difference can be entirely accounted for by the increased aid they were given, (i.e. there is a self-fulfilling prophesy at work).

Debt reduction is, therefore, essential and the World Bank needs to be resolute in encouraging official and commercial debt reduction and in coordinating this process. There is need modification in the mandate of the International Financial Institutions so that their paramount objective is to help unfold a workable debt strategy, rather than simply protect creditors. In particular, the Bank should help ensure that commercial creditors do not force debtors to accept more onerous terms than are offered by official creditors via the Paris Club.

Northern governments must play a coordinating role to urge the banks to be much faster in reducing their debts, and must penalize banks who refuse or are slow to join in debt reduction schemes. They must also do more themselves to reduce official debt burdens. One target for the debt strategy should be to reverse the present net transfer of resources from the South to the North for the seriously indebted countries. Multilateral creditors should themselves give much greater attention to refinancing and other schemes which enable reductions in debt service obligations due to them by debt distressed countries.

Donors should take greater responsibility for the debt burden. This means a much fuller programme of writing off official debt especially (but not only) to low income countries. Also the question should be raised about the responsibility for debts stemming from, for example, World Bank loans for projects which failed--the recent special Africa report admits that many Bank supported rural projects failed. Perhaps the Bank should write off a portion (perhaps 50%) of such debt in the spirit of shared responsibility.

Poverty

NGOs would agree with the Bank that poverty needs to be addressed partly by generating the right type of growth--that is labour intensive and directed towards ensuring the productive use of the labour of the poor (at reasonable wages) PLUS investment in human capital through widespread provision to the poor of basic social services, especially primary health care, primary education, family planning services etc, PLUS well targeted transfers and safety nets for those who do not immediately benefit from the above and who perhaps suffer shocks as a result of deteriorating circumstances (e.g. economic crisis).

The Bank rightly reports in the World Development Report that alleviating poverty should not be ghettoized into a number of discreet projects. There should be an economy-wide approach, including a scrutiny of the poverty implications of all government policies. For this reason NGOs would have been interested in seeing the "Core Poverty Programme" approach recommended by the Poverty Task Force of 1987/8 at least experimented with. This seems to have been stillborn.

NGOs are likely to welcome the World Development Report and its focus on poverty, and broadly agree with its analysis, but stress the need for an open debate about what the Bank is going to do to implement its ideas. The report contains virtually no policy recommendations for the Bank. There now needs to be a high level policy paper drawn up on how Bank operational policies and procedure should change in order for the Bank to make the fullest possible contribution to the strategy hinted at. This policy review needs to lead to a new mandate from governments. From this point Bank staff will have a major task in turning the new policies into practice--the implementation stage. Without these steps the report will remain rhetorical, or simply left as advice to others--advice which the author organisation may fail to follow.

Particularly important is to have some policy proposals as to how the world Development Report's important comments about the need for greater responsibility from Northern governments can be translated into new policies, and what the role for the Bank might be in this.

It was surprising that the World Development Report made no reference to the two volume report of the Poverty Task Force. Though insubstantial in many respects, that report contained fifteen pages of policy recommendations. If, as appears, the report was not approved by the Executive Board, what hope is there for the more sweeping ideas implied by the World Development Report? Has even the idea of experimenting with one or two trial Core Poverty Programmes been discarded?

Given what the Bank says about the limitations of GNP per capita figures, NGO readers might find an undue emphasis on this indicator throughout the report. Even the classification of who is poor was determined purely by income in dollars. Earlier Bank commissioned studies on the "ultra-poor" made a strong case for using nutritional as well as economic data, which makes good sense. (Lipton et al. suggest the ultra poor are those who spend 80% of their income on food, or who eat less than 80% of recommended diet.)

Even more important would be the need to reflect on what the poor themselves have to say about the meaning of poverty. They do not refer to it in terms of money, nor necessarily in terms of diet, but characteristically in terms of vulnerability (i.e. dependence on a single employer, having to sell their produce through a single outlet-usually their landlord, having to sell a high proportion of their harvest immediately after harvest, vulnerability to pests, plant disease etc.).

It is surprising that the World Development Report 1990 had virtually nothing to say about the issues of environment and democracy since both of these are of critical importance to the poor and both have been energetically raised in other recent Bank reports.

The World Development Report did, however, address the issue of wastelands, forests and other commons in a progressive way. It rightly criticised policies to privatize these resources (though NGOs would tend to stress the importance of giving traditional users of these commons clear useful rights). NGOs would agree with the World Development Report that "common property resources should receive greater attention. They need to be better protected and better managed. Investment in research on how to use these fragile resources would be money well spent." However we would stress that all such initiatives should be in the context of helping those who traditionally live in or depend on such properties to be responsible for the protection, conduct (or set the parameters for) the studies, and manage the resources themselves.

Aid

The purpose of aid must be more clearly defined. The World Bank has expressed that their "overall lending program has become increasingly focussed on poverty". This is a welcome sentiment, but much more attention is needed, as we probably all agree, to enable the poor themselves to have a powerful say in the design of these programmes, otherwise there is no room for complacency. Indeed the Bank itself recognises that a major cause for poor project performance is the failure to involve intended beneficiaries, to foster a participatory approach or to attend adequately to institution building. The World Development Report recognises that "involving the poor in the design, implementation and evaluation of projects in a range of sectors would make aid more effective." The World Bank NGO Committee paper on Popular Participation provides importance guidance on achieving such improvements.

Aid should concentrate on poverty alleviation, directly and indirectly, so countries whose governments have a good record in this respect should receive more aid, and elsewhere aid should be channelled through NGOs or those ministries and schemes which have a good track record in benefiting the poor.

There has been too much faddism in aid planning. As the Bank has commented: in the 80s there was "a sharp and simplistic swing of donor attention towards efficiency and away from equity concerns". The Bank is right to say this but should be more unequivocal in saying that this shift contributed to exacerbating social problems.

Equally, crude self interest in aid planning should be rejected. An overwhelming proportion of US aid is allocated with strategic or military (rather than humanitarian) objectives in mind. Only 8% of US aid went as development assistance to the poorest countries in 1986. Such records deserve international criticism as they help give the whole development sector a bad name.

There is a need to invest in human capital and environmental capital, in order to maximise the potential of these assets. This calls for, *inter-alia,* supporting micro-enterprise and developing the informal sector.

NGOs would agree with the Bank that population growth is a vital concern. Rapid population growth is a major cause of environmental, social and economic problems in many developing countries.

Aid is needed to support programmes of equity. These include agrarian reform, which has been discussed earlier. (This includes land-titling and improved tenancy practices, both of which are called for by the Bank, as well as land redistribution). Gender and the rural and urban divide are also areas in which we need to strive for equity.

Collaboration with NGOs

The agreed WB-NGO Committee paper on popular participation details some important common understandings on the need to foster participation at all stages of project planning and policy debate.

The Bank is successfully increasing the number of its projects in which NGOs are involved. This is important and--in so far as the objective is to involve NGOs earlier on in the project cycle so that they help identify and plan the project, not just implement components of it--could help improve the value of projects to the poor. Important caveats are the need to avoid "bogus" NGOs and the cautious NGOs must exercise to avoid becoming so swamped that they lose their own legitimate agenda.

NGOs should not just be involved in project implementation, but also in helping design the project, and shape plans and policies.

NGOs and other people's organisations can give governments and the World Bank the local knowledge they need for planning good programmes, and help "attune" the project to people's needs and aspirations.

The Bank now expects recipient governments to consult with local NGOs on environmentally sensitive projects, and should expect similar consultation on socially sensitive schemes (including adjustment programmes).

Adjustment

NGOs would agree that economic reforms, improvement of efficiency of directory and government departments, institution building, improving management and planning in government departments etc are often needed, but that this is not the whole picture.

Severely over valued exchange rates and inflation hit the poor hardest. Conversely cuts in government spending on services consumed mostly by the rich and currency devaluation may be ways of handling the unpleasant task of apportioning the cost of a recession so that it does least damage to the poor. (NGOs, however, should never stop asking why developing countries, who did virtually nothing to create the international recession, are now expected to bear all the costs. This comes back to the arguments of the need for Adjustment in the North). Increasing agricultural prices, curbing government deficits, improving efficiency of public spending are good for the poor and for the environment. Adjustment can be an unpleasant medicine, and sometimes it should not be administered in the doses given, or should be accompanied by other measures (such as increased resources, debt relief, programmes to help the poor etc.) to soften the blow, but the underlying problem is the disease (recession) more than the medicine.

Recognition by the bank that adjustment can bring unbearable costs to vulnerable groups and that this must be guarded against is welcome. The bank points out that food consumption per capita has stagnated in countries or declined in countries taking adjustment loans. This cannot be justified; it reveals that hostile economic forces (largely determined by Northern governments) is creating malnutrition in the South.

In the World Development Report the Bank recognises that adjustment in the '80s was often "at the cost of compressed consumption and wages, lower investment and output, and frequent recourse to inflationary financing of government deficits"--hence, as we agree, there is a need for a fresh generation of adjustment lending which is designed to avoid such problems inflicting the poor. It is clear from data elsewhere in the World Development Report that an important strategy for the reduction of poverty and inequality is the increasing of real unskilled wages.

The Bank agrees in its response to the NGO Position paper that "special programs to help the poor during a period of adjustment are less important than the poverty impact of the adjustment policies themselves." Hence it is critical to design adjustment programmes in consultation with the poor, and with the objective of improving their access to productive assets.

The Bank is right to look for internal shifts in terms of trade to favour poorer groups--this is how adjustment might promote equity (in particular increases in agricultural prices to favour the rural sector). However, such an approach has to be mindful (a) of the ability of the elite to annex all the benefits unless the latter are very carefully targetted, (b) the need for careful sequencing of interventions, for example, examining what has to be done first to enable the most vulnerable to take advantage of a price incentive (e.g. rural credit, attention to ensuring farm inputs are available to the poor, agricultural extension services targetted at women farmers etc.) and (c) economic and related shocks can have devastating impact to the poor (e.g. loss of health services), albeit those state services may have been inefficient. the withdrawal of a state subsidy might cost a poor person $1 and a rich person $10, and so appear to be a progressive way of meeting the state's objective of making a saving. However, the loss of the dollar may be enough to kill the poor person, while the rich person survives (though grumbling) the $10 loss. There is a Chinese proverb that says "if a man is up to his neck in water it only takes a ripple to drown him".

Also needed are efforts to improve social welfare, to invest in people, to build up institutions, to protect the environment, to foster more accountable, responsive, participatory governance and other policy initiatives. The achievement of "sound economic management" (i.e. correction of budget or current account imbalance) while neglecting these issues or perhaps even at the expense of them, is not good economics, It is only a pretence of a solution--as with a company which apparently overcomes a sticky period by running down its stock or selling off its equipment.

Most NGOs would agree with the Bank that there needs to be less dogmatism on the part of Northern funders in future, and a greater sense of "ownership" of the adjustment programmes and development projects by Southern governments. In theory these schemes belong to the Southern governments, but as the World Bank is bravely recognising now, one of the major reasons for project failure is that they are essentially donor's projects, lacking the commitment of the Southern governments (WDR 1990). As the Bank says, there is the need for more "internationalization" of aid processes, otherwise they will not be effective or sustainable. This should include responsibility for the governments to explain and discuss development processes with their public.

NGOs would agree with the "Poverty Task Force" report that there needs to be better integration of policy lending and projects (the "Core Poverty Program" approach). In particular parallel measures are needed to agricultural price increases if small farmers (especially women) are to be able to benefit from and therefore respond to the price incentive.

More attention both in research and policy planning is needed on how women are affected by economic crisis and adjustment.

Structural Transformation

The following is a tentative suggestion as to what might be necessary ingredients if we are to achieve the necessary transformation of adjustment:

For Northern Governments

a reversal in the present extraction of financial resources from the South
a reduction of 3W interest rates
a reduction of official debt for both low and middle income countries
action to stem and help return capital flight
action to coordinate commercial bank debt reduction
action designed to help improve terms of trade for the South.
removal of both tariff and non-tariff trade barriers
reform of protectionist agricultural policies
adequate funding for bold global initiatives to protect the environment official aid to become strongly poverty focussed
aid to stress popular participation, grassroots democracy and more accountable processes of governance.
greater weight to be given to southern voices in international fora
a reduction of defence spending to finance environmental protection, debt relief, peace initiatives and poverty alleviation programmes (this would be a truly "Strategic Defence Initiative")

For Southern Governments

The pursuit of a development model based on economic growth through equity, social justice and democracy.

Improvement in incomes and asset holdings of the poor (including land reform) and the protection and strengthening of sectors that are of critical importance to the poor (e.g. staple food production, essential industries). This might necessitate an emphasis on selective import substitution, and some regulation of foreign exchange investment in human capital prioritizing sustainable development.

Pursuit of sound economic management (i.e. curbing of imbalances etc.), but with overall objectives of guaranteeing the survival of the poor in the short term and ensuring their interests are prioritized in the long term.

Support for grassroots democracy (not just the exporting of a Westminster style of multi-party democracy, but an approach which helps foster widespread popular participation and a strong civil society. This includes affording citizens basic rights, such as freedom of association, the right to have a say in decision-making, accountability of the state, access to information etc.).

Guarantee of full human rights and social justice.

Peaceful co-operation with neighbours and the formation of strong regional groupings to achieve the above.

11

DEFINING GOOD INSTITUTIONS

It was a long felt need to prepare a list of good institutions under NGO's fold. Objective of developing conceptual clarity on the question of good, not so good, and bad institutions in KVI or NGO sector is basically the following:

1. For expansion of rural industries programme to have a list of good institutions which can be depended upon for the extension, servicing, raw material storage, training, marketing etc. of the cluster of villages around it.
2. As and when linkages are established with Education Department for imparting vocational training under 10+2 or any other programmes of Education Department our institutions can be the nodal centres in the vicinity of 5 to 10 km. depending upon the location.
3. Since many of the KVI Boards & NGOs have not been able to give satisfactory performance in the field of monitoring, extension, servicing these institutions may be developed by requesting them to take up new and new industries for acting as mini V.I. clusters for giving integrated service.
4. When the question of analytical data base for decentralised sector comes we may have to identify good institutions for helping us in monitoring, dissemination etc. in those areas.
5. Since annually many institutions are being funded by KVI sector through KVIC/KVIB and many more like minded decentralised industries are being developed through other funding institutions which we do not know because of lack of regular interaction or sharing of information. These informations may be circulated to other institutions so that at local level atleast some institutions are available for giving them help.

6. As and when rural industrialisation is accepted as essential aspect for rural development, these institutions should be centres for further growth within the area. For this also it is essential that our new institutions are kept informed about the parameters to become good institution so that they know in whcih area they must pay better attention for becoming good institutions.
7. A lot of institutions are being sanctioned and set up every year by State Boards. Unless there is a cover for backward/forward support for the individuals they could not survive in isolation. If we identify some of the good institutions we can ask them to give backward and forward linkages to the large number of individuals who are being sanctioned funds every year by Boards.

In this connection, E.C.R. Section has made an attempt to compile the list of good institutions, as suggested by different Industry Directorates. However, different norms were followed by these Directorates for determining good institutions. In this background it was felt necessary to evolve common criteria for determining good institutions. In view of this, a meeting was called in C.E.O.'s chamber on 6th August, 1991 for finalising the criteria to be adopted for determining the good institutions. The following officers attended the meeting:

1. Chief Executive Officer.
2. Jt. Chief Executive Officer.
3. Dy. C.E.O. (E.C.R.)
4. Dy. C.E.O. (Khadi)
5. Director (Training)
6. Director (Handmade Paper)
7. Dy. Director (Village Oil)
8. Dy Director (Hindi Cell)
9. Dy. Director I/C E.C.R.

After detailed deliberations on the issue it was decided to categorise the institutions by giving marks under various criteria. It was also decided to adopt the following criteria with the marks indicated against each.

Item	*Detail*	*Maximum marks*
1	2	3
1. Location	Rural location of the institution will be entitled for full marks if it is beyond 50 kms. from district headquarters and 5 marks for institutions in between 25 and 50 kms. However, the institutions in hill, border and tribal areas will be entitled for full marks irrespective of the distance of location.	10
2. Participation of SC/ST women and Ex-service man	If the institution is working exclusively for, or managed exclusively by any one of the said category will be entitled for full marks. For other institutions the marks should be proportionate to the participation of these categories.	10
3. Capacity utilisation. (We may study the capacity utilisation to know to what extent the good institutions could utilise the equipment and machineries provided to them when they achieve their targets of production & employment)	The institutions having cent per cent of utilisation of the installed capacity in the last 3 years will be entitled for full marks. For other institutions the marks will be proportionate to the average capacity utilisation for the last 3 years.	10
4. Internal resource generation. (Some village industries have surplus or	The ratio of internal resource generated by the Institution in relation to total resources available with them for their disposal will	10

1		2	3
	profits. Whether the institutions are repaying the loans fully and utilising these surpluses as reserves for expansion of their programmes further without coming to KVIC for additonal funds is intended from this study.	determine the marks on this criteria. However, the marks can be divided into 5 each and considered for (i) surplus and earned (ii) other internal resources.	
5.	Bank Finance (Whether schemes are bankable will be known by knowing the extent of Bank Finance availed by the Institution.)	Marks will be given as per the percentage share of actual availment of Bank Finance against the Eligibility Certificate issued.	10
6.	Training	Out of the total number of persons trained by the institution the percentage of trainees taken up self-employment will determine the quantum of marks on this item.	10
7.	Marketing/Export	The marks should be equally divided to internal marketing and export at the rate of 5 each and the marks should be determined as per the percentage share of export in the total volume of sales or the internal disposal in the total volume of sales.	10
8.	R&D Quality Improvement, New Products, Quality control facility, Product development etc.	Here an assessment may be made on the positive impact of these items in the functioning of the institutions and marks should be determined accordingly.	10

1	2	3
9. Accountability, Timely auditing etc.	Accountability of the institution will be decided by considering the utilisation of funds, repayment of loan, generation of new employment opportunity etc. Here full marks may be awarded to the institution who are earning profit for the last 3 years and whose utilisation of funds and repayment including payment of interest are as per norms.	10
10. Reporting	Regular reporting or any other special achievements made by the institutions may be put under this category. Regular submission of quarterly reports, annual reports and any other similar reports required by KVIC will be entitled for full marks. However, negative marks will be given appropriately, for irregular reporting.	10

PART-II

ARRANGEMENT ACTION BLUEPRINT RECOMMENDATIONS

12

FIELD VISITS
Tour Report of Ratnagiri District

(District chosen by Dr. (Mrs.) Najma Heptullah, Chairperson of Parliamentarians' Forum for Human Development)

A visit was made with Chairperson of the Forum to Ratnagiri District in May end to finalise the proposal under MPs Local Area Development Scheme.

Meetings were held with the Members of the Nagar Palika, district administration, beneficiaries, school teachers and distinguished members of the society. Various proposals were considered in consultation with the district administration and Nagar Palika for the construction of the school building, road, girls' college, computer training institute and other areas of pressing requirements.

It was also felt by the Chairperson that the possibilities may be explored for creating awareness among the women and training them in food processing as this area is growing mangoes on a large scale. Mangoes from Ratnagiri are considered to be very prized in India and abroad. This is the world famous variety of mango called 'Alfonso', and it commands a considerable premium in the market. This area is also growing cashew on a large scale. But unfortunately, this district lacks facilities of a modern food processing centre. It was felt that if proper training can be given to the women, substantive value addition can be done to the mango and cashew produce.

This area is located on the western coast of the Arabian sea and has a small port. The status of the port and facilities are not adequate. Since this city is located on way to Goa, it can be developed into a tourist centre for overnight stay after seven hours journey from Bombay by road. It is a small hilly area located on a scenic location. The main occupation of the people is fishing. The conditions for this occupation can also be modernised. Upgrading the transportation facilities, both land borne and sea borne would go a long way in bringing prosperity to the area.

The Chairperson felt that development plans can be considered on above lines. So far this district is not even linked by a railway. The Konkan Railway is under construction and would take some time before it is fully operational.

Dr. Najma Heptullah, Rajya Sabha (Hon. M.P.) for District Ratnagiri (Maharashtra)

- -- Multipurpose hall to be used for adult education, literacy and vocational training programmes.
- -- Drinking water
- -- Creche
- -- Roads leading to blocks
- -- Causeway linking with difficult terrains
- -- Sanitation

Interactions about Raghubir Nagar

During the last 16-17 days I have been trying to get the feel of the stàte of affair through various meetings and field visits. I also had the opportunity of attending a meeting with UNDP officials in Water and Sanitary project, World Bank. The meeting was hardly useful and I am sorry to mention here that there was utter frustration among the field officials due to directionlessness. My query about the total amount spent on consultancies remained unreplied.

As a last resort, I took time off despite my busy schedule to visit Raghuvir Nagar, had discussions, with Mr. Manjeet Singh, local officials and people and also exchanged views with Mr. Vidyarthi, head of a NGO. On 29 September I discussed for about one hour with Mr. Singh about various criticalities of initiating a short-term work.

The summary of the discussions is as under:

1. The traditional approach will not help and there is need of transparent, replicable, entrepreneurship led initiatives by involving women and senior citizens of the slums.
2. Some programmes like drinking water, hand pumps, schools, sulabh sochalayas, vocational centre, marketing led, bio-gas etc. could be taken up in the first phase. The infrastructure could be created by joint funding. Since, the beneficiaries would also be the incharge of running and managing it for which a nominal user charges must be in-built from the very beginning. List of existing under utilised resources must be prepared so that they could be utilised.

3. Philosophical base of intentions must rely on practical aspects of the *slum creations.* Simultaneously, efforts should be made to study why these people came from rural areas to such dirty, filthy places fit for pigs. Well meaning people have a challenge here if they are really sincere. Hence, I suggested that under Mr. Manjeet Singh, a steering group be formed including Mr. Kohli and others. This is to see that the golden opportunity offered by this synergistic effort is not lost off.
4. There is also a need to learn from past experience in Proyog Vihar and Ekta Vihar. Since, Mr. Manjeet has worked for about 14 years around this slum activities, it is high time he is requested to codify various issues to be kept in mind for developing learning to work together (LTWT) and issues in replication. This is essential to institutionalise experiments from cost effectiveness, organising the beneficiaries and developing overall culture etc. For next programme it would be better if PARCEL approach is adopted.
5. A surprising news came to me that in Delhi alone electricity worth *750 crores is stolen* per year. Roughly it is 2 to 3 crore rupees per day. But these are problems of multi-dimensional, well entranged inefficiency, lethargy and despirited servicing systems. Hence, it is worth if a modest beginning could be made as Father of the Nation used to say *one step is enough for me.*
6. About funding part we discussed that if replicable models have to be developed, then funds must come from various sources so that monitoring is also multi-institutional. Hence, we felt if two small projects could be taken up say worth 25 lakhs or so with people's contribution a modest beginning could be made. To carry out comparative analysis Bugla Matchi and Raghubir Nagar may be considered. This also offers multi party involvement of the Hon. MLAs and the MPs. This can be decided as per the experience and possibility identification by Mr. Manjeet.
7. Before I close, I would like to mention that probably the slums are direct creation of the industrial policies pursued so far. There are recorded warnings available since the last 125 years or so warning the long term losses to society, environment, morale and overall sustainability of the universe. The blend of multi dimensional and multi disciplinary, holistic plan of action may be able to show some rays of hope.
8. After meeting Mr. Manjeet Singh twice and discussing with

some of the role players my conviction is further cemented that this initiative of Parliamentarians' Forum and UN systems desire and urge and compulsion to learn to work together would definitely result in better sustainable output. Mr. Singh has agreed to head the planning-cum-action team for better results and coordination.

Tour Report to the Field Visit in the Constituency of Shri Saifuddin Chowdhary, MP, Lok Sabha--Katwa Constituency (District: Hoogli and Bardhwan)

The team from Delhi consisting, UNDP, Mr. Kamal Taori, IAS and Project Coordinator, Dr. Neeru Misra, left for Calcutta on 9th August, 1995 by Indian Airlines Flight at 10.00 a.m. After reaching Calcutta at around one O'clock, efforts were made to hold a meeting with the UNICEF office in Calcutta. The meeting was fixed with Officer In Charge, Shri Murlidharan and Mrs. Shikha Wadhwa, Project Officer at 3.00 p.m. During the discussion it was found that UNICEF Calcutta is involved deeply into the grassroot development plan with the Government of West Bengal, particularly in these two districts. UNICEF has already held demonstration beautifying class rooms, teachers motivation camp, parents teaching association, training of gram panchayat, sanitary mart scheme and other ICDS, DWACRA and many other programmes. Mrs. Shikha Wadhwa joined the team for the field visit which started on 10th August, 1995 around 9.00 a.m. from Calcutta along with MP Shri Saifuddin Chowdhary.

10.8.95

Approximately 123 kilometers from Calcutta the team halted at Kalna Tehsil where the meetings were held with SDM Kalna, Vice Chairman, Kalna Municipality; Chairman, Kalna Municipality; Deputy Magistrate, Kalna; Joint BDO, Kalna II block and other members of the Municipality. The visits were made to the following schools;

- -- Mahishamardini Uchcha Balika Vidyalaya
- -- Datta Dariyatan Swami Vivekanand Vidhyamandir
- -- Sanerdanga Ramakrishna Vidyamandir
- -- Shashibala Uchcha Balika Vidyalaya
- -- Shri Shri Migamananda Uchcha Vidyalaya

11.8.95

In the morning the first visit was made to site where a road linking Lichutula to Talbore More (75 kilometers) has been made into a pucca road. The total project cost is Rs. 2,12,000. After the visit a meeting was held in the BDO's office along with the local panchayat people, MLA, Shri Biren Ghosh (Dhatri Gram, Bardhwan Distt.) and with the engineer Mr. Devasis Nandi. MLA of Poorvasthali Shri Manoranjan Nath Bhattacharya accompanied the team to the respective schools in his Assembly Constituency. The team left for Katwa for the night stay.

12.8.95 (Katwa-Monteshwar)

The meeting was held with the local MLA Mr. Anjan Chatterjee and Gautam Banerjee, Sabhapati Shri Surat Ali, Katwa Panchayat Samiti. The team left for site visits.

-- Churpuri Village High School
-- Badla High School
-- Badla Girls High School
-- Akalpouse Saratchandra Uchcha Vidyalaya, etc.

Chandpur

The meeting was held with SDO Shri G. Bayan; BDO, Shri Shantanu Shah and MLA. MP has sanctioned his money for the pucca road which will connect to nine villages and in total a population of 14,000 will be benefited by this road. This is a predominantly minority area. Its main inhabitants are agricultural labourers, owners, blacksmith and carpenters. It was desired that if a metal road is made, it will protect transport etc. Presently, the Health Centres are also at the distance of three kilometers. The social forestry can also be developed in this area. A sum of Rs. 3,50,000 has been sanctioned from the MP's fund and Rs. 70,000 has been contributed by the beneficiaries. A visit was made to Dr. Panchanan Roy Vocational Training Institute, Monteshwar where a training of two wheeler, electrical, pump setting, repair, carpentry, pisciculture is being given to the desirous students. This has been made by an individual out of government loan of 7 lakh which is to be repaid. MLA of the area Shri Motilal Mohan, Sabhapati of Panchayat Samiti, Monteshwar also joined the group. The students in this training institute are mainly from the TRYSEM (Training of Rural Youth for Self-Employment-below poverty line). They are granted a stipend of

Rs. 350 per month.

A visit was made at Vaishnav Daga and Shri Gurango High School. The strength of the students is 575. Later that evening the team reached Bardhwan District and had the meeting with District Magistrate, Shri M.L. Meena; Sabhaadhipati, Shri Madan Ghosh; ADM, Shri Rajiv Dubey and BDO. The experiences of the visit were shared and advices during further discussion were taken from the government officials to prioritise the development programme for future. The district officials suggested the programmes which can be taken up in the area to promote local handicrafts, agro-based activities, jute production and processing, irrigation, particularly in the area of Katwa I and II, Kalna I and II and Poorvasthali since they being the agricultural based areas.

The Gist of the Discussion and the Observations

-- This area is agriculturally very rich. Paddy being the main crop is grown twice a year. Jute is also surplus in this area but presently it is being sent to the main industries and there is no local facility for promoting processing of jute at local level. It was felt if the promotion of jute at the local level is taken up then the growers will be benefited.

-- Agro based activities like animal husbandry, hatchery, sericulture, poultry, fishery should be taken up since the production of milk is low. West Bengal being the land of ponds and every village is having 4-5 ponds in their area, it was felt that fisheries can be promoted in more scientific and organised manner.

-- All women cooperatives to promote the loom and production of tangile (Taant) will be very useful since the villages in Kalna and Poorvasthali are having loom practically in every house and production of tangile saris is going on, but there is no benefit to the local population since the market is not locally available. If they are given proper training and more scope for marketing is explored, the local weavers will be benefited.

-- Another area needing attention is the lack of drinking water. The water level in West Bengal has gone very low and lack of hygienic drinking water is causing health problem

-- UNICEF representative suggested that their promotion of 'Sanitary Mart Programme' has been very successful in Hoogli district and DM expressed his willingness to promote the same programme in his area as well.

-- DM also suggested that some of his officers can visit the district of 24 parganas to learn from the experience of UNICEF activities done at Vishnupur area for ICDS Food Programme and the same programme can be implemented in his area as well.

Suggestions

-- DM was requested to identify 10 to 15 villages or 4-5 panchayat areas to take up the activities of the Forum/UNDP for the developmental programmes. This will enable us to monitor the activities in a proper way and also to take up the area as a model for further developmental programmes. The UNICEF representative was very encouraging and she was requested to send us her suggestions to achieve success in the areas of education, health, women, child programmes in which UNICEF has already done a great work in West Bengal.

-- As per the suggestions of the District Magistrate, it is suggested that agro-based activities will be very useful in this area and since the production of milk is low not due to any other reasons but all the land has been cultivated into paddy growing area, there is hardly any land left for animal grazing. Therefore, production of animal food and support to animal husbandry will be useful.

-- Jute being the local raw material if something can be done for the jute industry.

-- There are certain areas in Kalna which are very good for textile, carpentry and terra cotta work. If the production of the handicraft is developed through marketing, the production can go up at a higher level.

-- It was observed that the community based organisation is very strong in West Bengal. It has given kick to the ongoing literacy programme in the area. The gender balance in the schools is very encouraging and the involvement of the community people is shown in the construction work going on under MP's Local Area Development Scheme where Committee has been formed and each village is being supervised by block people/engineers/ panchayat committee/teachers/parents. Material is also being procured by this committee from the local market. The contribution and finances has been given by all the people and where it has not been possible, the local population have contributed by putting up the labour which is a very unique feature and successful instrument to develop other projects in the area.

Mr. Saifuddin Chowdhary, CPI (M), Katwa, West Bengal (Priority by Hon. M.P.)

- -- School building
- -- Library
- -- Roads leading to villages
- -- Girls School
- -- Rural electrification
- -- Bus stand
- -- Construction of sub station (electricity)

Action Lessons from "Katwa--West Bengal"

Strengths

(1) Grass-root Organisation and Transparency;
(2) Literacy rate Good;
(3) Multiplier and Contributory Systems prevalent;
(4) Rural Economy-with surplus paddy, Jute, Fisheries, Potatoes, Banana, Bamboo-Handloom Weavers in pockets-concentrated.
(5) Alternate-Para Teacher system prevailing;

Need for "Entrepreneurship"

Resources

(A) Tanks Everywhere

(1) Marketing, Production & Training Centres;
(2) Plantation;
(3) Rainfall;
(4) Fishery;
(5) Mango;
(6) Jackfruit;
(7) Minor Irrigation;
(8) Tourism;
(9) Beautification;
(10) Floriculture & Exnort Potential;
(11) Dairy;
(12) Bio-Gas;

(B) Tourism at Kalna

(1) Old 108 temples;
(2) Ganges;
(3) Tourist home of Panchayat;
(4) Hotel;
(5) Transport;
(6) Guide;
(7) Joint Literature;
(8) Bankable Servicing;

(C) Non Farm Sector

Effective Technology near school through M.P.T. Concept

(1) Paddy;
(2) Jute;
(3) Oil Seeds;
(4) Potato;
(5) Banana;
(6) Computer;
(7) Communication;
(8) Marketing;

(D) Linkage with on-going UNDP Programme

(1) HMP
(2) Jute;
(3) Leather;

(E) Internal Resource Generation Road Projects

(1) Internal Resource Generation-Cost Sharing;
(2) Plantation;
(3) Bunds;

(F) Role of Organised Sector in the Longer Run
(G) Role of ARTEP/I.L.O.-Past Project
(H) Model Building around school-Katwa

(1) Building Biogas, Plantation, Toilet, Computer.

About Jabalpur

World Food Programme has ambitious programme in Jabalpur district. Shri Sharavan K. Patel, Congress (I) Member of Parliament from Jabalpur (Madhya Pradesh) had given the following priority areas for Member of Parliament Local Area Development Scheme:

1. Multi purpose Hall (to be used for health centre, AIDs counselling, Library, Creche, Vocational Training Programme)
2. Drinking water
3. Roads leading to blocks
4. School complex
5. Sanitation programme
6. Post literacy centre

During discussions he mentioned lack of will power, need for self-employment, and sufficient input and thus motivation through vocational education on raw material based value addition. He also mentioned the massive misuse of funds in the construction programme and how there is total exploitation at all levels. After discussions the following action plan emerged:

1. Start rural entrepreneurial programme based on marketing potentials;
2. Dialogue with -- Local Office Bearers
   -- Rural Technology Providers
   -- Financiers

   For new innovations; - Action Plan
3. Integrate non-farm sector with nearby schools for income generation activities like Dairy, Nursery, Biogas, Tourism, Technology, Oil-Seed Crusher, Soap making, Jute Value Addition, *Neem*-Seed Collection.
4. Volunteers and low-cost practical consultants-(local thrust);
5. Study of watershed management initiatives with World Food Programme as Nodal Agency;
6. Thrust on tribals, basic education and other neglected spheres;
7. Joint Management areas.

13

MP/UN FORUM FOR INTEGRATED DEVELOPMENT

WFP-Assisted Tribal Development Projects

1. The projects operate in areas where people depend upon forest resources for their livelihood. These people belong mainly to tribal and low caste groups. They have limited agricultural facilities and employment opportunities. The RPDS and PDS systems are ineffective in most of these areas; and where they exist people cannot always afford to buy the food entitlements (that are in any case insufficient to meet needs). Combined with rapid deterioration of the forests, representing a decline of the resource base of the people depending upon them, these factors make such groups vulnerable to chronic food insecurity. Women and children are even worse off.
2. The main employers in such areas are the Forest Departments. WFP provides food to casual labourers employed by them. They may opt for a WFP family ration, for which part of their wages is deducted. As the value of the WFP family ration is higher than that of the wage deduction, the net effect is an income transfer to the labourers. Moreover, the availability of easily accessible food is a major attraction to the workers. Through this direct food assistance, the projects address short-term food insecurity.
3. The funds thus generated are put in a fund, administered and accounted for by the WFP Project Unit of each state's Forest Department. They are to be invested in a variety of schemes aiming at community development. The sectors in which schemes can be funded are indicated in the "contract" between the Government and WFP, which is called the Plan of Operations.
4. So far, there have been quite a number of sectors that were eligible for funding, like *education, road improvement, health,*

drinking water supply, irrigation facilities, plantations for fuelwood and fodder. Proposals for funding are submitted by the Divisional Forest Officers to the FD/WFP Project Unit. After a first screening, proposals are submitted to the State Level Coordinating Committee (SLCC) for approval. WFP, along with the FD and concerned Department, is member of the SLCC.

5. This approach has been very useful in providing villages with required schemes. It also has contributed to a better rapport between the villages and the Forest Departments. The latter are shifting progressively from a regulatory to a participatory role. They recognise that it is only through genuine people's participation in forest management can they hope enventually to achieve sustained forest protection. In this evolution of ideas and action the Forest Departments have found the availability of WFP generated funds to be a very suitable mechanism to win the villagers' confidence.
6. It is now time to build on the experience gained and to further improve fund investment. A couple of areas for that have been identified. One of these is to clarify the overall objectives of the WFP inputs, both food and funds. This has been absent until now, although tacitly understood. This can be seen from the multitude of sectors the funds can be invested in.
7. Some other area of concern is the following:
   Proposals for investment are mostly identified by the DFO rather than the villages and are in general of an infrastructural nature. They are submitted to the SLCC on an adhoc basis, and treated on a first-come first serve basis. This has led to:
   (i) the inclusion of schemes that were not always need based;
   (ii) a lack of a sense of ownership by the population resulting in a lack of maintenance; and
   (iii) the risk that equally poor and poorer villages have been left out due to a lack of scheme identification (less active DFO etc.) Moreover, as the investments are spread over the entire project area, the impact at village level is mostly rather limited.
8. As a result of successful experiments in Rajasthan and Gujarat, the following approach has therefore now been adopted by the Government and WFP in Orissa and Bihar, and it is expected that a similar approach will be adopted for the projects in Madhya Pradesh and Uttar Pradesh.
   (a) the investment of the fund is considered as a sub-project,

and focussed on improvement of sustainable household food security, as WFP's overall mandate. Thus, rather than a broad variety of sectors, only those would be eligible for investment that lead directly to improved and sustainable food security at household level, and for which no other source of funding is available;

(b) investments will no longer cover the entire project area, but a limited number of villages only;

(c) one of the criteria for the selection of villages will be the functioning of a JFM Committee. Through these committees, people will participate in all stages of project design and implementation, including maintenance also.

9. Through this concentrated investment strategy, both geographically and sector-wise, the impact of the investment at each village will be greater than would have been the case otherwise.
10. The basis for the investments will be micro-plans, prepared for and by those villages, based on identified needs. By involving people directly in identifying the requirements, a sense of ownership would be introduced, which would increase the chances for sustainability.
11. An important pre-requisite for success is proper training at all levels, i.e. Forest Department and villages, in development and gender issues and the like, which is all the more necessary as the focus of investments will move from infrastructure to development, with special attention to the needs of women.
12. Identified needs would include all sectors, but the generated funds would only finance the food security related ones. Other schemes might be taken up in some cases, but these should in principle be financed from other sources, e.g. government sources. Investment from the generated funds might in those cases be made conditional on the financing of the other items by the Government. In connection with the MP/UN Forum, however, these other schemes could also be provided by the other UN agencies, in addition to the MP's fund and Government funds such as those of the Collector, and private (local) financer. It is also important to ensure a contribution by the population itself, to increase their sense of ownership of the investments. This contribution could be in cash or in kind.
13. Dr. Taori asked what our spending level was in Jabalpur, and what we needed from other agencies. At a very rough estimate we may be able to spend about five lakh rupees in the district.

It is not easy to say how much more money is needed without a comprehensive development plan, along the lines described above. We can, however indicate some of the identified requirements for the forestry projects in general that may be difficult to introduce. These could be taken up by other agencies. One of these is the establishment of a marketing mechanism for forest and agricultural produce, once income generating activities at village produce a marketable product. Another possibility is the creation of a revolving credit fund for individuals or groups.

Coimbatore

Introduction

The basic requirement for take off *Gandhian model* of integrated replicable model is *available.* The strength, weakness, opportunity, threat analysis of working with Shanti Ashram need no elaboration. The following activities could be immediately considered.

1. Around BUND
2. Block Development Programme for resourceless.
3. Support services including low cost practical consultancies (LCPC), Data Storage, Rural enterprises Development-cum-Marketing Production Training Centres--all with special 'thrust target' groups.
4. A non-violent *waging of peace is possible* under the able guidance and supervision of Dr. Aram

Action Required

1. Clarification of Mission
2. Success Parameters both in short term and long term.
3. Steering team, Evaluating team and PARCEL team.
4. Other support systems and sharing of constituencies for example major UN systems like ILO, WFP etc. could be given one each to have compact, focused, comparable, competitive model development based upon pre determined objective criteria.
5. Evaluating some so called, widely acclaimed, successful models from various angles for drawing lessons for our effort. This means inviting major role players to decide what should be done and what should not be ventured.

Caution
For every ailment under the sun
There is a remedy or
There is none
If there is one
Try to find it
If there is none
Never mind it

Objectives

1. To assess the scope of synergyising the efforts of UN agencies and MP's Parliamentarians Forum (MP LAD scheme) in the development process of the MP constituency/*area.*
2. To develop a blue print/action plan for implementing the synergystic programmes for six identified MP areas/ constituencies, viz. Jabalpur, Kalna (Katwa), West Bengal; Coimbatore; Raghubir Nagar (Delhi); South Dunajpur, West Bengal, Ratnagiri, Maharashtra.
3. To provide an overview of the efforts needed for appropriate intersectoral linkages for implementation.

Methodology

The methodology adopted by the consultant as per the terms of reference were.

- Visit to few constituencies of the MPs alongwith the UN team, representative of the MP Forum and local district administration officials.
- Meeting with different UN agencies in Delhi.
- Meeting with various development agencies of Government of India.
- Collection of secondary data about the programmes of UN agencies and Govt. of India at the field level. (upto the extent available)

Observations and Analysis

(a) There seems to be total absence of knowledge about each other's programmes in UN agencies and Govt. of India agencies. This became apparent to the consultant during his field visits and interactions with various officials in and outside the UN Systems. Thus, the level of cooperation and coordination among agencies is very low. There is limited interaction and coordination even among UN agencies working on common programmes/areas of focus, resulting in wastage/under utilization of huge amounts of funds and loss of potential opportunities for area focused integrated development.

(b) Extremely limited data is available at UN agencies about their investment in programme at the district, block etc. level.

(c) Unlimited potential exists for synergysing the efforts of the UN agencies and MP LAD schemes for development by designing programmes based on the local resources, both natural and human, for solving local development problems.

(d) Efforts have been made to design a blue print and action plan for immediate implementation with an eye on the needs.

The basic foundation for my recommendations is in tune with the declaration adopted on 20 February 1995 by the MPs Forum for Human Development and is based on Gandhian model of development on area specific planning requirements. Development in their declaration adopted on 20 February 1995 at the conclusion of the pre-World Social Summit consultation.

(e) Therefore I have assessed, upto the extent possible within the time frame, the local strengths and weaknesses and opportunities and formulated plans which are reflected in the detailed blue print/POA presented in tabular form for three MP areas: Jabalpur, Katwa/Kalna and Coimbatore.

Proposal for the other three MP areas where the consultant had no opportunity for direct intervention with stakeholders or a site visit have actually been finalised upto the suggestive level only, based upon available information.

The Blue Print

Introduction to Blue Print/POA

The blue prints/POA in regard to local problems as perceived by M.P.s and others and recommended activities by the consultant have been prepared for Katwa, Jabalpur and Coimbatore and are appended after the end of the chapter.

The blue print has been divided under four different heads viz. (a) economic, (b) social, (c) socio-economic, and (d) management and control.

The introduction of each of the area, analysis of the programmes on the basis of Blue Prints etc are given below.

M.P. LAD Priority

The social and economic activities to be taken up on priority basis, as communicated by M.Ps to U.N.D.P. for Katwa, Jabalpur and Coimbatore are given below.

	Social	*Economic*
Katwa	1. School Building	1. School Building
	2. Library	2. Library
	3. Roads leading to blocks/villages	3. Road leading to villages
	4. Health	4. Girls schools
	5. Rural electrification	5. Rural electrification
	6. Bus stand	6. Bus stand
	7. Construction of sub-station (Electricity)	7. Construction of sub-station
Jabalpur	1. Multipurpose Hall (to be used for Health centre, AIDS coun-celling, Library, Creche and Vocational training programmes)	1. Multipurpose Hall
	2. Drinking Water programme	2. Drinking Water programmes
	3. Roads leading to Blocks	3. Roads leading to Blocks
	4. School complex	4. School complex
	5. Sanitation programmes	5. Rural electrification
	6. Post literacy centre	6. Bus stand
		7. Construction of sub-station
		8. Need of Women Entrepreneurship Development
		9. R&D Centre
		10. Basic Education
		11. Employment generation

		Social		Economic
Coimbatore	1.	Multipurpose Hall	1.	Multipurpose Hall
	2.	Drinking Water programmes	2.	Drinking Water programmes
	3.	Roads leading to blocks	3.	Roads leading to blocks
	4.	School complex	4.	School complex
	5.	Rural electrification	5.	Rural electrification
	6.	Bus stand	6.	Bus stand
	7.	Construction of sub-station	7.	Construction of Sub-station
	8.	Need of Women Entrepreneurship Development	8.	Need of Women Entrepreneurship Development
	9.	R&D Centre	9.	R&D Centre
	10.	Basic Education	10.	Basic Education
	11.	Employment generation	11.	Employment generation

It is obvious from above, that there are many activities which are categorised in both. The difference lies in absorbing or contributing capacity of the people. Even today in most of the areas school, hospital services, water facilities etc are available both through 100 per cent government funds and also through totally private initiatives. Best model would be that one shifted from social to economic. These activities fulfil from economic enterprises. As level of development and paying capacity of beneficiaries increases a shift from charity to creativity and conference building develops. The shift can never been sudden but with proper appreciation, policy support and holistic implementation. This means creating those conditions the people become their own master in the right sense to ensure this shift through planning, action, research, codification, extension and loaning model. The M.P. LAD schemes, U.N. systems and people's initiatives through Panchayati Raj with NGOs and state agencies could become an effective model for replication. It is obvious that with better convergence, pooling of resources with active involvement of beneficiaries both in supervision and knowledge, it is possible to have better impact in lesser time.

Introduction to MP Areas

Katwa/Kalna (W.B.)

(a) Information Source

1. Visit of the team consisting of UN officials, the consultant and

Dr. Neeru Mishra
2. Note on the Area by the District Magistrate
3. Interaction with the MP., Mr. Saifuddin Choudhury
4. Press clippings by Mrs. Nag. Divisional PR Manager, Tata Steel

(b) Analysis

As observed by the team, the area has strength in infrastructure, locational advantage, leadership with commitment and mass acceptance, alongwith natural resources, and weaknesses in ignorance, lack of entrepreneurial skills, lack of marketing orientation etc.

On the basis of the above and Blue Print for an integrated social and economic development, I recommend marketing of value-added products produced from,

- Local Resources by Local Population, By marketing at Local, Regional and National Market through the following programmes:

Social programmes, these are essential for developing the basic capacity of the vulnerable groups like children, mothers etc. and hence emphasis on basic education, drinking water, health etc. is very essential. UNICEF would be the obvious lead agency in these sectors (It has a number of ongoing programmes in the area) with possible technical comments and support by WHO/UNESCO/Water and Sanitation group.

However, as the primary problem that need to be solved on priority basis is *Ignorance* and *Mental Blocks* I recommend.

	Economic Programmes	Supported by UN Agency	Others
	1	2	3
1.	Jute-based Value added products	UNDP Spl programmes	
2.	Fishery	UNDP	
3.	Paddy	UNDP, APCTT	KVIC
4.	Leather	UNDP, APCTT	KVIC
5.	Bio-Gas	APCTT	NGOs
6.	Tourism	UNESCO	NGOs
7.	Hand-loom	UNDP	NGOs
8.	Plantation/forestry	WFP/FAO	NGOs
9.	Marketing (Exports)	UNDP (Limited involvement of other relevant UN specialised agencies to be explored for the above.)	NGOs

	1	2	3
10.	Field visits of opinion leaders to places like Wardha, Anand, Ralegaon etc. for MIND-OPENING and places of educational and cultural value	UNESCO/UNDP	Edn. Deptt
11.	Innovative Education programmes matching local needs, (Modifying the UGC-CBSE courses) Edn. Deptt.		UNESCO/ UNICEF
12.	NGOs for innovative Methods of learning	UNICEF/ UNESCO	Edn. Deptt.
13.	Assessment of Past Develop-mental Work	UNDP/WB UNDP/APCTT	All Con-cerned
14.	Technology needs assessment for women	(UNISOI/UNIDO)	DST & NGOs
15.	Preparation of literature on Kalna for family tourism.		Jointly by Chamber of Commerce, Kalna and UNDP

Jabalpur

Information Source

1. Visit of the team consisting of UN officials, the Consultant and Dr. Neeru Mishra
2. Visit of Mr. Ranjan Mohapatra (Provides project design support to Consultant) to Jabalpur
3. Note of WFP on Jabalpur Perceptions
   (No report from District Magistrate and District Forest Officer available despite reminders)

Analysis (Brief SWOT)

As observed by the team the strengths and weaknesses as recommended in the blue print, the socio-economic backwardness of Jabalpur can be tackled jointly through programmes based on Local Resources like.

- Forest products,
- Limited water resources,
- Wasteland etc. through Mass Participation, to generate (a) income and (b) Facilities for Social Development.

There is need to develop multi-diciplinary NGOS or self-help groups to take up various social, economic activities

	Programmes	*Supported by UN Agency: Others*	
1.	Social Programmes	Since the basic requirements for take off are not readily available, it is essential to develop models in all areas of POA.	
2.	Economic Activity		
3.	Value-added forest products marketing through cooperatives for mass participation to generate income and forest protection	WFP	Forest Dept. & Women's groups
4.	Mush-room cultivation	WFP	Forest Dept.
5.	Bio-Gas Plants	WFP	KVIC, Min. of Energy, Forest Deptt.
6.	Watershed Management for irrigation, fishery, Social Forestry etc.	WFP	Forest Dept. Irrigation Deptt.
7.	Wasteland Development	FAO	Forest Deptt. Wasteland Dev. Board, Neem Foundation, Corporate Sector, Drip irrigation.

However as the primary problem that needs to be solved on priority basis is *Ignorance and Mental Blocks,* I recommend.

8.	Field Visits of opinion leaders to places like *Wardha, Anand, Ralegaon* etc. for Mind-opening & places of Educational & cultural value	UNESCO/UNDP	Edn. Deptt.
9.	Innovative Education programmes matching local needs. (modifying the UGC-CBSE courses)	UNESCO/UNICEF	Edn. Deptt.
10.	NGOs for innovative Methods of learning	UNICEF/UNESCO	Edn. Deptt.

11. Assessment of Past Development work — UNDP/WB

Coimbatore

This area has greatest advantage in having Shanti Ashram as a nodal agency working for convergence of various components of sustainable rural development. There is 100% literacy and Dr. Aram, Hon. M.P., has proposed various activities leading to total poverty eradication in Perur Block.

Based upon the Gandhian model through Shanti Ashram and other women's groups working in these areas as well as recommended in the blue print, it is possible in a short time to develop models which can meet the tests of our time.

The following activities can be considered:

1. *Social Programmes*
   - (i) Schools with post literacy activities and UNICEF programmes
   - (ii) Informal sector activity including sanitation drinking water, etc. with requisite design inputs from UNICEF/Water & Sanitation Group etc.
2. *Economic Activity*
   - (i) There is need to start some marketing organisation like "Shanti Marketing Organisation" to basically have PARCEL type of action research to study issues in informal sector development.
   - (ii) Various economic programmes for empowerment of women can be started through better innovative training and marketing practices
   - (iii) A vocational education centre would also be useful.
3. *Programmes Around Bund*

This is a socio-economic programme which with proper coordination, integration and vision can be a very replicable and self employment generating programme. The details have to be worked out on the following lines:

Objectives of Bund Programme

Short Term – Combating Health Hazard
Long Term – Convergence, Income generation and hope multiplication
This model will need involvement of following:

- – Rotarians-NGO's Volunteers
- – Bankers
- – Administration
- – Industrialist
- – Trainers and Evaluators
- – Local bodies

Implementation

For implementing the above blueprint, we need to have a professional team/agency,

(a) to conduct bench mark studies,
(b) to fine tune the blue print/POA,
(c) to assist and guide the local authorities in implementing the programmes as catalysts or
(d) to take up the implementation task on contract basis,
(e) to develop control systems for monitoring the programmes.

These teams/professional development agencies/consultants can coordinate with Distt. administration, MPs Forum/MPs and UN agencies as nodal points/catalyst.

Interest shown by various agencies during interaction with the consultant:

(a) DST (Department of Science and Technology, Govt of India) has agreed to support a study on technology need assessment.
(b) CBSE and UGC have agreed to modify courses in specific rural schools for meeting local needs.
(c) APCTT has commissioned a study and bio-gas feasibility in Ambala which has a potential to be replicated nationally.
(d) A national workshop on corporate sector role in rural development will be organised by ASSED (Asian Society for Self-employment Development) and VISION FOUNDATION.

Recommendations

(i) Organise a Seminar with participation by members of the

Parliamentarians' Forum for HD and the Representatives of UN organisations with a view to share experience of implementation problems and broadly agree a two-year plan of action.

(ii) The outcomes of the Seminar should be codified into following categories:

- General observations--applicable to all
- Programme specific observations
- Financial and Non-financial aspects
- Tangibles and Intagibles
- Short-term and Long-term
- NGOs *Vs* Govt. Role
- Management, MIS Control Systems
- People's participation
- Commitment *Vs* ego of development officials
- The Gender and Social Issues
- Cost break-up of the programme
- Economic, Social, Technological issues.
- Recommendations for various above categories
- Impact of computers, liberalisation/prioritization process on development.

(iii) Development of a data-base of expenditure incurred by various UN agencies on different programmes/projects at the DISTRICT level over the LAST FORTY YEARS.

This is essential for finding out the unutilised infrastructure, for proper utilisation and other relevant analysis for future planning and effective use.

The cost of preparation of the report should not exceed Rs. 1 lakh.

(iv) The data about the investment made in each district by UN programmes over the last 20 years under various schemes also needs be prepared by NIC (National Informatics Centre).

(v) All Developmental Work in Future needs to be area focused, supported by a multi-disciplinary team with proper coordination, with an area budget.

(vi) A document needs to be prepared bringing out all the lessons of sucessful development models, with all relevant information as mentioned above, for guiding the development planning in future, and to avoid failures. Specific reference needs to be made to the following models.

(a) Carry out studies in value based models of economic,

social and environment friendly development

(b) Ralegaon Sidhi Model near Pune
(c) Anand model in Gujarat
(d) Pani Panchayat of Pune
(e) Lizzat model of KVIC
(f) SEWA model of Gujarat
(g) Raghurajpur village in Orissa Model
(h) Role of Panchayat in Economic Development

(vii) Some Programmes which are very relevant for masses but have failed miserably have to be critically examined to draw some conclusions and identify precautions for future programmes.

Women and Development with UN Systems Support within MPs Pilot Projects:

(1) There is need to earmark some of the programmes exclusively for this group. This identification would differ from place to place but may include education, marketing, sericulture, pump sets and the total services sector (within manageable proportions).

(2) Special projects can be undertaken, PARCEL type be taken together with DST, APCTT, and ILO.

(3) A panel of low cost practical consultants amongst women can be drawn up and consulted.

(4) Training of Panchayati Raj members with emphasis on quality issues needs to be conducted (UNICEF is already experienced in the area).

(5) Emphasis on empowerment through a policy action package is vital. Hence, marketing training technology and banking success parameters be studied through PARCEL.

(6) Informal activity generation should be considered through examination of models of women power started by Vinobaji in Wardha, Patna, Assam, Nagaland and near Pune.

(7) There should be codification of success models developed by various institutions both national and international to locate areas of special thrust especially from the replicability and sustainability view points. This must be done by UN systems.

(8) Effective and Appropriate Technology along with women power, Science and Technology also plays a very important role. This aspect has to be another thrust area in learning to work together in selected pockets.

Policy Power

There is no need to reiterate again various segments in the policy planning and correcting issues. Whether it is about coordination, marketing economics or monitoring and control-various role players have to be involved to come out with widely acceptable policy package.

Panchayati Raj institutions and their role in Social Economic betterment of their area needs to be studied with reference to comparative, competitive advantageous the SWOT analysis of people, raw material, infrastructure etc. offers. Many new relevant programmes like NEEM, HERBAL, etc. are developing as economically viable propositions.

There is need to involve existing institutions like NABARD, KVIC, SIDBI, various boards, development commissioners etc. in the process of short and long term success of these efforts. Here the role of Capable Volunteers on cost effective basis needs to be accepted.

Various ongoing programmes within UNDP like agri-business, leather, handmade paper, jute, area development, macro-enterprises and institutional building, reforms in public administration etc. must be on experimental basis be studied in these areas.

Some Success Parameters

Even before the programme is launched it will be better to consider some aspects essential to its success. After all working together by the two very apex institutions has to have a broader and longer vision. The consultant would like to suggest that more discussions should take place to identify the parameters and essentials which will be required to call this project a success.

However, some of the aspects like empowerment, shifting from charity to creativity capacity and confidence building (CTOCCCB), transparency, viability, replicability, self propulsion etc. may have to be looked into. In this process everybody will have a role to play and contribute. Even the corporate sector can have a very active and fruitful role.

Precaution

This is only a gist of some of the recommendations made in the chapters. There are and will always be various types of suggestions keeping in mind the variety of the local conditions prevailing in different constituencies. A well considered flexibility must be offered to the implementing personnel so long as basic objectives and principles are achieved. In a multi-disciplinary and multi-dimensional programme of this nature transparency, clarity and viability would be some of the basic essentials with which no compromise can be permitted. Obviously, cost effectiveness at every level would be the other component of replicability.

CHART-1: SOCIAL–KATWA

Local problems as perceived by MP & others	Recommended activities by the consultant (Titles)	Plan of Action (POA) 6 months: Activity	Plan of Action (POA) 6 months: Cost	Outcome	12 Months 24 Months ACO/ACO	Total Cost	Synergetic UN System input in POA	Balance contribution of other sources	Stake holders or Beneficiaries	Critical parameters for monitoring and control
1	2	3	4	5	6	7	8	9	10	11
Lack of School Building	Basic Education	School Building Furnitures	Rs. 100,000 per school on cost sharing basis (C.S.B) including shramdan, land & transport	Replicable School building system	Extends upto a period of 2 years	Rs.2,00,000 for 10 schools on reducing scale	UNICEF W.F.P.	50% of the total investment Rs. 1,00,000	Students, Parents, Teachers, Edn. Admn. and Society	Enrollment, Pass out, standard of the programme, quality of respect
Lack of Primary Health Care	Primary Health care & drugs	Medical assistance, medicine, vaccines, surgical facility	Rs. 500,000 per centre on C.S.B.	Decrease in child mortality rate, population, control, Mother Health care	Extends upto a period of 2 years	Rs.2,00,000 for one centre	UNICEF W.F.P.	25% of the total investment Rs. 500,000	Social. impact for People's contribution, Mother & Child, family planning Deptt., Medical professionals, medical equipments & pharma industry	Percentage of immunisation, impact mortality rate, death rate of pregnant mother percentage reduction of patients
Availability of drinking water	Drinking water programme	Facilities for providing handpumps, wells, and water tanks	Rs. 20,000 per village on C.S.B.	Increase in productivity control of waterborne diseases, replicable model possible	Extends upto a period of 2 years	Rs. 2,00,000 (for 10 villages)	UNICEF W.F.P.	25% of the total cost Rs. 50,000	Local population and Public Health Deptt. Water Mgt., profiles, manufacturer & distributors	Availability scarcity of water relative to population, Reduction in water borne diseases

Note: Problem perceived by MPs are not specifically according to MP lad priority as communicated by them

CHART-I (Contd.)

1	2	3	4	5	6	7	8	9	10	11
Lack of Roads leading to villages	Road Infrastructure development	Construction of Roads	N.A. unit cost may vary	Economic development Improvement in rural communication	Extends upto a period of 2 years	N.A.	UNICEF	50% of the cost	Rural masses	Percentage increase in rural commuiation - Percentage increase in economic development - Percentage increase in export of raw material - Improvement in health care - Easy monitoring of programmes implemented in rural areas
Lack of Rural Electrification	Provision of electricity in rural areas	Rural electrification	N.A. unit cost may vary	Power generation for running of V.I. activities in the complex Fulfilling requirement of rural resort increasing percentage of irrigation in rural areas	Extends upto a period of 2 years	N.A.	UNDP World Bank	50% of the total cost domestic commercial tourist etc.	Farmers Entrepreneur setup and institution	% increase in the output of V.I. activities % increase in irrigation % increase of courts % increase in frequency of utilizing rural records

CHART-1 *(Contd.)*

1	2	3	4	5	6	7	8	9	10	11
Agriculture and Tourist based resources under utilised	Plantation and social forestry	10 acres	Rs. 25,000 Per acre i.e. Rs. 2,50,000 on cost sharing basis	Soil Conservation, women entrepreneurship Ecological Balance	Extends upto a period of 2 years	Rupees 12,50,000 for 5 plots	World Bank	50% of investment Rs. 6,25,000	Planters, Ecologist and Society	Number of Plants planted during the year, % of Land Area covered
Lack of Active Participation and Resource sharing by beneficiaries	Information Bank	One computer for each village	Rs. 75,000 for per each village	- Development of reliable data monitoring system, - self-employment - The trained person become the resource person, project making	Extends upto a period of 2 years	Rs. 7,50,000 for 10 villages	UNDP	50% of total investment 3,75,000	All villagers, Govt. system Entreprenures Bankers and Market organisation	Number of existing information bank in the particular surrounding, areas with respect to functioning and success rate
Lack of integrative knowledge	Book Bank (library chain)	Supply Reading room, Arrangement and Management vocational books	Rs. 1,00,000 per library book bank	Reading habit formation, confidence awareness and knowledge	Extends upto a period of 2 years	Rs. 5,00,000 for 5 library	UNICEF	25% of the total investment Rs. 1,25,000	Traders, students society, publishers, printers & all concerned	Availability of book/ journals with respect to number of book bank users

CHART-1 *(Contd.)*

1	2	3	4	5	6	7	8	9	10	11
	Learning to work together (LTWT) and awakening	3 workshops to be organised	Rs. 1,50,000 per village on C.S.B.	Health, leaving and working atmosphere	Extends upto a period of 2 years	Rs. 6,00,000 for 12 workshops @ 3 workshops in 6 months	ILO WFP	25% of the investment 1,25,000	Team builders potential and village HRD profile	Number of team based activities undergoing and underwent in the area.
Lack of Advancement of women	Empowerment of women, justice system and proper training programme	Training Exposure, Field work, case study and a leadership development workshop	Rs. 1,00,000 per workshop on C.S.B.	Healthy living, working atmosphere, employment and contribution to family & child harmony	Extends upto a period of 2 years	Rs. 10,00,000 for 10 workshop	UNDP	25% of the total investment Rs. 2,50,000	Women and the society, milk producers, cattle development of intra personal skills as well as general awareness of laws relating to women rights and upgradation of moral values.	Percentage of women graduate in the area with respect to women population, No. of conflict resolved locally

CHART-2: ECONOMIC--KATWA

Local problems as perceived by MP & others	Recommended activities by the consultant (Titles)	Plan of Action (POA) 6 months: Activity	Plan of Action (POA) 6 months: Cost	Outcome	12 Months 24 Months ACO/ACO	Total Cost	Synergetic UN System input in POA	Balance contribution of other sources	Stake holders or Beneficiaries	Critical parameters for monitoring and control
1	2	3	4	5	6	7	8	9	10	11
Under utilisation of available resources	1-Jute programme 2- Leather programme 3-Handmade paper programme (These are ongoing) 4-Paddy Processive 5-Biogas & V.I. Cluster as per KVIC Model (organic manure & Health Food) and Rural Resort Cluster (Women oriented)	* Identification of resources in terms of skills. * Provision of paper technology infrastructure * Training programmes * Building and workshop etc * Field Works * Training	Rs. 60 lakhs	- Increase in productivity - Self-employment - Upgradation of skills - Employment and contribution to family - Likely export oriented units.	Extended upto a period of two years	Rs. 60 lakhs	ILO U.N.D.P. A.P.C.T.T.	75% of total Rs. 45 lakhs	Local activities and craftsmen, their employees and customers, raw materials suppliers, entrepreneures, chamber of commerce, vocation educators	- By integrative UNDPs "Project tried tech" of product making and marketing and training, it could be easily replicated - By developing export policy planning & market led dev., jobs will be created

CHART-2 *(Contd.)*

1	2	3	4	5	6	7	8	9	10	11
		* Arrangement & management of resources. * Building & Land * Clusters can be commissioned								
Resource sharing by beneficiaries	Milk and Animal husbandry (Women oriented)	* Provision of veterinary services * Training arrangement & management of resources * Development of specific projects	Rs. 20 lakhs	- Increase in productivity - Generation of enriched manure - Supply of feed material for biogas plant - Alternate renewable energy	Extends up to a period of two years	Rs. 20 lakhs	A.P.C.T.T.	25% of total cost Rs. 5 lakh	Milk producers, cattle herbs, local milkmen and their dependents, Rural research cluster	Diversification Data base and codification - Bank finance/ loans from other sources - Repayment of financial loans.
	Export oriented Handlooms & Development programmes	* Exposure to potential buyers making available new products and avenues * Identify entrepreneurs		Export opportunity -Upgradation of standard of living through cost effective model	Extends upto a period of two years	Rs. 25 lakhs	I.T.C. UNDP	25% of Total cost Rs. 6.25 lakhs	Export opportunities Upgradation of standard of living and productivity of concerned individuals	- Regular & effective monitoring of data and analytical factor - Overall MIS

CHART-2 *(Contd.)*

1	2	3	4	5	6	7	8	9	10	11
				Increased productivity achieved						
	Rural entrepreneurship and skill upgradation centre with stress upon technical centre and self employment survey/ selection of entrepreneurs, feasibility and technical need assessment	* By utilising existing infrastructure carry out training programmes and skill upgradation * Exposure * Arrangement and management resources of training programmes * Development of intra personnel skills in entrepreneurs * Income generation case studies and experience sharing	Rs. 15 lakhs	A blue print for effective technology, based upon past experiences, useful for future need and for existing and future reference. Identification of equipment suppliers	Extends upto a period of two years	Rs. 15 lakhs	I.L.O. (NGO) UNDP	25% of total cost Rs. 3.75 lakhs	Entrepreneurs self-employed individuals, students, teachers, small industries, Distt. admns. & local governing body & residents	

CHART-2 *(Contd.)*

1	2	3	4	5	6	7	8	9	10	11
	Tourism/ Hotel Transport guide "in Kalna"	Interaction of different role players at the initiative of local Panchayat * Utilise available Hotel facilities * Preparation of joint literature * Monitoring system	Rs. 50 lakhs	-Employment generation and use of existing infrastructure. -Protection of temple, arts and crafts and their development -Income and confidence generation	Extends upto a period of 2 years	Rs. 50 lakhs	UNICEF UNDP	25% of total cost Rs. 12.5 lakhs	Travellers & Tourists Local skill potential in terms of productivity Employers and Employees	-Self supporting & Self-propelling system & programmes - Entrepreneurship dev. - Development of intra personnel skills
Lack of School Building	Basic Education	School building furnitures per school on CSB	Rs. 1 lakhs	Replicable school building system	Extends upto a period of 2 years	Rs. 20 lakhs per 10 schools on reducing scale	UNICEF WFP	50% of total investment Rs. 10 lakhs	Students, Parents, Teachers, Edu. Adm. Society	Enrolment, pass out, standard of the programme, social impact, people's contribution
Roads leading to villages	Road infrastructure development	Construction of roads	N.A. unit cost may vary	Economic Development improvement in rural	Extends upto a period of 2 years	N.A.	UNICEF	50% of the cost	Rural masses	Percentage increase in rural communication, percentage increase in economic development.

CHART-2 *(Contd.)*

1	2	3	4	5	6	7	8	9	10	11
		Hotel facilities * Prepar-ation of joint lite-rature * Monitoring system		communi-cation generation						Percentage increase in export of raw material, entre-preneurship dev. - Development of intra personnel skills
Lack of School building	Basic education	School building furnitures	Rs. 1 lakh per school on CSB	Replicable school building system	Extends upto a period of 2 years	Rs. 20 lakh for 10 schools on reducing scale	UNICEF WFP	50% of total investment Rs. 10 lakhs	Students, parents, teacher, Edn. Admn society	Enrolment, pass out, standard of the programme, social impact, peo-ple's contribution
Roads leading - Percentage to villages	structure development	Road infra- of roads	Construction cost may vary	development improvement in rural co-mmunication	N.A. unit upto a period of 2 years	Economic	Extends	N.A. cost	UNICEF masses	50% of the Rural increase in rural communication - Percentage increase in eco-nomic develop-ment - Percentage increase in export of raw material - Easy monitoring of programmes implemented in rural areas.

CHART 3: SOCIAL–JABALPUR

Local Problems as perceived by MP & others	Recommended Activities by the consultant (Titles)	Plan of Action (POA) 6 Months		Outcome	12 Months 24 months ACO/ACO	Total Cost	Synergetic UN Systems input in POA	Balance contribution from other sources	Stake-holders or Beneficiaries	Critical parameters for monitoring and control
		Activity	Cost							
1	2	3	4	5	6	7	8	9	10	11
Lack of Integrative knowledge	Information bank	One computer in a suitable rural setup and assign a trained person who finally become the resource person	Rs. 75000 per place	Self-employment, Awareness and knowledge through development of reliable data, project making facility, confidence, general awareness	Extends upto a period of 2 years	Rs. 3,75,000 for 5 places	World Bank	50% of total cost Rs.1,87,500	All villages Govt. system Entrepreneurs. Banker market organisation	Number of existing information, Bank in the particular surrounding areas with respect to functioning and success rate
	Book bank (library chain)	Supply, Reading room arrangement and management and vocational books	Rs. 50,000 per library book bank	Reading habit, formation confidence, Awareness and knowledge	Extend upto a period of 2 years	Rs.5,00,000 for 10 library and book bank	UNICEF	25% of total cost Rs.1,25,000	Traders students, society, publishers, printers and all concerned	Availability of Books/Journals with respect to number of book bank users

CHART-3 *(Contd.)*

1	2	3	4	5	6	7	8	9	10	11
Agriculture and tourist based resources under utilised	Plantation and social forestry	10 acres	Rs. 25000 per acre that is Rs. 2.5 lakhs	Soil conservations women entrepreneurship, Ecological Balance	Extends upto a period of 2 years	Rs. 12.5 lakh for 5 plots	World Bank	50% of total cost Rs. 6.25 lakhs	Planters Ecologist and society	Number of plants planted during the year. Percentage of land area covered
Lack of Availability of Drinking Water	Drinking water programme	Facilities for providing handpumps, wells, water tanks	Rs. 20,000 per village on C.S.B.	Increase in productivity, Replicable models possible	Extended upto 2 years	Rs. 200,000 (for 10 villages)	UNICEF W.F.P.	25% of total cost Rs. 50,000	Local population & Public Health Dept. Water Mgt. Profile, manufacturer and distributors	Availability/ scarcity of water relative to population
Lack of Sanitation	Providing basic service to the poverty ridden masses in the area	Sanitation programme	N.A. unit cost may vary	Disease control	Extends upto a period of 2 years	N.A.	W.F.P.	50% of the total cost	villagers livestock	Disposal of waste, cleaning of drainage, percentage decrease in diseases
Lack of primary health care	Primary Health care, medical provision to villages	Medical assistance, Medicines, Vaccine, surgical facilities	Rs. 200,000 per centre on C.S.B.	Fall in child mortality rate, control, mother & child health care, population control	Extends upto a period of 2 years	Rs. 400,000 (for 2 centres)	UNICEF WFP WHO	25% of total cost Rs. 100,000	Mother & family planning Dept., Med. Equip & Pharma Ind.	% decrease in infant mortality rate, Percentage of immunisation. Percentage decrease of prevalence of diseases.

CHART-3 *(Contd.)*

1	2	3	4	5	6	7	8	9	10	11
										% decrease in prevalence of diseases. % decrease in mortality of pregnant mothers. % reduction of patients
Lack of Roads leading to blocks	Road infrastructure development	Construction of roads	N.A. unit cost may vary	Economic development improvement in rural communication	Extends upto a period of 2 years	N.A.	W.F.P.	50% of the total cost	Rural masses	- Percentage increase in rural communication - Percentage increase in economic development - Percentage increase in export of raw material - Improvement in health care - Easy monitoring of programme implemented in villages
Lack of post literacy centre	Literacy centre be established	Implementation of literacy programme under N.L.H.	N.A. unit cost may vary	Removal of illiteracy socio-economic development Improvement in peoples	Extends upto a period of 2 years	N.A.	UNICEF UNESCO	50% of the total investment	Rural masses students, teachers, parents	Social improvement, peoples contribution enrolment pass out standard of the programme

CHART-3 *(Contd.)*

1	2	3	4	5	6	7	8	9	10	11
				participation for human development						
Lack of multi-purpose hall (to be used for health centre AIDS councelling library, creche vocational training programme)	Basic education	Infrastructure development (building, blackboards, furniture and facilities etc.)	Rs. 10 thousands per school on C.S.B.	Replicable school building system	Extends upto a period of 2 years	Rs. one lakh (for 10 schools)	UNICEF W.F.P.	50% of the total cost Rs. 50 thousands	Students, parents, teachers, Edu. Adm. and society	Enrolment Pass out standard of the programme Social impact People's contributions.
Lack of Advancement of women	Empowerment of women, justice system and a proper training programme	Training Exposure, Field work case study and a leadership development workshop	Rs. 100,000 per workshop on C.S.B.	Healthy living working atmosphere, employment and contribution to family and child harmony	Extends upto a period of 2 years (workshop in 6 months)	Rs.6,00,000 (for 6 workshops)	ILO	25% of Total cost Rs. 1,50,000	Families Entrepreneuers, women, society and bankers - Development of intra-personal skills as well as general awareness of laws relating to women right and upgradation of moral values	Number of educated women in the area relative to the illiterate ones, record of cases resolved locally

CHART 4 : ECONOMIC–JABALPUR

Local problems as perceived by MP & others	Reommended Activities by the consultant (Titles)	Plan of Action (POA) 6 Months: Activity	Plan of Action (POA) 6 Months: Cost	Outcome	12 months 24 months ACO/ACO	Total Cost	Synergetic UN Systems input in POA	Balance contribution from other sources	Stake-holders or Beneficiaries	Critical parameters for monitoring and control
1	2	3	4	5	6	7	8	9	10	11
Lack of Multi-purpose hall, health centre, AIDS counselling, library, creche, vocational training	Basic education	Infrastructure Development (building, blackboards, furnitures & facilities etc.)	Rs. 10,000 per school on C.S.B.	Replicable school building system	Extends upto a period of 2 years	One lakh (for 10 schools)	UNICEF WFP	50% of the total cost Rs. 50 thousand and society	Students, parents, teachers, Edu. Adm. social impact,	Enrolment Pass out standard of the programme, people's contributions.
Lack of Basic education & school complex	Schools for basic education be provided	Building furnitures	Rs. 100,000 per school on C.S.B. including shramdan, land & transport	Replicable school building system	Extends upto a period of 2 years	Rs.20,00,000 for 10 schools	UNICEF W.F.P.	50% of the total investment 10,00,000	Students parents teachers Edu. Admn & society	People's contribution, standard of programme, enrolment passout, quality respect, social impact
Lack of Rural Electrification	Provision of electricity in rural areas	Rural electrification	N.A. Unit cost may vary	Power generation for running of V.I. activity in the complex, fulfilling requirement	Extends upto a period of 2 years	N.A.	UNDP World Bank	50% of total cost	Farmers, entrepreneurs domestic set up & commercial institutions, tourists etc.	% increase in the output of V.I. activities % increase in irrigation, % increase of tourists

CHART-4 *(Contd.)*

1	2	3	4	5	6	7	8	9	10	11
				of rural resort, -Increasing percentage irrigation facility in rural areas						% increase in frequency of utilizing rural resorts
Construction of Sub-station										
Under utilisation of available resources	Leather programme, handmade paper programme (These are on going, paddy processing	Identification of resources in terms of skills, provision of paper technology infra-structure, -Training programme, building & workshop etc.	Rs. 60 lakhs	-Increase in Productivity - Self-employment - Upgradation of skills - Employment and contribution to family -Likely export oriented units.	Extends upto a period of 2 years	Rs. 60 lakhs	ILO UNDP APCTT	75% of total cost Rs. 45 lakh	Local activities & craftsmen, their employees & customers, raw material suppliers, entrepreneurs chamber of commerce, vocation educators	- By integrative UNDPs "Project tried tech" of product making & marketing & training it could be easily replicated -By developing export policy, planning led dev., jobs will be created.
	Biogas & V.I. clusters as per KVIC model (organic manure & health food) and	Field work Training, Arrangement & Management of resources, building &	Rs. 2 crores	-Useful technology transfer - Power generation for running the V.I. activity	Extend upto a period of 2 years	Rs. 2 crores	UNDP World Bank	25% of total cost Rs. 50 lakhs	Farmer Entrepreneurs, Rural Dev. Boards, Domestic set up and commercial	-Value addition of rural raw material - LTWT (Learning to work together) - Transparency & viability

CHART-4 *(Contd.)*

1	2	3	4	5	6	7	8	9	10	11
	Rural Resorts Cluster (Women oriented)	land clusters can be commiss-ioned		in the comp-lex, fulfilling requirements of Rural Resort Cluster - Generation of enriched manure. - Alternate renewable energy - Increase in productivity					institutions, tourists etc	- Marketing - Gender
Need of women entrepre-neurship development	Milk & Animal Husbandry (women oriented)	Provision of veterinary services, Training arrangement & manage-ment of resources, Develop-ment of specific projects	Rs. 20 lakhs	- Increase in productivity in terms of commercial aspect - Supply of feed material for biogas plant	Extends upto a period of 2 years	Rs. 20 lakhs	APCTT UNDP	25% of total cost Rs. 5 lakhs	Milk produ-cers, cattle herds, local milkmen, their depen-dents & Ru-ral Research Cluster	- Diversification -Data base & codification - Bank finance/ Loan from other sources. - Repayment of financial loans.
Employment generation	Tourism/ Hotel/	* Interac-tion of	Rs. 50 lakhs	- Employ-ment gene-	Extends upto a	Rs. 50 lakhs	UNICEF UNDP	25% of total cost	Travellers & Tourists,	-Self supporting & self-propelling

CHART-4 (*Contd.*)

1	2	3	4	5	6	7	8	9	10	11
	Transport guide "in Kalna"	different role players at the initiative of local panchayat - Utilise available Hotel facilities * Preparation of joint literature * Monitoring system		ration and use of existing infrastructure. - Protection of temple, arts and crafts and their development - Income and confidence generation	period of 2 years			Rs. 12.5 lakhs	Local skill potential in terms of productivity Employers and employees	system & programmes. - Entrepreneurship dev. - Development of intra personnel
	Export oriented Handlooms & Development Programmes	* Exposure to potential buyers making available new products and avenues * Identify entrepreneurs		Export opportunity - Upgradation of standard of living through cost effective model increased productivity achieved	Extends upto a period of 2 years	Rs. 25 lakhs	I.T.C. UNDP	25% of total cost Rs. 6.25 lakhs	Export opportunities Upgradation of standard of living and productivity of concerned individuals.	- Regular & effective monitoring of data and analytical factor - Over all
	Rural entrepreneurship and skill upgradation centre with	* By utilising existing infrastructure carry out training	Rs. 15 lakhs	A blue print for effective technology, based upon past experie-	Extends upto a period of 2 years	Rs. 15 lakhs	I.L.O. (NGO) UNDP	25% of total cost Rs. 3.75 lakhs	Entrepreneurs self employed individuals, students,	

CHART-4 *(Contd.)*

1	2	3	4	5	6	7	8	9	10	11
	stress upon technical centre and self-employment survey /selection of entrepreneurs, feasibility and technical need assessment	programmes and skill upgradation * Exposure * Arrangement and management of resources of training programmes * Development of intra personnel skills in entrepreneurs. * Income generation case studies and experience sharing		nces, useful for future need and for existing and future reference. - Identification of equipment suppliers					teachers, small industries, Distt., admns. & local governing body & residents	

CHART 5: SOCIAL–COIMBATORE

Local problems as perceived by MP & others	Recommended Activities by the consultant (Titles)	Plan of Action (POA) 6 Months		Outcome	12 months 24 months ACO/ACO	Total Cost	Synergetic UN Systems input in POA	Balance contribution from other sources	Stake-holders or Beneficiaries	Critical parameters for monitoring and control
		Activity	Cost							
1	2	3	4	5	6	7	8	9	10	11
Lack of Integrative knowledge Lack of active participation and resource sharing by beneficiaries	Information Bank	Computer for each village	Rs. 75,000 for each village	Development of reliable data, monitoring system, self-employment, project making facility	Extends upto a period of 2 years	Rs. 7,50,000 for 10 villages	UNDP	50% of total investment Rs. 3,75,000	All villagers Govt. System Entrepreneurs Bankers market organisation	Number of existing information bank in the particular surrounding area with respect to functioning and success rate
	Book bank (library chain)	Supply Reading room arrangement and management vocational books	Rs. 100,000 per library book bank	Reading habit formation, confidence, Awareness and knowledge	Extends upto a period of 2 years	Rs. 5,00,000 for 5 Library	UNICEF	20% of the total investment Rs. 1,25,000	Traders, students, society Publishers, printers, all concerned	Availability of books/journals with respect to number of book bank users
Agriculture and Tourist based resources under utilised	Plantation and social forestry	10 acres	Rs. 25,000 per acre that is Rs. 2.50,000	Soil conservation women entrepreneurship	Extends upto a period of 2 years	Rs.12,50,000 for 5 plots	World Bank	50% of total cost Rs.6,25,000	Planter, Ecologist and society	Number of plants planted during the year percentage of land area covered

CHART-5 *(Contd.)*

1	2	3	4	5	6	7	8	9	10	11
				Ecological Balance						
Lack of Advancement of women	Empowerment of women, justice system and a proper training programme	Training Exposure Field work case study and a leadership development workshop	Rs. 1,00,000 per workshop on C.S.B.	Healthy living working atmosphere, Employment	Extends upto 2 years	Rs. 5,00,000 (for 5 work shops)	UNDP WFP	50% of total cost Rs. 250,000	Families Entrepreneurs, women, society and bankers	Number of educated women in the area relative to the illiterate ones, record of cases resolved locally
Lack of multipurpose Hall (To be used for Health centre, AIDS Counselling, Library, creche and vocational training programme)	Basic Education	Infrastructure development (buildings, black boards, furnitures facilities etc.)	Rs. 10 thousand per school on C.S.B.	Replicable school building system	Extends upto a period of 2 years	Rs. one Lakh (for 10 schools)	UNICEF WFP	50% of the total cost Rs. 50 thousand	Students, parents, teachers, edu. adm. & society	Enrolment passout standard of the programme social impact, people's contribution
Lack of Drinking Water	Drinking water programme	Facilities for providing hand pumps wells & water tanks	Rs. 20 thousand per village on C.S.B.	Increase in productivity replicable model possible	Extends upto a period of 2 years	Rs. two lakhs	UNICEF WFP	25% of total cost Rs. 50 thousands	Local population, public health Deptt., water Mgt. profile, manufacturers & distributors	Availability/ scarcity of water relative to population

CHART-5 *(Contd.)*

1	2	3	4	5	6	7	8	9	10	11
Lack of Rural Electrification	Provision of electricity in rural areas	Rural electrification	N.A. Unit cost may vary	Power generation for running of V.I.activities in the complex fulfilling requirement of rural resort, increasing irrigation facilities in rural areas	Extends upto a period of 2 years	N.A.	UNDP World Bank	50% of the total cost	Farmers entrepreneurs domestic setup commercial institutions, tourists etc.	% increase in the output of V.I. activities % increase in irrigation % increase of tourists % increase in frequency of utilizing rural resorts
Lack of basic education & school complex	School for basic education be provided	Building furnitures	Rs. 100,000 per school on C.S.B. including shramdan, land & transport	Replicable school building system	Extends upto a period of 2 years	Rs. 20 lakh (for 10 schools)	UNICEF WFP	50% of the total investment	Students, parents, teachers Edn. Admn. & Society	Enrolment, pass-out, quality of respect, social impact standard of programme, people's contribution
Lack of Roads leading to blocks	Road Infrastructure development	Construction of roads	N.A. Unit cost may vary	Economic development Inprovement in rural communication	Extends upto a period of 2 years	N.A.	UNICEF	50% of the cost	Rural masses	% increase in rural communication % increase in economic development % increase in export of raw material

CHART-5 *(Contd.)*

1	2	3	4	5	6	7	8	9	10	11
										% Improvement in health care, Easy monitoring of programmes implemented in rural areas
Lack of Primary Health care	Primary Health care Medical provisions to villages	Medical Assistance Medicines Vaccines Surgical facilities	Rs. 200,000 per centre on CSB	Fall in child mortality rate, diseases control, mother & child Health care, population control	Extends upto a period of 2 years	Rs. 400000 (for 2 centres)	UNICEF WFP WHO	25% of the total cost Rs. 100,000	Mother & Family planning Deptt. Med. Equip. & Pharma Industries Medical Professionals	% decrease in prevalence of diseases % decrease in mortality of pregnant mothers % decrease in infant mortality rate Percentage of immunisation % reduction of patients

CHART 6 : ECONOMIC – COIMBATORE

Local Problems as perceived by MP & others	Recommended Activities by the consultant (Titles)	Plan of Action (POA) 6 Months		Outcome	12 Months 24 months ACO/ACO	Total Cost	Synergetic UN Systems input in POA	Balance contribution from other sources	Stakeholders or Beneficiaries	Critical parameters for monitoring and control
		Activity	Cost							
1	2	3	4	5	6	7	8	9	10	11
Under utilisation of available resources	Leather/ Handmade Paper processing units. Fruit & Food Processing Unit, Godowns, Tourist Dev., Rural Industries Cluster	Case study, field visit, market survey and dev. project, preparation for market led dev. programmes, Exposure	Rs. 20 lakhs	Employment generation in various segments, contribution to the local economy, Entrepreneurship Dev. & confidence building	Extends upto a period of 2 years	Rs. 20 lakhs	ILO UNDP APCTT	25% of the total investment Rs. 5 lakhs	Regional & local population, Entrepreneurs Consumers Trainees & Management consultants	a) The level of dev. b) Policy pakages c) Demonstration model to achieve overall objectives of the programmes d) Replicability factor e) Monitoring cost effectiveness f) Perceptions g) Quality control h) Long-term spread effect.
		Infrastructure dev. & activity starting Technology trans. Technology Dev. Publicity & Mkt. tie up	Rs. 10 lakhs	Initiation of a culture of viable, transparent eco. activities	Extends upto a period of 2 years	Rs. 10 lakhs		50% of total investment Rs. 5 lakhs	Govt. Deptt. Panchayati Raj Institution Team builders & village HRD Profiles Women and	i) Technical servicing & spare parts j) The No. of team based activities underwent in the area k) Percentage of women graduates

CHART-6 *(Contd.)*

1	2	3	4	5	6	7	8	9	10	11
									the society Milk producers Cattle Dev. of intra personnel skills as well as general awareness laws relating to women rights & upgradation of moral values	in the area with respect to women population, number of conflicts resolved locally. l) no. of existing book banks in the particular area and surrounding with respect to functioning and success rate.
Employment Generation	Marketing Corporation to be called (SMO) SHANTI Marketing Organisation	Increase in the viability and marketing Resource sharing	Rs. 5 lakhs	Upgradation of standard of living & social status of	Extends upto a period of 2 years	Rs. 5 lakhs	World Bank UNIDO	25% of the total investment	Local population, Entrepreneurs, consumers, society, marketing personnel (and all concerned)	
	Women Development oriented programmes	Leadership Dev. programme Admr. & Mnt. by	Rs. 1.5 lakhs	Employment and contribution to family and child	Extends upto a period of 2 years	Rs. 1.5 lakhs	UNICEF WFP		Note all the points mentioned above are applicable to all the	

CHART-6 *(Contd.)*

1	2	3	4	5	6	7	8	9	10	11
	Anti-poverty programmes	Expert Imparting training		harmony					activities	
	Training Programmes		Rs. 2 lakhs	Awareness about the programme Monitoring & Evaluation of the programme project formulation						
	Vocational Education	(Note: these activities are applicable for all proposed project by the consultant)	Rs. 1 lakhs	Self-employment income generation improvement in the socio-economic condition of the trainees.						
	Milk Value Added products		Rs. 1.5 lakhs	Income generation self-employment						
	Introducing N.R.I. in Rural Development		Rs. 2 lakhs	Development of reliable data provi-						

CHART-6 *(Contd.)*

1	2	3	4	5	6	7	8	9	10	11
				ding monitoring style & project making feasibility						
	Book banks		Rs. 1 lakh per library	Acquirement of knowledge contribution in the socio-economic development of the society Human Development A certain degree of providing a social justice & a sense of belonging.	Extends upto a period of 2 years	Rs. 1 lakh	UNESCO	All concerned	No. of book banks relative with No. of books	
Post Literacy Programme			Rs. 1 lakhs	Removal of illiteracy, socio-economic development, improvement in people's part-						

CHART-6 *(Contd.)*

1	2	3	4	5	6	7	8	9	10	11
				icipation for human deve-lopment						
Lack of Rural Electrification	Provision of electricity	Rural electri-fication	N.A. Unit cost may vary	Power gene-ration for running of V.I. activ-ities in the complex fulfilling requirement of rural resort, increasing irrigation facilities in rural areas	Extends upto a period of 2 years	N.A.	UNDP World Bank	50% of the total cost	Farmers Entrepren-eurs dom-estic set-up comm-ercial insti-tution Tourists etc.	% increase in the output of V.I. activities % increase in irrigation % increase of tourists % increase in frequency of utilising rural resort
Lack of Basic Education and school complex	School for basic education be provided	Building furnitures	Rs. 10 thousand per school on CSB in-cluding shramdan, land and transport	Replicable school building system	Extends upto a period of 2 years	Rs. 20 lakhs (for 10 schools)	UNICEF WFP	50% of the total invest-ment	Students, parents, Teachers, Edu. Adm., and society	Involvement passout, Quality of respect, social impact, standard of programme, people's contri-bution
Lack of Roads leading to blocks	Road Infrastruc-ture deve-lopment	Construc-tion of roads	N.A. unit cost may vary	Economic development Improvement	Extends upto a period of 2 years	N.A.	UNICEF	50% of the cost	Rural masses	% increase in rural commu-nication % increase in

CHART-6 *(Contd.)*

1	2	3	4	5	6	7	8	9	10	11
				in rural communication						economic development % increase in export of rural material % improvement in health care, easy monitoring of programmes implemented in rural areas
Lack of Primary Health Care	Primary Health care Medical provision to villages	Medical assistance, Medicines, vaccines, surgical facilities	Rs. 2 lakhs per centre on CSB	Fall in child mortality rate disease control mother & child health care Population control	Extends upto a period of 2 years	Rs. 4 lakhs (for 2 centres)	UNICEF WFP WHO	25% of the total cost Rs. 1 lakh	Mother & family planning deptt. Medical equipments pharma industries medical professionals	% increase in prevalance of diseases % decrease in mortality of pregnant mothers. % decrease in infant mortality rate % of immunisation % Reduction of patients

14

SOCIO-ECONOMIC PROGRAMMES
Common to All

(A) Bio-gas Integrated-organic Manure and Marketing Led Development Plant

It is proposed:

(a) In selected location.
(b) Through right entrepreneurs
(c) After market survey and financial tie-up
(d) An integrated programme be taken

Outcome

(a) Surplus generable, replicable, health, food, light, sanitation and increased agriculture yield programme.
(b) Planning action research codification extension and loanable programme with multi-disciplinary group like experts in sanitation, human resource, economists, technologists, overall health improvement, role players.
(c) Learning from experience of past and issues in its implementation for better model development.
(d) Bringing out issues and areas of weakness for further development.

Financing

(a) With support of ongoing programmes of MNES Government of India, Banks and entrepreneurs including corporate sector it will be possible to install a programme costing not more than 5 lakhs rupees for bio-gas plant. There are some subsidies, training programmes already available. Hence a token expenditure of about 3 lakhs may be enough.

Major Role Players and Stake Holders

Women
Villagers
Entrepreneurs
Equipment manufacturers
Diesel pump set makers (with mix of diesel and gas pump sets upto 10 horse powers can be operated)
Health groups
Family and eco groups
Increased productivity, soil improvement, sanitation and quality of overall education.

Critical Parameters for Monitoring and Control

(1) Conviction of the entrepreneurs about the utility.
(2) Timely marketing and recording
(3) Surplus generation
(4) Pulling with multi-disciplinary group like chemist, market producers and consumers.

(B) Central Board of Secondary Education (CBSE) Modified Academic Syllabus.

(1) Justification

The consultant had discussion with various groups about experiments in education field to meet the challenges of development in a country like India. Chairman, CBSE, Shri Khandelwal, an eminent educationist was very receptive to the idea of an experiment in the Parliamentarians' constituencies to carry out bold innovative corporate sector involvement in this field. This will have the following advantages:

(a) Based upon the synergised need of sustainable development, integrative syllabus to prepare citizens of tomorrow through cost effective systems could be developed.
(b) Vocational education is the priority of the day. But replicable models where the students could have placement demand right at the schooling stage and based upon systems of inter-locutary

nature vision are missing.

(c) Education at this level should be able to develop into economic programme. With better integration and usefulness it should be possible to do so.

(d) Even UNESCO Country Director, felt the need for such an experiment to meet the challenges of time.

Stake Holders

1. Students, Parents and Teachers
2. Educationists and administrators
3. Employment Planners
4. Bankers

Critical Parameters and Monitoring Points

(1) Low cost practical consultants
(2) Policies towards small enterprise and management development
(3) Cost of training
(4) Enrolment, pass out and demand.
(5) Social behaviour and sensitisation to the unorganised
(6) Corporate sector involvement.
(7) Overall newness and privatisation points and activities.
(8) Bank finance and return on investment.

15

MANAGEMENT AND CONTROL

(a) Recommended Activities

(1) Bench Marking

Development of data base relating to the existing developmental conditions through collection of secondary data and conducting empirical sample studies.
Activities--Appointment of professional consultants to develop and get implemented the studies with long term implementational issues. Rough cost 1 lakh.

(2) Policies and Plans

Activities-- The consultant should be able to study concurrently various policy prescription which hinder or help the success of social and economic programme implementation. The policies are framed by different groups including society and state. The plans, the training activities must cater impact assessment of policies on overall activities. Rough cost Rs. 1 lakh
Developing detailed time bound plan of action (POA) for completion of the project. Developing the proposals for necessary policy changes to make the plans implemented successfully.
Follow up with the policy making authority/agencies for necessary policy changes within the available time frame.

(3) MIS and Control

Developing practical field oriented management Information System for effective monitoring and control.

We recommend project monitoring to be done at, (a) at the field level--the point of the project implementation, and (b) at the central monitoring point like Parliamentarians Forum/UNDP at Delhi. The timely reports submitted by the MIS system need be analysed and review meetings to be organised at regular intervals participated by all concerned.

Activities--Developing MIS and control system both in the field and HQs on cost effective systems ensuring compilation, collation and presentation of findings to all the stake holders for taking up various decisions for the success.

Giving criticalities to all stake holders for quality and punctuality in the programme.

Cost can be decided as per the work load and expectation of integrated MIS control mechanism to be developed.

Organisation, Management, Communication and Control Workshop for Stake Holders including Visits to Selected Models both within and outside the State

Keeping in mind need to sensitize, expose and widen overall attitudes to multi-disciplinary and at times conflicting requirements of learning to work together for a common objective, it is essential that the training and visits of the type mentioned above are organised at the earliest. This will help a lot in bringing various role players and actors including development planners on a common platform.

Activities--Basically it involves selecting participants based upon their capacity to assimilate and transfer lessons of developmental issues.

Visit to selected models near Pune in Raile Gaon Siddi, Wardha, Tamil Nadu for replicability of socio-economic type models.

This also involves brain storming and open discussion about strengths, weaknesses, opportunities and threats alongwith actions required for replication and implementation in their area based upon local needs.

Role of finance, entrepreneurship, leader organiser, communicator, team spirit builder and overall initiative and spirit sustainer with reference to local conditions have to be holistically and critically examined. Special emphasis will also be on institution building essentialities.

Rough estimate--3 exercises could cost roughly two lakh rupees each depending upon the size of the participants and the distants. This is only indicative.

(b) Criticalities in Management and Control Systems

(1) It is important that the monitor and the monitoring system must be acceptable to all and impartial.
(2) Computers can be the best arbitrator
(3) Emphasis on all the programmes will be on gender, social marketing, accounts and openness. Hence, system must be transparent.
(4) Reports must be timely with critical analysis and current policy issues etc.

Stake Holders

(a) All UN Systems and agencies
(b) MPs forum
(c) Beneficiaries and their organisations
(d) District Development organisations
(e) Bankers and fiinancial institutions
(f) Trainers and marketing agents
(g) All interested in developing replicable sustainable models.

Activities

Since management and control systems are very important for overall sustainable viable and transparent and replicable model development, it is essential that *flexibility* with autonomy and accountability is provided.

In unorganised sector lot of precautions and transparencies are required. Like in economic programmes brand image, glamourization issues in organisation development and on the whole developing self supporting and mutual confidence building would require a very high degree of appreciation in the issues involved. For example even the corporate sector has important role to play in the unorganised sector which is hardly realised. Hence, integrative and holistic appreciative role will call for hard work and self discipline.

PART-III

CLARIFICATIONS, ISSUES AND ANALYSIS

16

WOMEN AND SCIENCE

Technology with special reference to U.P.--Role of State Textile Corporation Limited

The Corporation was started in 1970 and today it has 24 mills in some of the most backward districts of U.P. and has about 40,000 people working in this organisation. Due to various reasons the corporation is incurring heavy losses, but the management has taken the following important decisions:

1. The first priority is to turn about mill from loss to profit.
2. To improve socio-economic condition in the area where the mills are located by involving the families of officers and the workers and also the adjoining Panchayati Raj Institutions.

Priority Areas for Socio-economic Development fow Women in U.P.

Traditionally U.P. has been a very conservative backward State. This has resulted in over dependence on State for every activity. This resulted in over exploitation of women and children on the home front resulting in various problems of malnutrition, early marriages, poverty, destitution and such. These are all compounded because of illiteracy.

What can State Textile Corporation do to improve situation through better technology and income generating activity

Some of the major activities which the State Textile Corporation mills and the Consultancy Cell could do include the following:

1. The Consultancy Cell has Memorandum of Understanding with Goshalas, prominent NGOs and Academicians. The low cost

multi-disciplinary projects could be developed for capacity enhancement of women in the backward pockets of districts like Jhansi, Banda, Ballia, Ghazipur, Allahabad etc. Impose self regulation. The condition will be created where decision taking process is to become transparent and justifiable. The Panchayati Raj holds a promising future. The backward and forward linkages required for sustainable economy/human development calls for integration with the local programme. By involving local people, local priorities and even Member of Parliament local area development scheme (MP-LADS) it would be possible to develop better model.

What is the enterprise led development and whether it will help in reawakening of entrepreneurship?

Enterprise led development is nothing but creating those well organised conditions where through self-employment and urge of masses to do something, a plan is implemented with others cooperation. Thus there is a need for organiser enterprise for help, support, marketing, export where convergence could take place.

How can UP State Textile Corporation Limited give a lead--SWOT analysis

Tex Fed Group (consisting of UPSTC, UPSSC, UPSYC, UPCSMF) has five senior IAS officers. All of them have worked in the development and district administration fields. Even if the UP State Textile Corporation has priority in generating profit, the experience has been of losses. Hence with the better integration and by convergence of on-going development plans, it is possible and also essential to develop a synergistic initiative. U.P. State Textile Corporation Limited has very qualified people in the mills. These belong to technical, managerial, clerical, labour, security and marketing fields. They have infrastructure and solid investment. If they have been losing in the net profit, the potential to integrate is immense. With the five very senior IAS officers of Commissioner rank and above, it should be possible to take a broad view of developing requirements of the State with integrating on low cost and high impact (LCHI) system development. It is possible to devise methods for the benefit of all. This calls for clarity and urge. The resources are not difficult to pool. What is required is only model building and clear action plan on the following lines.

Action Plan

U.P. State Textile Corporation Limited can contribute in the rural enterprises development in the following way:

(a) By ancillarisation in the selected districts where mills are located.
(b) Developing powerloom, handloom, eco-friendly dyes, industrial cotton, hand knitted items.
(c) *Rural entrepreneurship development:* This is through better planning, monitoring, marketing so that sustainable and viable models can be developed.
(d) For development of data base around mills.

Linkages with Science and Technology Department, Government of India and the States

For rural development technology plays very important role. Departments like Science and Technology have been funding through non-governmental organisations for programmes of technology research and training activities. Whether it is Textiles, Leather, Pottery, Fruit Processing, Hand made paper or any type of technology development, coordinated efforts have been missing. The linkages between organised and unorganised sector have always been hampered by wrong mind sets. Various on-going programmes or so called implementable programme have hardly resulted into replicable programme.

Thus Member of Parliament Local Area Development (MPLAD) scheme and convergence of UN systems had offered golden opportunity to precisely identify those reasons, take concerned action and by involving local institutions, corporate sector take these projects which would make the job of human resource development for sustainable development easier.

17

SOME ISSUES

(1) What is the strength, weakness, opportunities, threats (SWOT) analysis of India?
(2) Urban vs Rural India
(3) Organised vs Unorganised India
(4) Masses vs Elite
(5) Educated vs Uneducated
(6) Male vs Female
(7) Upper Caste vs Lower Caste
(8) Govt. vs Non-Governmental and Private Organisation
(9) Poverty vs plenty

This part is included to throw some light and to understand clearly need for redefinitions, re-engineering and restructuring to formulate better cost effective, replicable and widely acceptable Plan of Action with Convergence.

FIG. 17.1: ORGANISING ISSUES & UN SYSTEM

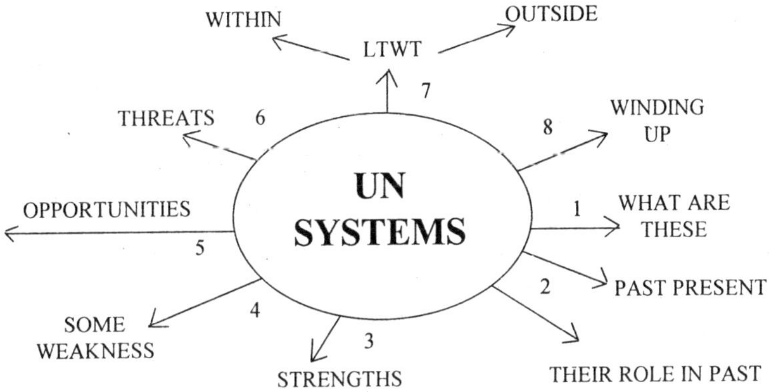

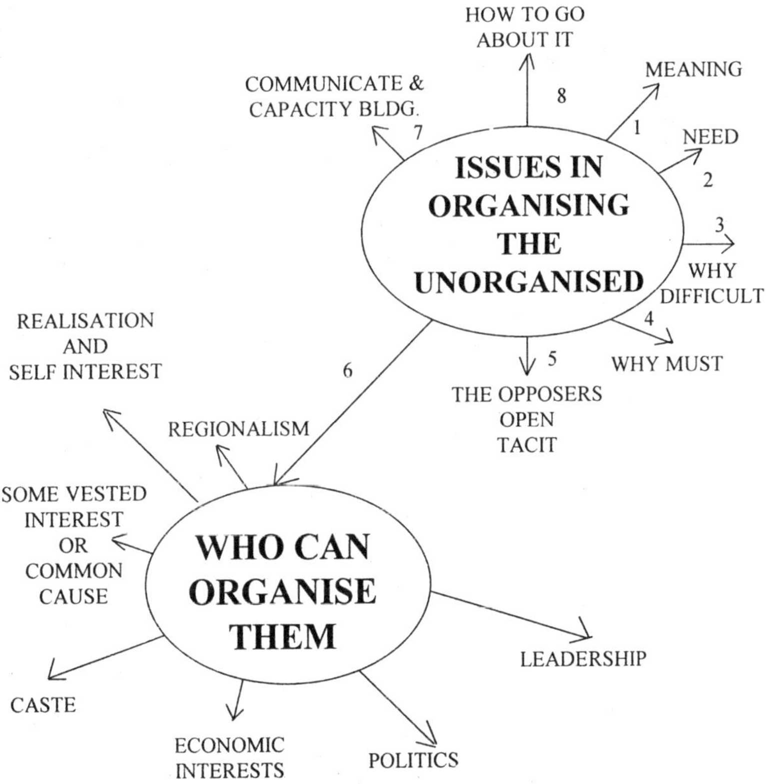

FIG. 17.2: MARKET LED DEVELOPMENT

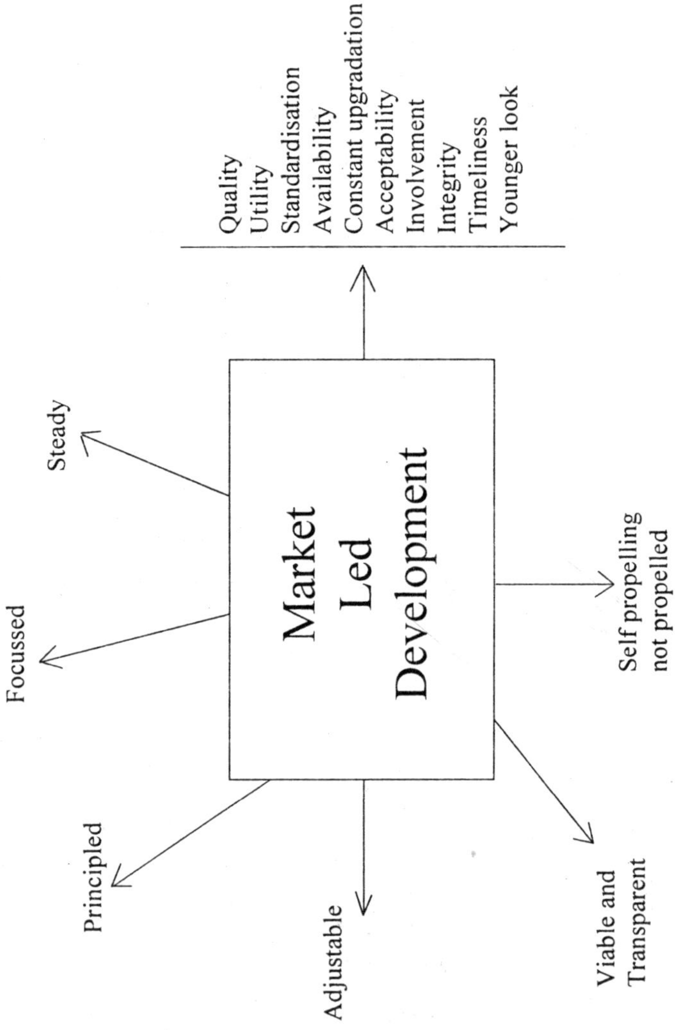

FIG. 17.3: CONVERGENCE AREAS

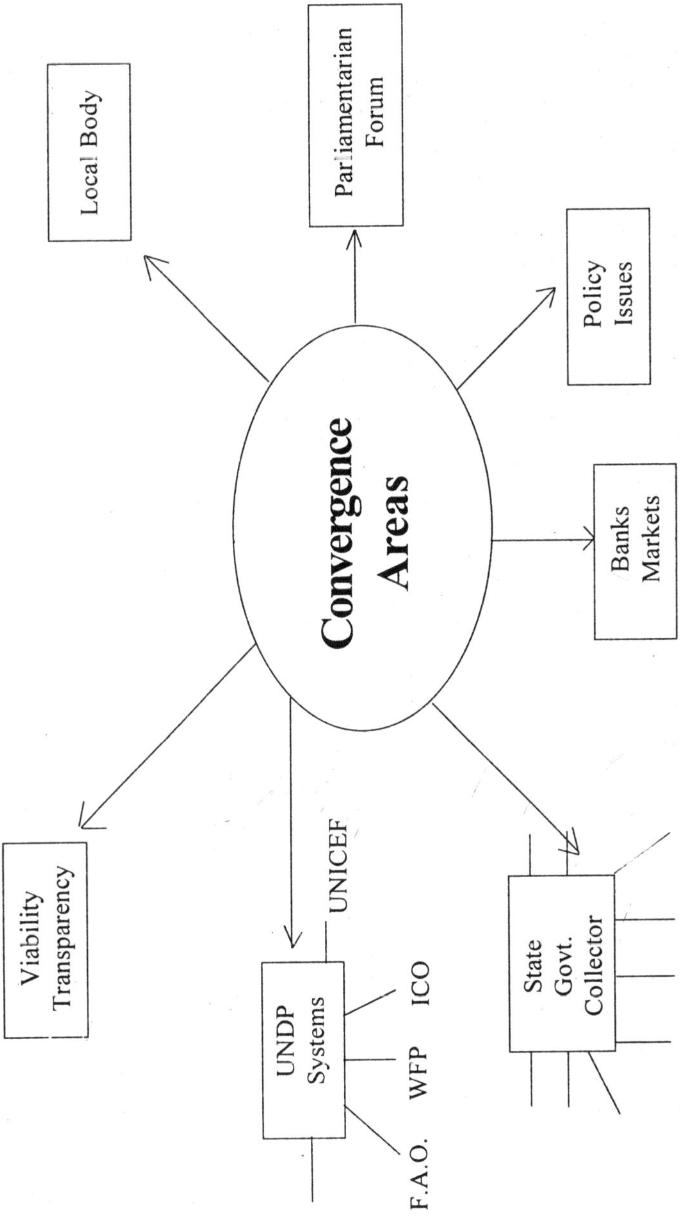

FIG. 17.4 : WDR-94-ANALYSIS

ABOUT PAST POOR PERFORMANCE

Manage

- Infrastructure like Business and
- As Service Sector
- Concretise objectives
- Pay for use
- Involve All
- Costs
- Orientation
- Self-help
- Competition
- Accountability

Incentive Providers Application of

(a) Commercial Mngt.

(b) Competition

(c) Stakeholder Involvement

Redefining

- Role of State
- Private & Public Sector
- Motivators
- Technology
- Experiments & Research

Need to have Parcel

- Organise Beneficiaries
- Design, Operate, Finance
- Fix Performance Indicators
- Policy Issues Study
- Private Involvement

FIG. 17.5 : UNDERSTANDING SOME CRITICALITIES

1.	Involve People	--	Why-how-where-when- Cost-lessons
2.	Long Term Vs Short Term	--	Gains Vs Losses
3.	Shortages	--	Concepts, Models, Ideas, People, Workers, Resources or Funds. Faith-Doners, Goods & Services, Food, Water, wealth, Education, Jobs
4.	Dependency Syndrome	--	On God, On Govt. On Society, On Charity-on self-Techno
5.	Attitudes	--	Role, formation, implications, Factors, Parents, Teachers, Society
6.	Resources	--	Economic, Human, Technology, Skills, Natural, Manmade, Long & Short term
7.	Replicability	--	of Concepts, Principles, Programmes
8.	Viability		
9.	Convergence		
10.	Model		
11.	Holistic-Human Development		
12.	Self-Propelling	--	Systems

FIG. 17.6: SUSTAINABLE

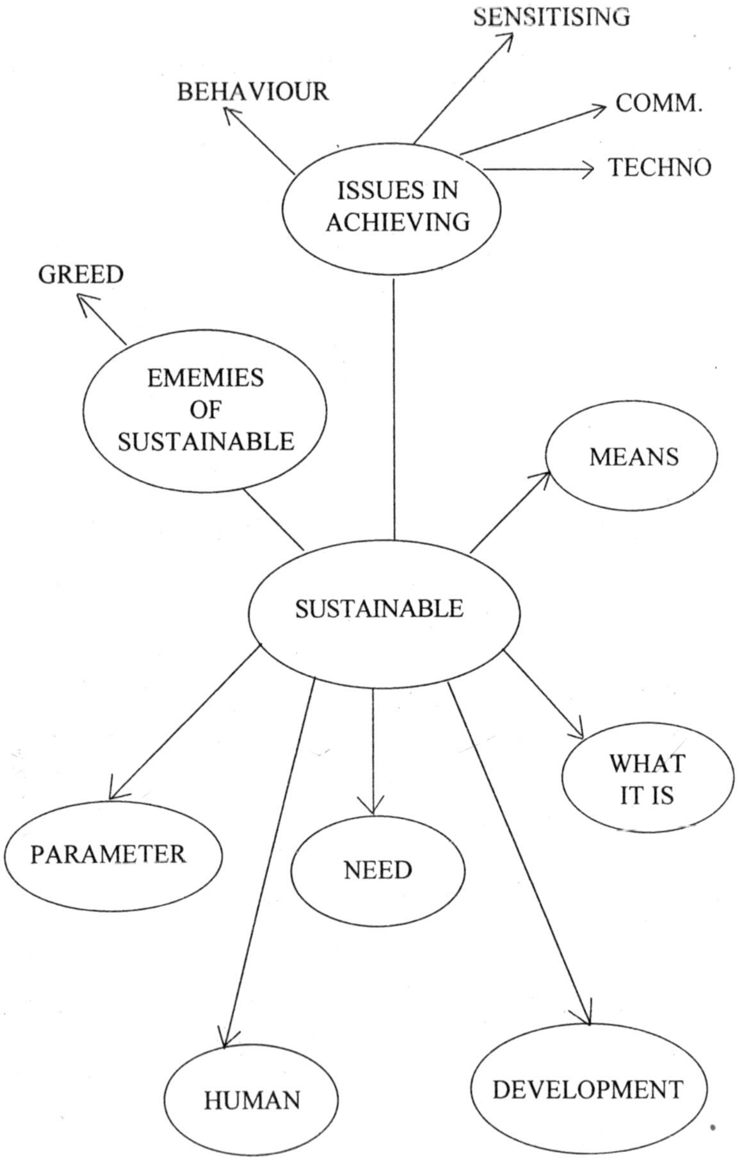

FIG. 17.7 : POLICY PERSPECTIVES FOR INDIA

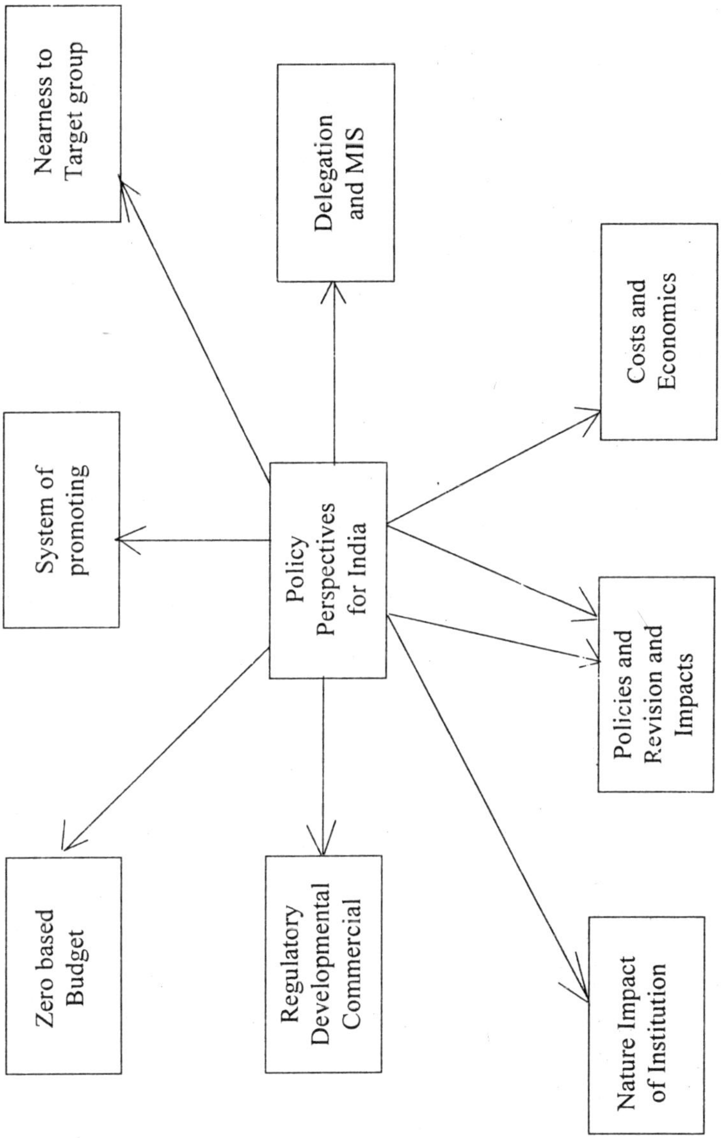

FIG. 17.8 : MODEL MAKING LINKAGE

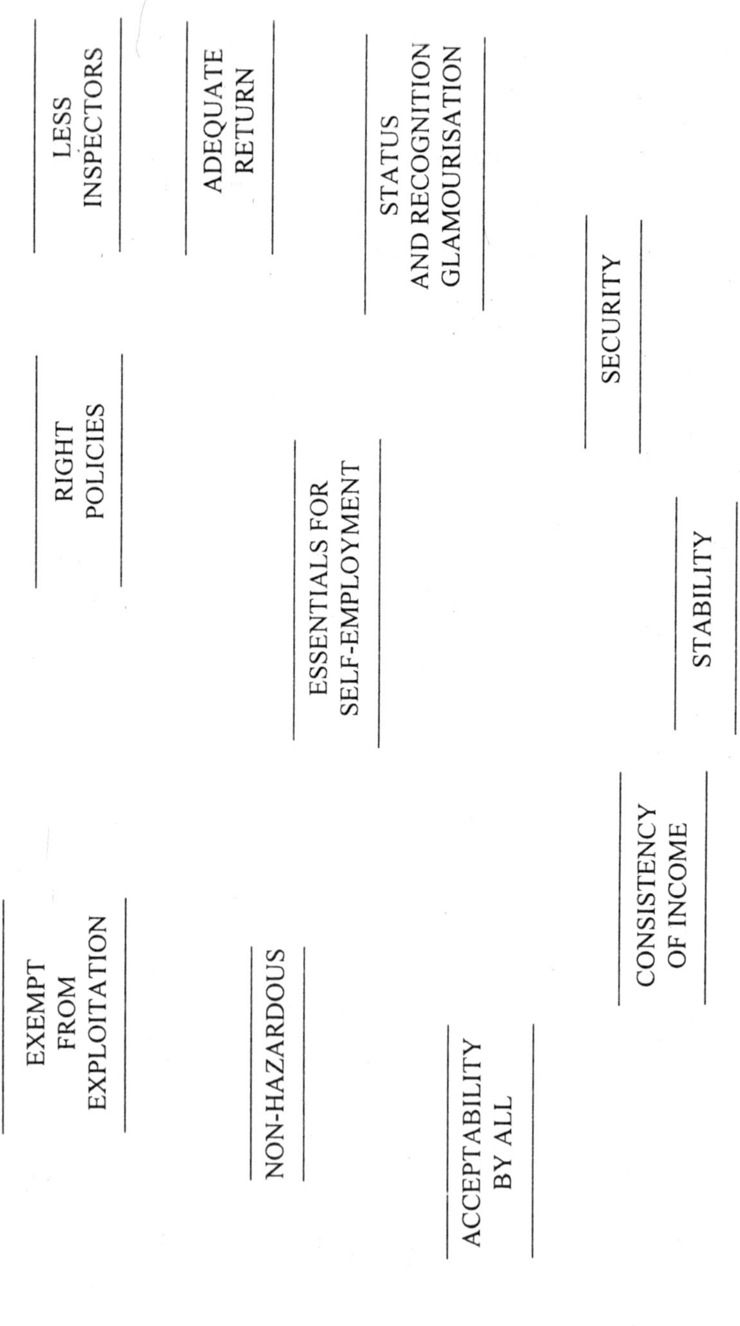

FIG. 17.9 : ADOPTING VIABLE MARKET APPROACH

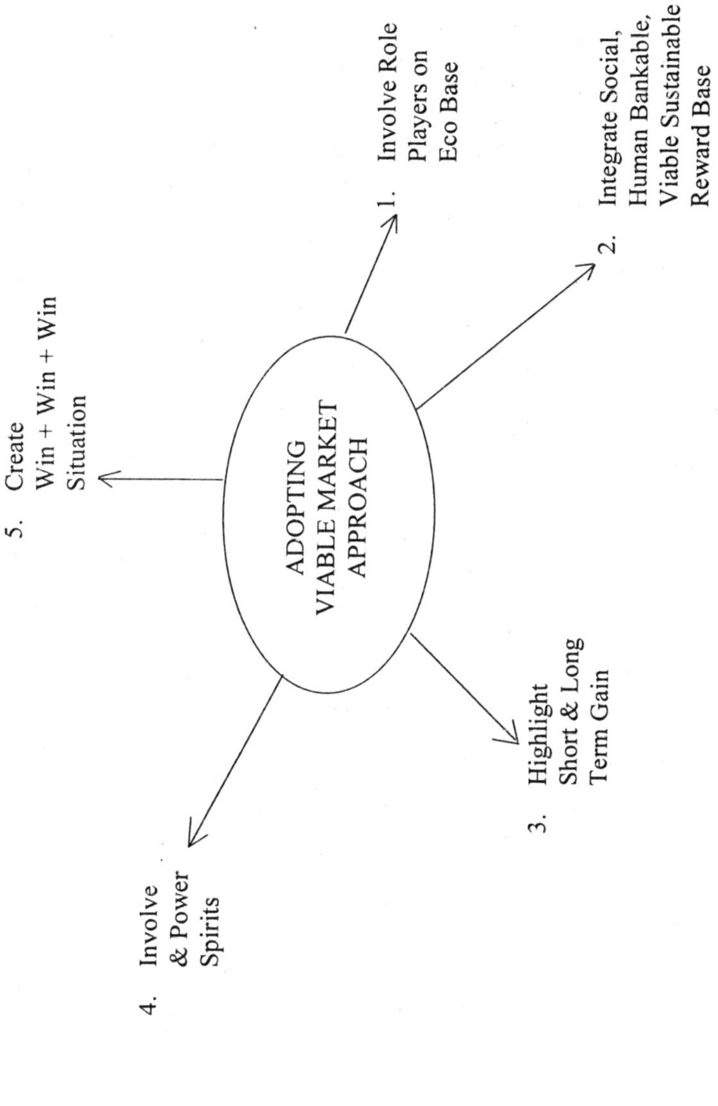

FIG. 17.10 : ESSENTIAL FOR SUCCESS OF THE PROGRAMME

1. Adequate reports to all
2. Bankability of the project
3. Linkage/tie-up.
4. Regular research
5. Dissemination of all information including marketing potential etc.

FIG. 17.11 : LESSONS OF THE PAST

1. How Programme has been run?
2. How funds have been spent?
3. How recruitments have been made?
4. How linkages broke down?
5. Whether coordination was minimal or nil?
6. Was the transparency absent?
7. Why achievement could not be spread?
8. What was the net result?

FIG. 17.12 : UNDERSTANDING RURALITIES OF OUR TIME

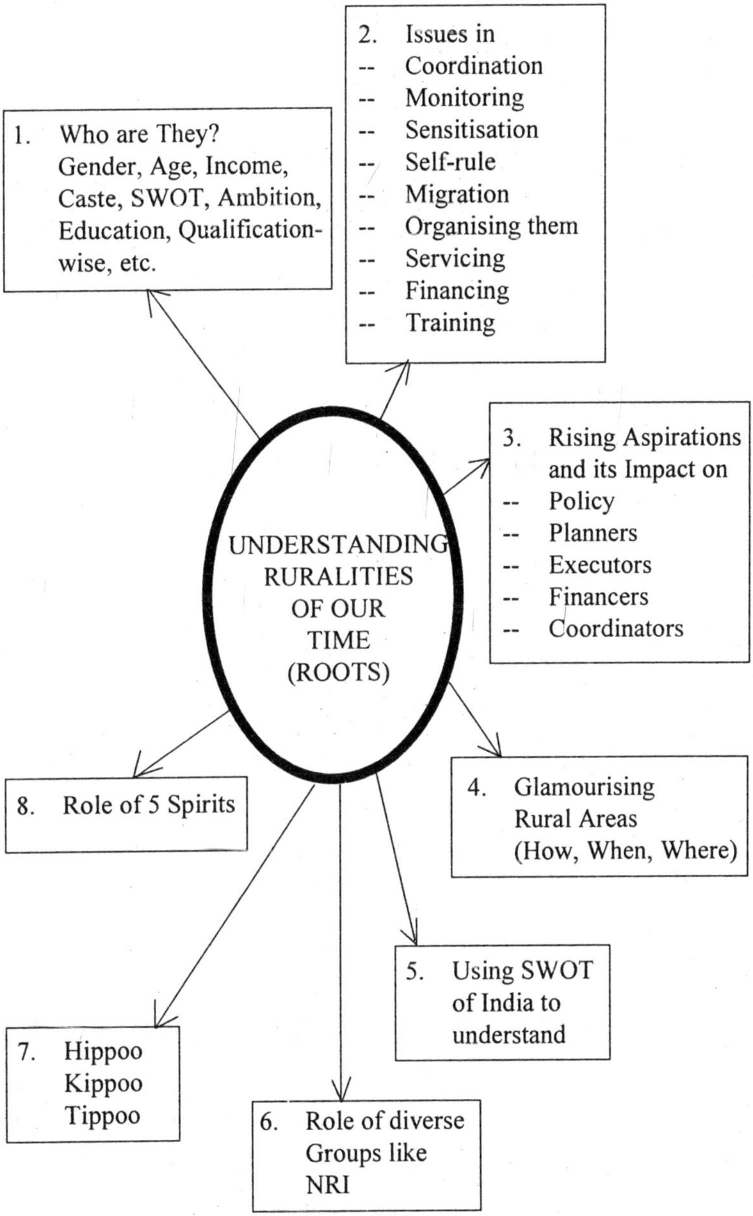

HIPPOO--Hidden Investible Potential Power of Organisation
KIPPOO--Known Investible Potential Power of Organisation
TIPPOO--Threatening Investible Potential Power of Organisation

FIG. 17.13: INTERNAL RESOURCE GENERATION BY

(a) Market Approach

(b) Pooling of Resources

(c) Better Servicing Systems

(d) Attitude Changes

(e) Proper Appreciation:

(i) Immediately Bankable

(ii) Gradually Bankable

(iii) Requiring Some Incentives

(iv) Better Systems for Confidence Building

FIG. 17.14 : HOLISTIC MODEL FOR DEVELOPMENT

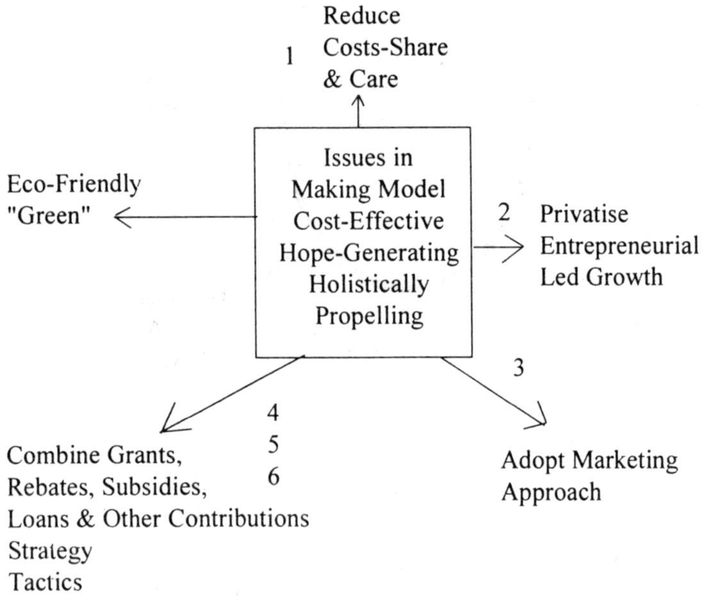

FIG. 17.15 : KVIC ACTIVITIES

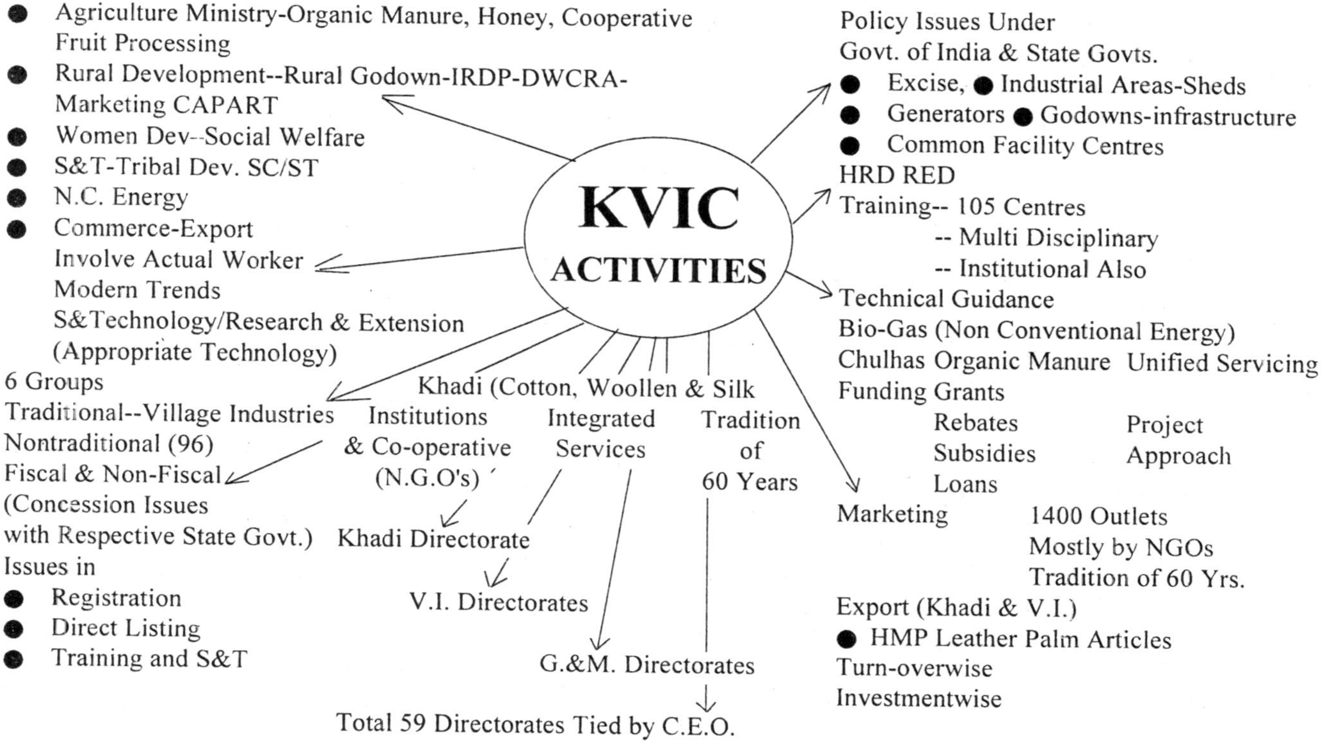

FIG. 17.16: WHAT TO DO?

1. Short Term Measures
2. Long Term Measures

SHORT TERM MEASURES--

Objectives--Immediate results
Immediate results with maximisation
of utilisation of existing infrastructure,
Manpower, investments made on
replicable, self supporting basis,
i.e. involve technology, women force,
economic principles, spirituality and faith

LONG TERM MEASURES--

Objectives--Will need attention to

A. Financial and administration
B. Academic
C. Marketing
D. Monitoring
E. Overall attitudinal change
of functionaries for self
supporting programme development

FIG. 17.17 : ACTIVITY CHART IN AND AROUND WARDHA

Institution & Location	What to See	Potential addition for replicability and multiplicity of such centres for sustainable employment generation through rural development programme
1	2	3
Brahma Vidya Mandir, Paramdham Ashram, Paunar	Dairy, Biogas, Organic Manure, Farming and Plantation, value added dairy products, marketing, tourism. historical temple, spirituality, meditation with special emphasis on development, simple living, ideal atmosphere and health oriented visionary development. Please contact: Smt. Kusum Deshpande, Shri Gautam Bajaj Tel. 2583	With proper marketing and replication activity by their exposure to foreigners, city dwellers and like minded organisation working for sustainable rural development, training centres for women, extension work and overall interaction with those interested in economically viable models may be taken up
Maharogi Seva Samiti, (Leprosy Service Centre), Dattapur	Leprosy, self employment, confidence building, cotton growing, ginning. spinning, weaving, marketing, oil ghani, tailoring, farming, biogas, community kitchen, dairy, leather footwear manufacture, sericulture, treatment of lepers. Dr. Ravi Shankar Sharma Tel. 3563, 2714	With total marketing and exposure it is possible to establish sustainable linkages with vocational education and social welfare institutions, production of environment friendly products, workshops, studies research and training programmes for various groups including bankers
Centre of Science for Villages, Dattapur	Biogas, Low cost housing. Handmade paper, pottery, Sanitation, Low cost irrigation and experiments on Rural Economics Shri Devendra Kumar Tel. 2956	With proper marketing approach and the linkages with ongoing programmes, excellent institutions for training, workshops, research codification could be replicated.
Gram Seva Mandal, Gopuri	Silver Plant, spinning, weaving, dairy, carpentry and Blacksmithy workshop, Charkha making, village oil, Agriculture, waste silk spinning. Secretary, Tel. 2749	There is a need to involve youth to make programme attractive and rural oriented with better cost effective system

1	2	3
Leather Institute, Gopuri	Tanning, Footwear, Marketing of leather goods, training	To replicate such model there is a need to involve beneficiaries specialised in traditional practice of flaying, vegetable tanning, packaging besides better exposure of non-violent leather products.
Gosamvardhan Goras Bhandar, Maganwadi	Cow Milk, value added milk products like Goras pak, Peda, Ghee, Shrikhand butter milk, and unique bakery products, aggressive marketing with Low Cost High Effect (LCHE) working since 1940s. Shri Ramkrishan Date.	With better marketing outlet at Railway station, Bus station at Wardha and Nagpur and popularising the value of cow milk, by exposing to conscious keepers of society with linkages between animal husbandry on the one hand and rural development including women development on the other, bankable projects with assured replication is possible besides better insemination practices, self-employment programmes, animal feed and fodder and selective linkages with leather industry. This may become a covered model related to cow development programme having linkage with biogas.
Bhartiya Kutir Udyog, (Indian Cottage Industry) Dahegaon	20 Km from Wardha, Excellent model of rural development involving women (about 150) producing Khowa based Rajmalai Chocolate, Peda, Bar-powder, Mangoes, Awala, Pickle, Garlic Paste, Chilli paste, spices, engaged in this activity since 1931. Shri Arun Kelkar.	Excellent marketing, production, training. consultancy and overall replicable model which had stood the test of time. It epitomises total integration of trusteeship concept and economic self sufficiency with absolutely no funds or facilities from government. It is an ideal model for the country's entrepreneurship which emphasises on women employment in rural areas through value addition to rural raw materials. Special attention is needed for replication, diversification in dairy, training and research. It is an excellent centre for multifarious studies on rural industrialisation.
Rural Food Industry Training Institute, Wardha (East), Railway Station	Spice, Noodles and Papad making, popcorn, rice milling, dal making, Bakery, Marketing, production and Training Centre which markets the products manu-	Run jointly by Shiksha Mandal and KVIC, this centre has a lot of land in the proximity of important railway junction. If aggressive marketing is taken on priority basis it would prove to be a centre

1	2	3
	factured by trainees to build up their confident for self employment. Hostel and library facilities available.	of excellence for internal resource generation, low cost high impact publicity and an effective communication for self employment. Since the Shiksha Mandal has various institutions like Commerce and Science College, Polytechnic and industrial cluster, it would be possible to develop it as an ideal cooperative venture where corporate culture and development of rural entrepreneurship on food based industries would be evolved through policy changes.
Jamnalal Bajaj Central Research Institute, Maganwadi.	In 1935 All India Village Industries Association was formed here and subsequently since 1956-57. Handmade paper, M.D. Workshop, Village pottery, Soap. Dal processing, Village oil, Biogas, Lime activities are going on. It is a well known Centre for proper and effective instrumentation for rural industrial activity and marketing.	Endowed with about 11 acres of land and with better coordination and marketing approach, training, research, codification, consultancy and instrumentation, rural industrialisation could be possible with special thrust on Vidarbha. In adtion, activity like Computer Training for disabled and SC/ST could be taken up and direct linkage for sustainable rural development could be established.
General Institutions Gandhi Gnyan Mandir, Wardha.	Very old library with excellent literature on Gandhian philosophy	There is a need to have more popular and useful books to youth by holding workshop, Diverse books relating to Gandhian philosophy abroad are also to be got.
Gagan Sangrahalaya, Wardha	A Museum of Khadi and Village industries and items presented to Gandhiji are exhibited there	To collaborate jointly with like minded organisation abroad is utmost required
Geeta Mandir, Gopuri,	18th Chapter of *Geeta* has been carved on stones. It is a memorial of Late Shri Jamnalal Bajaj. Also Buddha Stupa funded by Japanese Fuji Guruji, Vinoba exhibition, guest house, library are nearby.	
Chetana Vikas, Gopuri.	It is working for the development of women in rural areas creating awareness in the rural	

1	2	3
	women about overall health, education, agriculture, integrated programme, etc.	
Sevagram Ashram, Wardha	Gandhiji's cottage activities started by Gandhiji like Nai Talim (Basic education). prayer hall, guest house, book stall and Gandhian literature, medical college, yoga centre	
Leprosy Foundation Wardha	Research centre for leprosy having hospital for indoor treatment.	
Khadi Bhandars and Emporia, Wardha.	For marketing of Khadi and V.I. Products in and around Wardha.	
Sharad Samagra Grameen Sanstha, Wardha	Experiment on sustainable development, through oriented institution, physical education, youth technical education and linkages with vocational education for rural entrepreneurship development and involvement of corporate sector like Llyods Steel to meet rising aspirations of youth.	
Rashtrabhasha Prachar Samiti, Wardha.	A viable institution in the field of propagation of national language (Hindi)	
Sreeman Narayan Smruthi Sanstha, Wardha.	An excellent centre for intellectual. spiritual, codification of experience of by-gone year with futuristic era. Smt. Madalsa Narain Tel. 3175	
Swamy Satyabhakt Ashram	It preaches on spirituality and religion.	

FIG. 17.18: AREAS OF CO-OPERATION WITH OTHER DEPARTMENTS

-- HUMAN RESOURCES DEVELOPMENT
-- RURAL DEVELOPMENT
-- NON-CONVENTIONAL ENERGY
-- FRUIT PROCESSING AND PRESERVATION
-- HEALTH
-- EDUCATION
-- EXPORT PROMOTION
-- FOOD PROCESSING
-- SCIENCE & TECHNOLOGY
-- C.S.I.R.
-- ALL INDIA BEEKEEPING BOARD
-- AGRICULTURE
-- LEATHER DEVELOPMENT BOARD
-- TRAINING

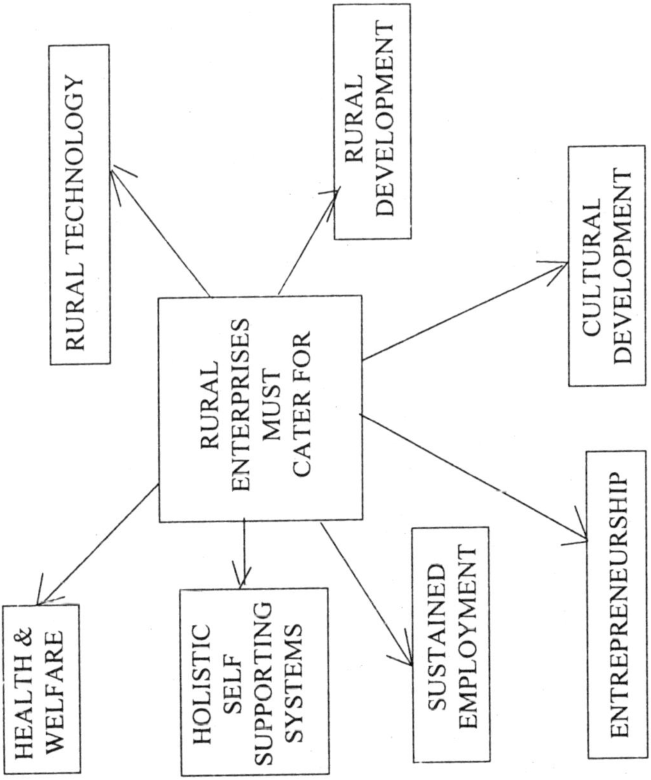

FIG. 17.19: WOMEN UNEDUCATED VS EDUCATED

FIG. 17.20 : CONCEPTS OF MODELS

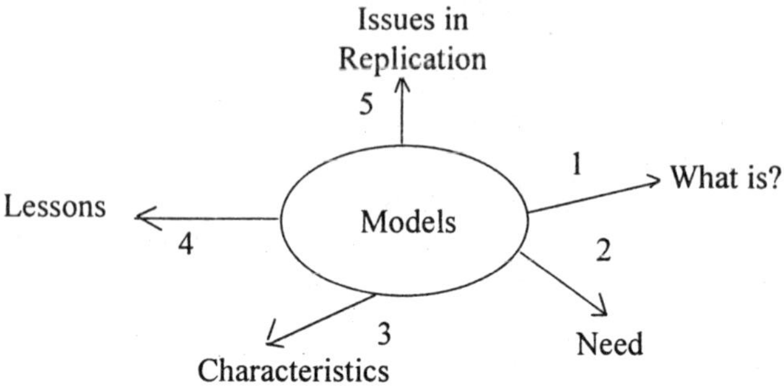

FIG. 17.21: LTWT–LEARNING TO WORKING TOGETHER

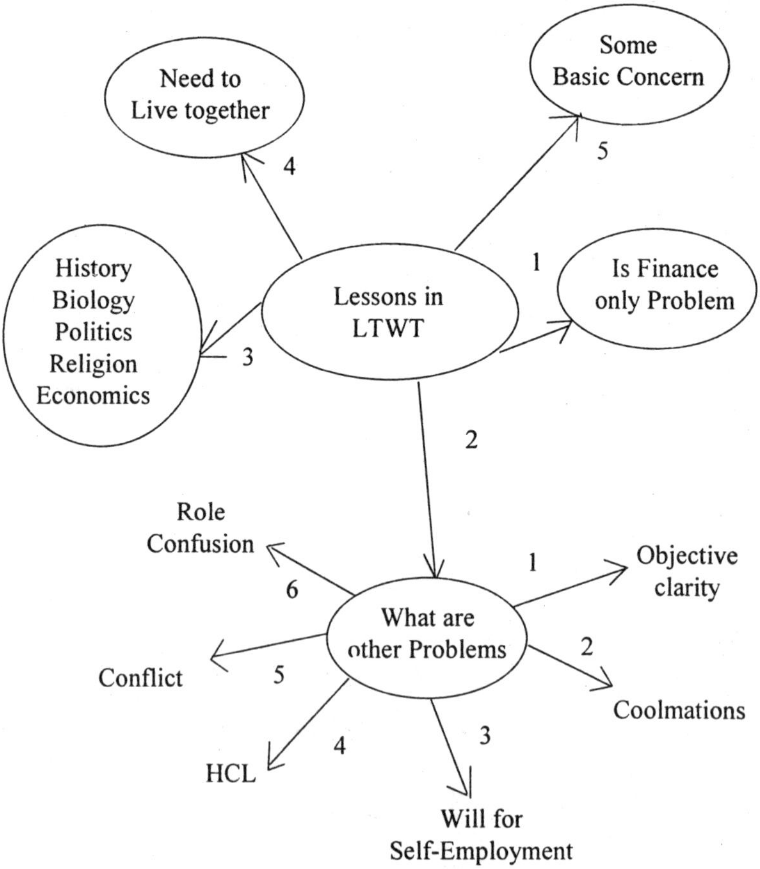

FIG. 17.22 : FACTORS AFFECTING BUREAUCRATS DECISION TAKING

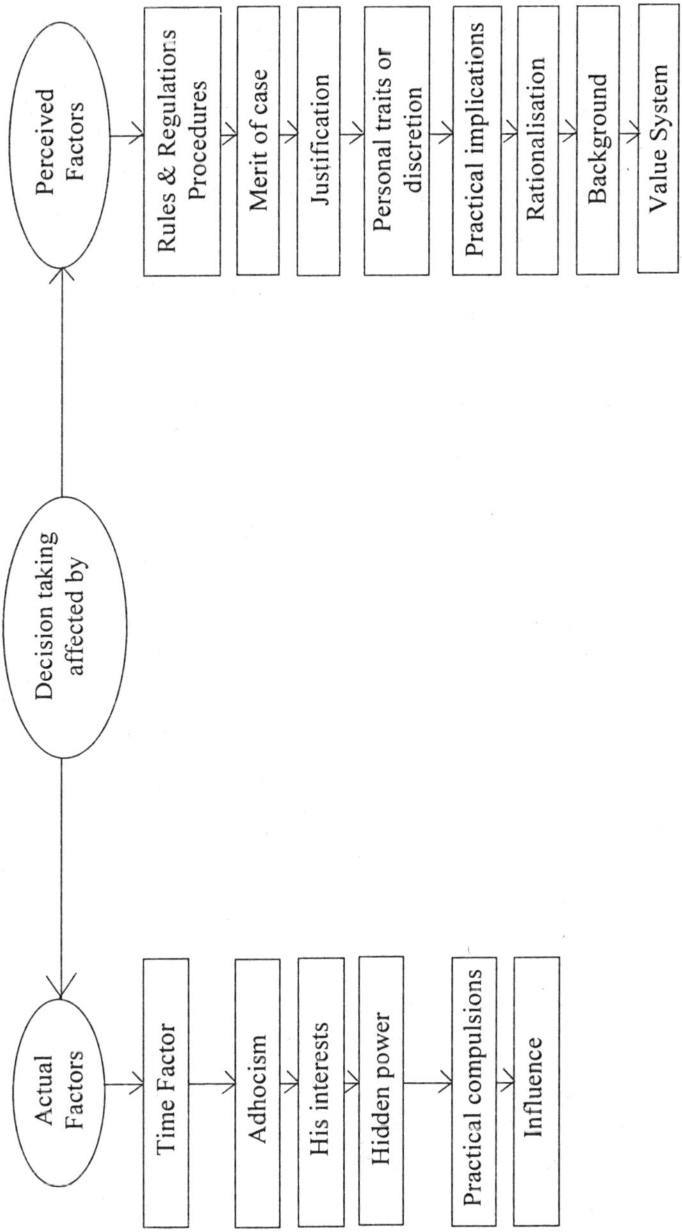

FIG. 17.23: ADOPTING VIABLE MARKET APPROACH

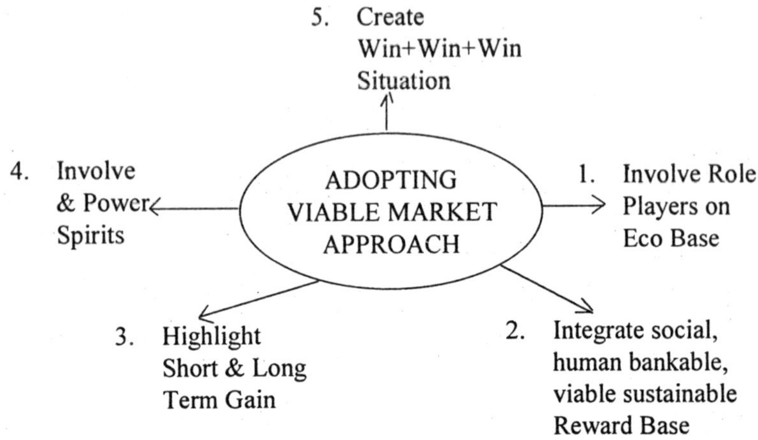

FIG. 17.24: FACTORS IN RURAL DEVELOPMENT MODEL (REDM)

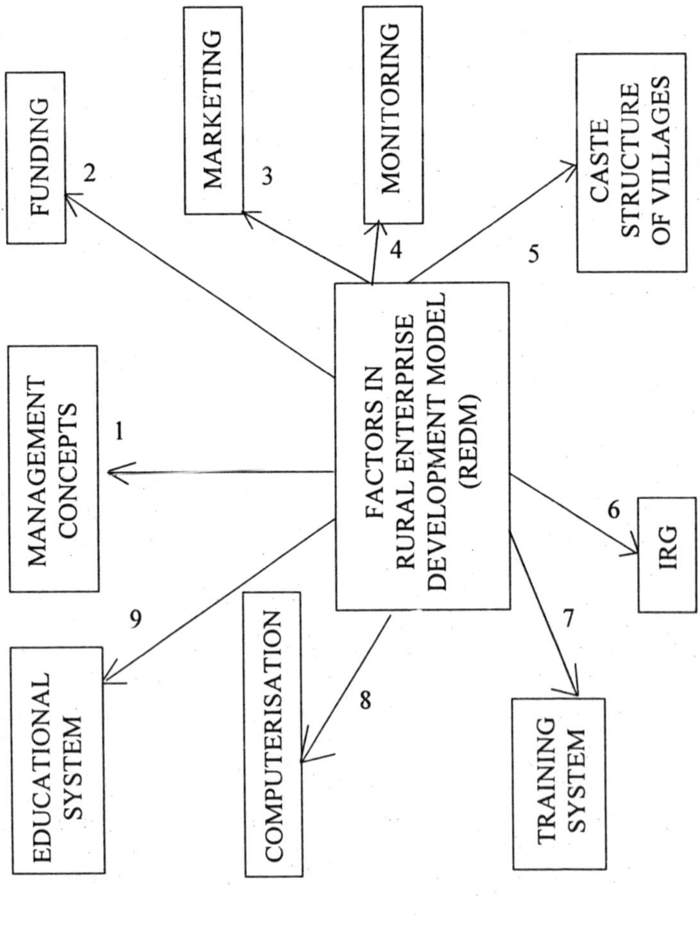

FIG. 17.25: PROBLEMS AND IMPLICATIONS

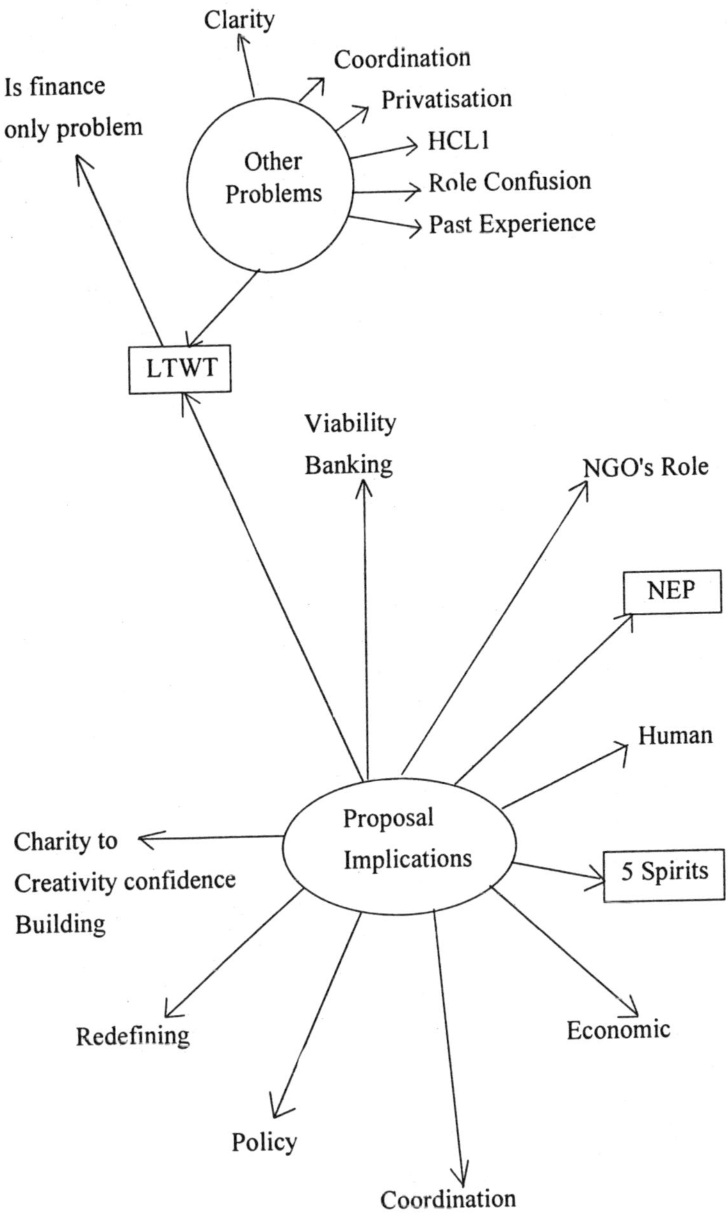

LTWT - Learning to work together

NEP - New Economic Policy

FIG. 17.26: ANALYSIS SERIES

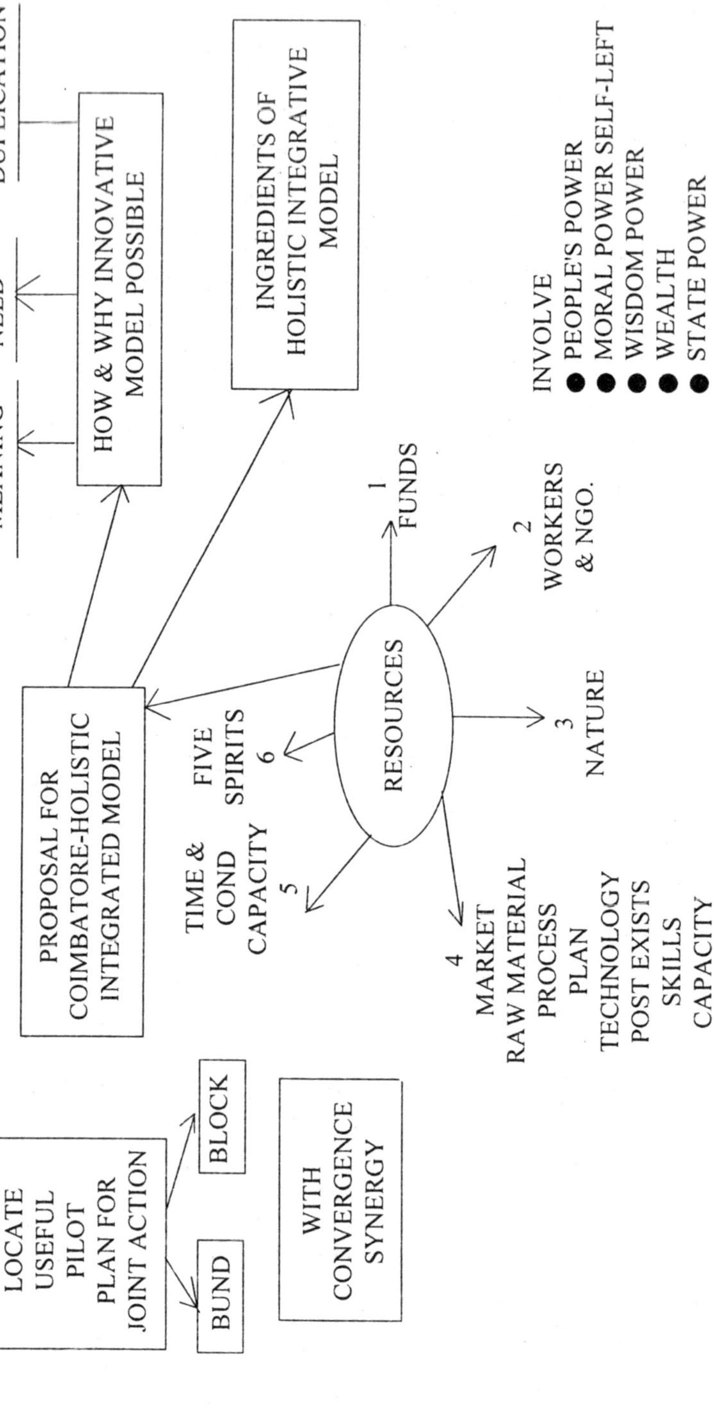

FIG. 17.27: ROLE OF BUREAUCRATS

1. Is he sensitised to serve the target group in question?
2. His role as

   Planner

   Monitor

   Motivator

   Finance provider

   Problem solver

   Market solver

   Market developer

   Codifier

   overall propagator & sympathiser

FIG. 17.28: MONITORING SYSTEM

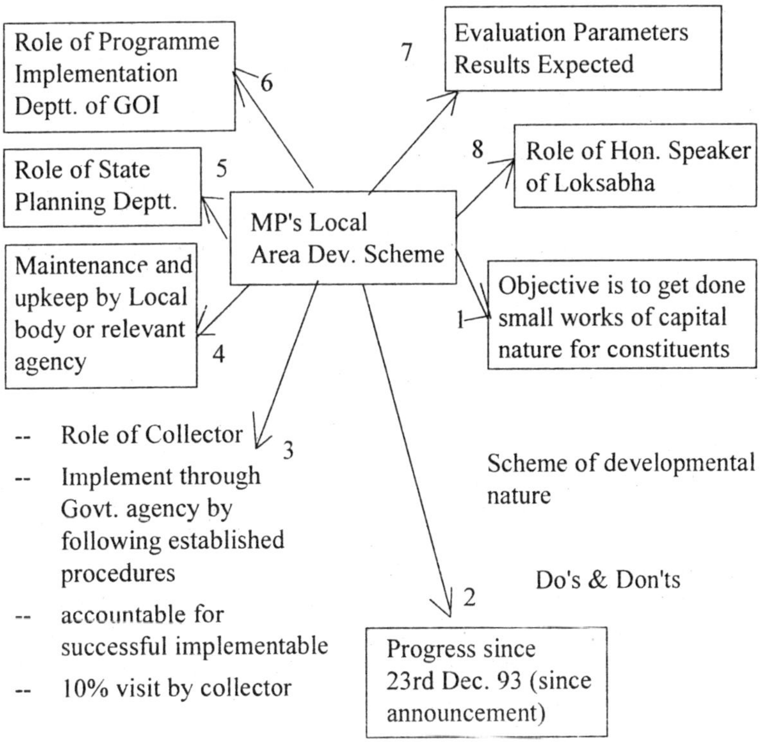

18

GLOBALIZATION AND SELF-RELIANCE
Understanding of Principles

Globalisation many fear may kill self-reliance. After all one should not forget that in many parts of Latin America, Africa, globalisation has genuinely killed the self-reliant societies. They have become totally dependent on western concepts and have hardly been left with anything which they could call their own.

The fear of India also losing its self-reliant nature of development or life style or society at large definitely has to be looked with apprehension. Despite the fear that India has been a self regulated, self-propelled, self-sufficient, sustainable, humanist, comparative village economy in the history--the future does call for a realistic re-assessment. Globalisation has mind boggling implications. The aggressive technology, glamourised life styles, expensive power structure and indifference of masses it call for concern on this front.

When we look at some of those principles or commonly applicable factors to various aspects of human behaviour and lessons of history we have to approach every conscious, transparent, examinable and rationally analysable principles. The need to examine through principles or some tenets or commonly applicable communities to basically to draw centre key point. For example we can look at the various aspects divided into subjects through which man passes. He has basic needs then education, marriage, job, sex, family, society, social security, love, affection, fraternity and then ultimately lessons of history. Hence to examine issues of globalisation and self-reliance a phased subject-wise study has to be undertaken as we bring out in the various subjects, commonalities, communities.

Common Issues

While looking into the principles there are bound to be some common principles. For example simplicity, fruitfulness, sensitivity, respect for each other, dignity, tolerance, truth, non-violence, equal opportunities for growth etc. prepared to be common points irrespective of religion, place, age, education. These have to be imbibed and taught by teachers, society, family and the state. There can hardly be any compromise. But the regional variance about eating non-veg or killing animals or status of women or number of children etc. may vary as per the level of knowledge of the individual and his personal religion.

Capacity of the state to be logical, rational and intelligible. There cannot be uniformity. But here also rationality, scientific analysis, judicious approach can definitely be common.

Coming back to the principles subject-wise we may take up this matter for examination. Hence for our discussion the following may be important areas:

1. Economics,
2. Politics,
3. Science,
4. History,
5. Geography,
6. Religion,
7. Sex & Human Behaviour,
8. Trade & Commerce.

The most important subject which has developed for good or bad in the last century is economics, whether it is applied economics or econometrics or any other specialised field. Probably economics has helped increasing the value of money and this has created all the problems in the world.

It has fuelled the greed aspect for money in the human beings. All other subjects have become secondary and discardable. We have to observe around us to see how every one has become money minded. How do we understand scientifically, rationally various developments. We have to only observe our own behaviour if doubts persists we may observe our friends behaviour. Even though we are all basically selfish and the fact remains that there is nothing like un-selfishness the over emphasis on creation part makes our life miserable and behaviour devoid of sensitivity. These becomes the crux of the problem. This is how it works. Leading to individualism, lack of transparency in decision making, secretiveness, suspicion and on the whole exploitative, the psychological, social, organic, temperamental, law and order and other related aspects have to be integrated to draw valid conclusions. Economics as it becomes dominating over other aspects of life say culture, art and so in final aspects the results are bound to be devastating to social equilibrium. Ultimately it is the balancing which is sustaining the life. The problems of economy, devastation of nature, unbridled growth of imbalanced industries and towns, wrong policy planning and usurping of the state by the manipulators make the life for simple, honest, God fearing, humble citizens, difficult. The happenings around us make it very simple to observe. Economics has to be redefined to meet the taste of sustainable human development. Only earning more money and spending more money and consuming more electricity and exploiting more natural resources can never be the ultimate objective of any society. The economic development can only be a part of sustainable human development. As we all know human beings are only one part of the nature's creation. They have no right to think, act, work and plan in isolation. Same way economics is also only one aspect of ultimate happenings. The conglomeration of various inputs may be made available easily through money but that means only acting as facilitator, hence money cannot be the end. It is here the HDI Report prepared by UNDP since last 6/7 years helps us in redefining the established definitions. The evolutionary development so wide and in such a short time make our job of drawing principles much easier.

The economics of tomorrow has to meet the following taste:

1. Does it really lead to sustainable happiness.
2. Does it promise self-propelled growth and equitable distribution.
3. Does it empower people by taking them away from charity to creativity, capacity and confidence building.
4. Does it ensure area, time, culture, oriented development planning process.
5. Does it ensure role of various role players.
6. New economic order has to be more humanistic and broader in vision.
7. Capital intensive has to be replaced by senstivity. From exploitative it has to shift to expropriative. This is not possible so long as capital intensive programmes and projects remain the priority of the State. There has to be emphasis on natural resources and gifts of God. So long as manual work is not recognised and accounted for properly in the so called GDP calculation the definition of economics would be topsyturvy.

Economics had very limited role in the past. Today it has become the most SWOT after but very destructive subject. The human aspect of economic development can no more be neglected.

This calls for the following action.

1. Re-defining multi-dimensionally various definitions.
2. Demistifying various concepts.
3. Developing suitable models to suit vision of tomorrow.
4. Relying more on rationality, scientific analysis, analytical approach, rather than borrowed implanted concepts.
5. Developing regional local models with emphasis on replication and pulling of wisdom and resources and involvement of all and Panchayati Raj system.
6. Decentralised Governments.

The concept of the farther the state but better the government has been replaced by accountability and nearness of citizen. The concept of state being well meaning has not stood the test of time. The problem of human nature relating to greed, exploitation, dictatorial behaviour remains as good or bad. The only difference visible is in terms of awakening of the masses making arbitrariness difficult. There are many developments which bring out the irreversible nature of development which make the coming decade as that of masses. The state will face tough competition from other competitors and it is only with transparency, viability that better alternatives may emerge and survive. The socialism, capitalism and humanism issues are bound to lead to totally new approaches. The un-utilising infrastructure will find aggressive users. In this process the mind sets will be getting transformed and re-structured. These are the challenges which time has to face.

19

LOW COST PRACTICAL CONSULTANCY AND SUSTAINABLE HUMAN DEVELOPMENT

The concept of consultancy has been unknown to rural development programme. Traditionally consultancy has been a high cost business affordable for only organised sector with high investment. But now time has come when rural development programme do have benefit of services of experts. Retired people, freedom fighters, volunteers from other organisations, experimenter have role to play in this process. What is required is acceptance of the fact that everybody has important role to play and working in isolation, individualistic, nuisance mind sets have accelerated the process of collapse. It is here not only man as a part of the Society but also society itself should have system of low cost practical consultancy. Due to problem of CTB, law and order problem was rampant, stock exchange failure became common. It is essential that new investment potential with stability and security are identified in small towns and rural area. The field of consultancy is bound to open up. How do we go about it? This question which this project tries to address itself. This is golden time to implement various reports of international and national bodies. Lessons of various efforts need to be suitably adjusted with the local conditions. This project by adopting evolutionary, humanistic approach to the whole developmental process did try to come out with implementable plan of action. Needless to say there cannot be soft options.

20

NEED TO STUDY DEVELOPMENT OF ENTREPRENEURSHIP FOR BACKWARD POCKETS

This opportunity of linking up Member of Parliament, Local Area Development Scheme and UN Systems also offers a challenging opportunity to study how entrepreneurship has developed and sustained. Punjab, Gujarat along with Kerala are well known for their capacity to migrate. Even from backward state like Uttar Pradesh there are pockets like Jaunpur district from where thousand of people have migrated to place like Bombay and earned name, fame and wealth for themselves. How it has happened? Cannot same thing, may be on minor scale, be tried as an opportunity of entrepreneurship development in the scheme? Has any sincere effort been made to také up a village or a block to study evolutionary process of masses trying to explore their full worth? Cannot this be an opportunity to locate those missing linkages whether of policy, technology, financing or overall social structure which hampered this upward shift? How its training, vocationalisation, technology and other back up and social value system change the whole system from charity to commerce? How the communication termed effective? What are the issues in financing, recoveries, shaping of attitude and overall personality development not only of individual but also of the community?

A case study system may help in identifying those reasons and the following aspects may help in total appreciation.

To make this point more clear we may take example of district like Jaunpur in Uttar Pradesh from where many people have migrated to Bombay for exploring their potential in the economic development field. Why have these people gone from Jaunpur? How have they performed? What is the past, present and vision for future? How they have integrated with the people of that area? Who compelled and supported them? What are the lessons for others to learn from them? What are the social, political, economic lessons?

This is not something new as it happens all over the world. We should try to understand the various aspects through this effort to understand fully the process involved in the sustainable human development efforts.

21

LINKAGES WITH PANT NAGAR UNIVERSITY HILL CAMPUS, RANICHAURI

There is a need to develop linkages with all the local infrastructure expertise manpower and on-going programmes within the areas.

Traditionally Agriculture University has worked in collaboration only with district administration and government department. It is high time linkages and joint work culture is developed with non-governmental organizations, private sector and entrepreneurs for extending the benefits of research, technology and new innovations.

Local Institutions of people, NGOs, Panchayati Raj, market linked developmental initiatives and local business enterprises could benefit from value addition effort on the raw material from agriculture including forest, horticulture, floriculture etc.

The campus has infrastructural, transport, training, communication facilities alongwith expertise in the traditional field. In the new emerging fields of enterprises development, privatisation, marketing effective technology and linkages with Panchayati Raj, new initiatives are required.

By establishing linkages, the facilities of Library, communication network would easily be possible.

It is pity that traditionally different groups working even in difficult areas have worked in isolation. This has resulted in distress on the one hand and ignorance about each other. The Himalayan Community had various traditional knowledge, expertise and way of life which has sustained over centuries. All these have been working with efficiency and providing quality of life.

The Himalayan NGOs have also been working since long though in their own isolated areas. There has been tradition, pilgrims, servicing, plantation, charity, dharamshalas, but in the last about ten years NGOs have come in new areas like soil conservation, plantation, water management, health, sanitation, family planning, empowerment, education etc. etc.

This is the right time where case studies could be developed keeping in mind the following aspects:

1. Cost of implementation of programme/project by government and NGO. This study can be in any field since it will be based on common parameters of expenditure and results. For example plantation, drinking water facility, education, roads etc. could be comparatively analysed both for fixed and running expenditure.
2. There are areas of cooperation as applicable to Himalayan communities and NGOs. By taking up area based integrated development plans this partnership could be studied with replicability aspect.
3. In the field of self employment, vocational education, skill up-gradation on traditional industries, self sufficiency, organic manure, eco-friendly products, effective technology, selected programmes implemented are being considered for implementation could be jointly examined from various angles.
4. There are many missing areas in communities. Low cost practical consultants, traditional based datas and technologies, arts and crafts, vocational trainings and nurseries etc. could be taken up jointly for developing case studies on the earlier initiatives or new areas for action.

Schools, Inter Colleges, Media and Parents have lot of role to play in sustainable human development. In Hill areas where communication is still difficult and transport expensive, the local institutes of learning and the families and communities could have low cost practical consultants staying in the villages and sharing the knowledge base. Even though T.V. and Radio have made this job easier still there is need to involve schools, families and parents in overall extension of developmental initiatives. A single window servicing system by government departments could also help a lot in developing cost effective systems.

PART-IV

CORRESPONDENCE, LETTERS AND READING MATERIALS

Letter to Shri Mani Shankarji, Hon'ble M.P. dated 20th April 1994 by Dr. Kamal Taori

D.O. No. CEO/Pub/96/94-95 20th April, 1994

My dear Shri Mani Shankarji,

I had the opportunity of reading in Sunday your Mani-talk on "My Own one crores"--Largesse parsimony--or bloody nuisano?.

It makes a very interesting, frustrating and also concern sharing, but one sided story. There are many missing areas because of which this well intentioned scheme may not receive proper justification.

While the objective of this funding must be to take up those programmes which are hitherto neglected with proper planning, co-ordination and priority setting, it should be possible to not only multiply the monetary value of this money, but also to take up really socially useful programmes for improving, competitive compatibility of the beneficiaries.

This letter I am writing in my personal capacity. But it has social implications. It has a fact that traditionally this sort of money should have been spent on sweet will and adhoc priority of the recipient. This will necessarily lead to unpleasant situation where very few will be quiet, many will be discontented and vocal. This may ultimately lead to halo and mauls and the concern of the Hon. writer is fully understandable. But today because of the rising expectations and possibility of linking up with other initiatives it should be possible to develop better systems of increasing the utility of this fund. For example, some priority programmes can be identified which can be made economically viable. Hence, the Banks, the loans, the grants and even foreign investment can be pooled to create jobs on self-employment basis with better policy prescription. The policy needs to understand that self-help, principled allotment right prioritation and long term output from the investment have to be given priority. There may be weightage to social, gender and traditionally neglected issues while giving these weightages. But the new wave of cost effectiveness have to be built in even in these allotments. Can it be taken as an investment which must pay after some time? Instead of proportionate distribution or duress distribution or calamity distribution, some principles can be developed so as to achieve the following objectives,

(1) Pulling the resources and infrastructure
(2) Involve big schemes of investors
(3) Develop marketing approach through these investments
(4) Ultimate aim of developing enterprise concept must be in-built, in-distribution programme.

Letter dated 7 November 1994 from Shri Nawal Kishore Sharma, Chairman, Khadi & Village Industries Commission, Bombay to Dr. Man Mohan Singh, Union Minister of Finance, Government of India, New Delhi

No.CEO/Up. Govt./162/94-95 7th November, 1994

My dear

I have been given to understand that various International Organisations have carried out studies on the question of involvement of NGOs in the development of unorganised sector, especially in the rural area.

As you are aware, KVI Sector has come of the oldest NGOs working in the field of income generation. They are not only spread all over India but also have contacts in the rural areas. In this connection, KVIC has received a letter from UNDP, a copy of which is enclosed for your information with this letter.

I would like to take this opportunity to offer on behalf of the KVIC and all those Institutions that they can be helpful to the Govt. in extending on a cost effective basis programme for sustainable employment generation.

I need not mention that in the longer run, for making effective contribution to Rural Development Programme, the role of KVI Sector will have to be suitably recognised by the Govt. of India.

Yours Sincerely,

(Nawal Kishore Sharma)

Encl. Copy of a letter dt.
9.12.1992 from programme
officers, UNDP, New Delhi

Dr. Man Mohan Singh
Union Minister for Finance
Govt. of India,
New Delhi

Letter dated 14 July 1995 from Resident Representative, UNDP to Chairman, Khadi & Village Industries Commission, Bombay for KVIC link-up with pilot UN system initiative in support MPs Local Area Development Schemes

Account Code : 2DA-5IND-490 (Into Activities) 14 July 1995
IND/PRO/300 (INF-HDRPF)
IND/PRO/300 (INF-Coordination)

Dear Mr. Sharma

KVIC Link-up with pilot UN System Initiative in support MPs Local Area Development Schemes

Encouraged by the progress being achieved in the country by the Khadi and Village Industries Commission (KVIC) in creative employment generation, appropriate rural technology and social development activities at the grass-roots level under your dynamic and progressive leadership, we are writing to seek your support in synergistic collaboration over a pilot initiative being undertaken by the UN system in India under UNDP co-ordination, in co-operation with the Parliamentarians Forum for Human Development.

Under the able leadership of Dr. (Mrs) Najma Heptullah, Deputy Chairman, Rajya Sabha six-members of the Forum have agreed to try and formulate and implement model plans for sustainable human development in their constituencies with UN System support and to devote funds under the MPs Local Area Development Scheme to this cause. As you are no doubt aware under this scheme an amount of Rs. 10 million per year (non-lapsing) is available to each MP who is empowered to direct the district administration in his/her constituency to utilise these funds for development projects according to certain criteria. A short description of the way the scheme operates is attached for reference. An important consideration is that no individual project should exceed an allocation of Rs. 10 lakhs.

The aim of our collaboration with the MPs (Terms of Reference attached) is to try and catalyse a synergistic approach bringing together capacities and resources from different sources to produce a multiplier effect and implement an innovative developmental approach at the village level which could be replicable on a wider scale. Towards this end, we feel that a link up with KVIC experience and initiatives could yield promising results which would be beneficial to all the actors in the enterprise.

With the project having completed the planning phase and reached the stage of site visits and concrete project formulation, we would request that Mr. Kamal Taori CEO of KVIC may kindly join an important inter Agency meeting at the UNDP office in New Delhi on 19 July at 10 a.m. where the second action phase will be launched.

We would also request that Mr. Taori kindly participate in the initial site visits by the UN team to Jabalpur (the constituency of Mr. Shravan Patel, Lok Sabha MP) from 20-22 July and to Coimbatore (the constituency of Dr. M. Aram, Rajya Sabha MP) on 26-27 July to review the proposals on the ground and explore the feasibility of a holistic collaborative approach. We are aware of the short notice and that the above itinerary may indeed clash with some KVIC meetings, but we very much hope positive for my roam to join the meeting and visits at this very vital formative stage. This would then greatly ease the way towards reaching a decision on any follow-up involvement of KVIC and Mr. Taori in a more formal way.

We believe that Mr. Taori with the values instilled in him owing to his upbringing in Wardha and his Army background together with his substantive published works on relevant subjects and 25 years experience in the Indian Administrative Service (including as Secretary, Rural Development and Secretary, 20-point programme, at the state-level, and ten years stewardship of KVIC, where he is also National Project Director of two UNDP-assisted projects) would be an ideal guiding partner in taking this innovative experiment further. Needless to say, we would ensure that KVIC does not bear any financial burden for Mr. Taori travel to Delhi. Jabalpur and Coimbatore for these initial meetings and planning visits.

We very much look forward to receiving a positive response in this matter, we thank you in anticipation of your very kind co-operation.

With best regards,

Yours sincerely,
Renato Fornocaldo
Resident Representative

Ms. Nawal Kishore Sharma
Chairman
Khadi & Village Industries, Commission (KVIC)
Bombay

Mr. Kamal Taori
CFO, KVIC Bombay

Declaration adopted by Parliamentarian Forum for Human Development published in Human Development News, Volume 3, Issue 1 of August 1995

First Sensitization Meeting and Declaration to WSSD-95

A one day National Consultation-cum-Sensitization Meeting on Human Social Security and Sustainable Development was held in New Delhi on 20th February, 1995. The Meeting, organized by the Parliamentarians' Forum for Human Development, in collaboration with the UNDP and two leading NGOs--Action Aid (India) and Working Women's Forum (India)--examined critical issue relating to the World Summit for Social Development held in Copenhagen from March 6-12, 1995.

In her opening remarks, Dr. Najma Heptulla, Deputy Chairperson, Rajya Sabha and Chairperson of the parliamentarians Forum for Human Development called for a new social compact between different actors in society in order to tackle the problems of poverty, employment and social integration--the three main themes of the World Summit.

Setting the theme for the Meeting, Mrs. Jaya Arunachalam, President, Working, Women's Forum (India) outlined the many unresolved issues at the end of the Third prepcom for the World Summit. She called for measures to protect the poor and the women in the informal sector from the impact of structural adjustment policies.

The Meeting was inaugurated by Shri Shivraj Patil, Hon'ble Speaker, Lok Sabha, who called for global reduction in military spending and increased expenditure on meeting basic needs. "To live is not sufficient. Human beings should lead healthy good lives" he said while emphasizing the need to prioritize food, health, shelter, employment, and the freedom to develop.

In his Key Note Address, the External Affairs Minister and the Deputy Chairman, Planning Commission, Shri Pranab Mukherji called for a twin pronged poverty eradication strategy involving organizing the poor at the grassroot, in which he said that NGOs had a major role to play, and through a well defined and implemented development strategy.

The inaugural session was also addressed by Dr. Amitava Mukherji, Director (Operations), Action Aid (India), As Chairman of the South Asia Caucus a loose coalition of NGOs from the subcontinent who have been active in the preparatory meetings held for the Summit in New York he outlined the work of the Caucus and in particular its success in getting South Asia mentioned in the official UN documents of the Summit. Summing up, Dr. Nandini Azad of the Indian Cooperative Network for Women hailed the new vision of Human Social Security and Sustainable Development as an integrated model combining equity, growth, empowerment, sustainability, participation and gender justice.

Several Members of Parliament, former Ministers and leading NGO representative spoke integration. It was regretted that even though the world has progressed technologically, economically and scientifically, it has retarded socially and morally.

Participants called for democratization of the UN. Human democracy, it was stressed, was more important than the market democracy that developed countries were promoting. The need to eliminate gender bias that was prevalent on a large scale was emphasized.

On the issue of debt, there was a demand for an audit of "who owes what to whom" in the context of the plunder that the colonial powers resorted to and established mechanisms for the transfer of resources from the North to the South.

NGO leaders raised the problems of full employment and the need to focus on women's self employment as a means of poverty reduction. Concern was expressed that structural adjustments is impacting negatively on the poor and hence the need to protect social expenditures from budgetary cuts. The need to eliminate child labour and provide basic education to child labourers was highlighted. The need to publicize Gandhiji's approach of promoting indigenous technology and self sufficiency as an alternative development paradigm to the market led one was emphasized. It was also recognized that Gandhiji's non-violent approach was most effective for promoting social integration.

The meeting was attended, among others, by Shri Natwar Singh, former External Affairs Minister; Shri Jagmohan, Member of Parliament and former Governor of Jammu and Kashmir, Members of Parliament, such as Shri Prithviraj Chavan, Dr. M. Aram, Shri Nilotpal Basu, Shri S.K. Singla, Shri Virendra Kataria, Shri S.S. Surjewala, Shri J.V.S. Drona, Shri Satish Pradhan, Shri Iqbal Singh, Smt. Veena Verma, Shri T.N. Chaturvedi, Shri Vyalar Ravi, Shri Murlidhar Chandrakant Bhandare, among others.

We the Members of the Indian Parliament, NGO representatives and academics having met in New Delhi on 20th February, 1995 under the aegis of the Parliamentarians' Forum for Human Development and deliberated upon the critical issues of Human Social Security and Sustainable Development in the context of the World Summit for Social

Development to be held in Copenhagen from March 6-12, 1995 do hereby declare the following:

Acknowledg the considerable interest shown in the Summit by the Members of the United Nations through active participation in the three official preparatory meetings held in New York as also the efforts of the Inter Parliamentary Union and various non-Governmental Organizations to draw attention to, inform and participate in the important event,

Appreciating the efforts made in the post cold war era in reducing conflict and promoting peace and opportunity this affords to all nations to reduce military spending and use the peace dividend to increase expenditure on social development,

Recognizing that over one billion people continue to live in grinding poverty, nearly half of them in South Asia, that hunger is widespread, and access to food, health, education, shelter, work, and a clean environment remains a distant reality for millions of poor,

Considering that women constitute the most disadvantaged group among the poor and that eradication of poverty would be impossible without eliminating all forms of discrimination against them,

Expressing concern at the growing gap between the rich and poor within and between countries and the need for ensuring growth with equity and distributive justice,

Conscious that the market-led development paradigm being promoted by the developed countries excludes the poor and alternative development models need to be promoted that would enable the poor to participate with dignity,

Reaffirming the right to livelihood and the need to provide work to all those having the capacity to work and are willing to do so,

Aware that structural adjustment programmes adversely affect the poor and need to be recast to ensure that social development is promoted,

Noting with regret developed countries refuse to commit new resources for financing the Summit's Programme of Action and in particular to set a time frame within which to reach the 0.7% GNP target for development aid they are committed to achieve,

Mindful that democratization at all levels is essential to promote social development and the need for democratizing the United Nations and the Bretton Woods institutions so that they become representative bodies of not nations but of people's,

Considering all the above concerns we call on the United Nations' World Summit for Social Development to take steps and measures do:

Pledge to ensure that the moral and social retardation that has accompanied the technical, economic and scientific advancement of our times and is a problem of civilization and culture be arrested through promoting a people-centred approach to development,

Undertake to achieve full equality between men and women, and take all measures necessary to eliminate discrimination against women. States that have yet to rectify Convention on Elimination of Discrimination Against Women should do so at the earliest.

Affirm that the highest priority be accorded to elimination of hunger and to meeting the basic needs of the billion people who continue to live in abject poverty,

Resolve to provide full employment, promote self-employment and eliminate the problems associated with jobless growth,

Promote human social security which includes but is not restricted to emotional and mental security,

Restore human dignity which can be done by democratic society only, noting that such democracy has to be human democracy and not market democracy which is being advocated by some of the developed countries,

Provide social and legal protection to the informal sector workers as 70% of all workers are from the informal sector and over two-thirds of these are women,

Address the problems or release of child labour, of their education and of compensation to the families of the released child labourers for loss of income,

Adopt the Gandhian model of development, which includes against other curbing consumerism, promoting self sufficiency, decentralization of development and governance and reliance of indigenous knowledge of technology as an alternative model to the market-dominated paradigm that is being advocated by the developed countries,

Impress upon each country the need to develop its own model of social integration, based on, but not restricted, to religious tolerance and removal of discrimination based on caste, class, colour and language,

Mandate that each country sets up a transparent and accountable National Commission on Social Development as a constitutional body, with constitutional safeguards and powers to ensure and promote social development,

Urge that on the issue of debt there be an audit of "who owes what to whom" in the context of the plunder that the colonial powers resorted to and establish mechanisms for the transfer of resources from the North to the South.

The Meeting also calls upon all Parliamentarians' Legislators and elected members of the local bodies who represent the aspirations of the people to come forward for a more active participation in social development, and act as a communication link between the people, the NGOs and the Government, to facilitate a realistic formulation and implementation of the Government policies.

Letter dated 07 August 1995 from Chief Development Coordinator, UNDP to Ms Marty Rajendran, UNICEF for their cooperation

IND/PRO/300 (INF-HDRPE) 7 August 1995

Dear Ms. Rajendran

Parliamentarians Forum Initiatives

I have been trying unsuccessfully to contact you on the telephone all day. I saw your letter of 2 August this morning on return from an official trip to Bangalore.

As you must have heard from Ms. Jaya Gokulmani from your Madras Field Office, her joining in the planning visit to Coimbatore by Dr. Neeru Misra, Mr. R. Sudarshan and Mr. Kamal Taori proved very useful indeed and was welcomed by Dr. M. Aram, MP. Dr. Misra has been in contact with Ms. Gokulmani to seek her ideas on what it might be possible for UNICEF to assist with in concrete terms on the ground in Dr. Aram's district. We can put our heads together when her submission is received.

It is most heartening to learn that in principle UNICEF could serve as a lead agency for the Parliamentarians Forum initiative in Ratnagiri district of Maharashtra. With respect to the specific queries and comments from your state representative, our response, ad seriatim, are as follows

We work through the Parliamentarians Forum, i.e. the MP and MLAs and the Project Coordinator. The Forum specifically, but certainly at the implementation level through the Collector, Zila Parishad and Panchayat officials. The collector has already been involved and consulted by the MP (Dr. Najma Heptulla herself in this case) and the Project Co-ordinator Dr. Neeru Misra.

Inputs from other agencies (only UNICEF is actually represented on the ground in the State) will again be organised via the Project Co-ordinator and UNDP through site visits, follow-up meetings, project documentation etc.

The workshop is an excellent idea and can be part of a site visit by a team comprising MP, MLA, Project Co-ordinator, UNDP representative, UNDP consultant for this initiative and the UNICEF Bombay team. The dates can be agreed as mutually convenient.

On a more immediate note, we are in urgent need of UNICEF asistance with participation in a planning visit to West Bengal to the Lok Sabha constituency of CPI(M) Member of Parliament Saifuddin

Choudhary. This visit has been firmed up at short notice for 9-12 August to cover two Assembly areas in Hoogli District (Pandua and Balagarh) and four in Bardhaman District (Kalna, Poorvasthali, Katwa and Monteshwar). Dr. Neeru Misra, UNDP Projcct Co-ordinator at the Parliamentarians Forum and Dr. Kamal Taori, ex-CEO, KVIC, will undertake this visit together with Mr. Choudhary, with the involvement of the relevant MLAs, and district and Panchayat officials.

Since Mr. Choudhary is specifically seeking UN System assistance with rural education, especially for girls, as linked to the school buildings, library and girls school he has proposed under his Local Area Development Scheme funding plans, UNICEF Calcutta no doubt is well placed to play an important role in the initiative. I am fully aware of your current preoccupation with other pressing matters and would be happy to discuss direct with Mr. Murlidharan, faxing him the necessary documentation, if UNICEF Delhi could only give us the go-ahead to do so. UNICEF Calcutta has been very supportive on previous occasions of UN System activity in West Bengal, most recently during the Pre-Copenhagen Summit regional consultation process. Our request, in this case, would be that a UNICEF staff member join the visit to Hoogli and Bardhman districts from 10-12 August (after initial discussions in Calcutta on 9 August).

I look forward to an urgent word of confirmation from your office.

With best regards.

Yours sincerely,

Bhaskar Bhattacharji
Chief. Dev. Coordination/Ext. Relations

Letter dated 23 August 1995 from Mr. Bhaskar Bhattacharji, Chief Development Coordinator to Dr. Kamal Taori for starting the assignment as time is essence

IND/PRO/300 (INF-HDRPF) 23 August 1995

Dear Dr. Taori,

Please find enclosed a Terms of Reference as discussed for a short-term Consultancy on the Parliamentarians Forum for Human Development Project which we very much hope you will be able to accept.

I shall be away on mission travel and return to desk on Monday 28 August. It would be most helpful if you could telephone me that morning to confirm your acceptance. The necessary papers can then be drawn up for signature and you could commence the assignment as planned from 4 September 1995. As discussed, time is of the essence.

Mr, Von Sponeck sends you greetings!

Yours sincerely,

Bhaskar Bhattacharji
Chief. Dev. Coordination/Ext. Relations

Dr. Kamal Taori
No. 2 Abhishekh Row
Co-op. Housing Society Ltd.
Behind D.N. Nagar Police Station
D.N. Nagar
Andheri (West)
Bombay-58

Parliamentarian's Forum for Human Development Project

Terms of Reference for Short-term Consultant

After completion of the initial visits to a number of Members of Parliament constituencies, the consultant, with the support of senior UN officials aware of the issues and logistic operations and requirements, is expected to (1) produce (2) individual blueprints for (3) UN System support to the (4) Six chosen project areas. The blueprints should include:

(1) Identification of a lead activity by a lead UN agency which may commence in direct support of or in parallel to the MP's chosen areas of focus in their Local Area Development Scheme Plan;
(2) Identification of more mid-term/long-term synergistic inputs from one or more other UN System agencies working together;
(3) Identification of a costing chart scenario for some innovative initiatives linking to other government/NGO civil society on-going programmes in the area.

The process of putting a practical blueprint for action together is envisaged to involve.

(a) a summarisation of stated expectation on the ground at the project site by the concerned MP along with District administration and beneficiaries;
(b) detailed discussions on the above with relevant UN agencies:
    (i) with ongoing programmes in the area and/or who may wish to start programmes; and
    (ii) those who can only provide design/training inputs
(c) Matching outcomes of (a) and (b) above in a practical time bound stepwise action plan

This document would then need to be discussed with the MPs and the Forum Chairperson for analytical guidance as to practicability and then as necessary with the UN System again to reach a consensus approach paper.

It is envisaged that the entire consultancy would not take more than three working weeks starting from 4 September 1995 and will involve the consultants' relocation to Delhi on a partial DSA basis (Rs. 2000 per day) plus a total consultancy fee in the range of Rs. 50,000 being agreed upon acceptance of terms of reference in principle. UNDP will provide basic logistic support.

Note dated 29.8.95 from Mr. Bhaskar Bhattacharji, Chief Development Coordinator, UNDP to Dr. Kamal Taori

IND/PRO/300 (INF-HDRPE) 29 August 1995

Dear Mr. Taori

Further to our detailed discussion with respect to the Terms of Reference for the short-term Consultancy on the Parliamentarians Forum for Human Development project enclosed with my letter of 23 August. I am pleased to inform you that the UN Resident Coordinator has agreed the attached revised Terms of Reference. We very much hope this addresses all your concerns and you will now be able to accept and commence the assignment from 6 September 1995 for three weeks. It is proposed to offer a consultancy fee in the range of Rs. 50,000 plus a negotiated DSA rate, as relocation to Delhi for the period in question is involved.

Kindly send us as soon as possible a formal acceptance letter enclosing evidence of leave to do so from the Uttar Pradesh Government. Meanwhile, we are requesting our Personnel section to draw up the necessary Special Service Agreement for signature.

With best regards

Yours sincerely,

Bhaskar Bhattacharji
Chief. Dev. Coordination/Ext. Relations

Dr. Kamal Taori I.A.S.
No. 2 Abhishek Row
Co-op. Housing Society Ltd.
Behind D.N. Nagar Police Station
D.N. Nagar,
Andheri (West)
Bombay-58

Parliamentarian's Forum for Human Development Project

Terms of Reference for Short-term Consultant

Having completed the initial visits to three Members of Parliament constituencies, the Consultant, with the support of senior UN officials aware of the issues and logistic operations and requirements, is expected to produce a blueprint, in relation to the ground realities, principally to identify possible UN System support to potential development possibilities linked to the MPs Local Area Development Schemes in the six chosen project areas. It is understood that the blueprint will include a detailed proposed plan of action for Jabalpur, Coimbatore and Hoogly/Burdwan (areas physically visited by the Consultant), and general proposals for possible follow-up and UN system support to Ratnagiri, Raghubir Nagar (Delhi) and South Dinajpur on the basis of discussions documentary information made available to the Consultant. The blueprint should include;

(1) Identification of a lead activity by a lead UN agency which may commence in direct support of or in parallel to the MP's chosen areas of focus in their Local Area Development Scheme Plan;

(2) Identification of more mid-term (within six months)/long-term (1-2 years) synergistic inputs from one or more other UN systems agencies working together;

(3) A rough estimate of costs for some innovative experimental initiatives linking to other government/NGO/stakeholders on-going programmes in the area.

The process of putting together a practical blueprint in consultation with the MPs and other role-players should involve:

(a) a summarisation of stated expectation on the ground at the project site by the concerned MP along with District administration and beneficiaries;

(b) detailed discussions on the above with relevant UN agencies: including

  (i) those with ongoing programmes in the area and/or who may wish to start programmes; and

  (ii) those who can only provide design/training inputs

(c) Matching outcomes of (a) and (b) above in a practical time bound stepwise action plan

It is envisaged that the document would be ready within three working weeks after the commencement of the consultancy from 6 September, 1995. It would then be presented to the Resident Coordinator for further discussion with the Forum Chairperson and MPs in a formal interaction to reach a consensus project document.

Letter Dated 31 August 1995 from Dr. Kamal Taori to Chief Development Coordinator; UNDP intimating willingness for consultancy on an honorary basis.

Dr. Kamal Taori IAS
No. 2 Abhishek Row
Coop. Housing Society Ltd.
DN Nagar, Andheri (West)
Bombay-58

29 August 1995

Dear Bhaskar,

Thanks a lot for your letter of 29 August with the revised terms of reference for the short-term consultancy on the UN Parliamentarians Forum initiative.

Keeping in mind the urgency and time compulsions to initiate action immediately on the lines discussed, I deem it as a part of my duty in the national awakening and integrative process to accept this challenging assignment.

As you are aware, I am currently on two months leave from KVIC from 20 July before having to report to Lucknow. It may take quite some time to obtain the formal permission of the Government of Uttar Pradesh as suggested in your letter. However, in the interests of immediate progress with the initiative I am willing to undertake the consultancy on an honorary basis, provided all other permissible support expenses (including DSA, transportation etc.) are incurred by UNDP, I believe this arrangement would then obviate the need for official secondment from the UP Government.

Before I close, I would once again like to reiterate what I said during the discussions with the UN Resident Coordinator--that this is a very complex terms of reference and will require total support and active cooperation from all UN System officials in general and UNDP programme officers in particular. I therefore trust that the Resident Coordinator will issue the necessary instructions in this regard and extend total support.

I am endorsing a copy of this letter along with your letter to the Chief Secretary, Uttar Pradesh Government, for necessary action. Thanking you once again for offering me the consultancy for a very difficult but challenging project,

Best wishes to you and please convey my regards to Mr. R.R.

Yours sincerely
Kamal Taori

Mr. Bhaskar Bhattacharji
Chief, Devpt. Coordination/Ext. Relations UNDP, New Delhi

Letter dated 05.09.1995 from Mr. Hans-C von Sponeck Resident Coordinator, about Parliamentarians' Forum Pilot Local Areas Initiative with UN System Support addressed to all UN System institutions in Delhi briefing the progress of Inter-Agency meeting of 19 July 1995 and proposed plan of action including honorary consultancy by Dr. Kamal Taori and terms of reference for short term consultancy.

IND/PRO/300 (INF-HDRPE) 5 September 1995

Dear Colleague,

Parliamentarians' Forum Pilot Local Areas Initiative with UN System Support

I am very grateful to Michael Ellis for taking forward, with agencies' support, the above effort during my absence in July and early August. To bring you up-to-date, the following action has been taken:

1. An Inter-Agency Meeting on this subject alone was held on 19 July where it became clear that the following agencies could provide direct support at the field level in the six specific districts under discussion--Jabalpur, Madhya Pradesh; Coimbatore, Tamilnadu; Raghubir Nagar, Delhi; Hooghly and Bardhaman, W. Bengal, South Dinajpur, W. Bengal; and Ratnagiri, Maharashtra:

WFP, UNICEF, UNDP/WB Water & Sanitation Group, UNDP and ILO, UNESCO, FAO, UNFPA, UNDCP & UNIFEM all expressed interest in the initiative but felt their contribution could mainly be in the design of projects, when agreed, and with expert advice and possibly training inputs, as relevant, once implementation was under way.

WHO and APCTT did not attend but can no doubt contribute in specialised areas. The World Bank was also not represented at the meeting but have a great deal to contribute.

2. A site visit was undertaken to Jabalpur (constituency of Mr. Shravan Patel, Lok Sabha MP, Congress-I), from 20-22 July by Mr. Ellis, Mr. Emmanuel (WFP), Dr. Neeru Misra, the Project Coordinator at the Parliamentarians' Forum and Dr. Kamal Taori, IAS, ex-CEO, Khadi & Village Industries Commission. Dr. Taori is currently on leave from the Uttar Pradesh Government and has agreed to assist us as a short-term honorary Consultant on this initiative.

3. A site visit was undertaken to Coimbatore (Constituency of Dr. M. Aram, Rajya Sabha MP, Independent) on 26-27 July by Mr. R.

Sudarshan, UNDP, Ms. Jaya Gokulamani (UNICEF, Madras), Dr. Misra and Dr. Taori.

All Heads of UN Agencies
(as per list attached)

Mr. Peter Rosenegger, Representative, FAO
Mrs. J. Karavasil, Director, ILO
Mr. Christopher Ronald, Director, Regional Office, UNDCP
Dr. Jurgen Bischoff, Director, UN/ESCAP APCTT
Dr. John V. Kingston, Director, UNESCO
Dr. Jon E. Rohde, Representative, India Country Office, UNICEF
Dr. N.K. Shah, WHO Representative to India.
Dr. Richard O. Wada, Chief, ADB/Delhi
Ms. Denise Leonard, Chief, IFC/Delhi
Mr. Richard Hemming, Senior Resident Representative, IMF/Delhi
Mr. Javed Khalilzadeh-Shirazi, Director, Resident Staff in India, The World Bank/Delhi
Mr. Wasim A. Zaman, Chairperson, IAWG on Population and Development
Mr. P.J. Brenn Chairperson, IAWG on HIV/AIDS
Mr. Richard Young, Chairperson, IAWG on Gender and Development
Mr. Ridley Netson, Chief, Agriculture Unit, World Bank/Delhi
Mr. Adriaan Verspoor, Education Advisor, World Bank/Delhi
Mr. Mansoor Dailami, Principal Economist, World Bank/Delhi
Mr. Anthony Measham, Advisor/PHN (Health), World Bank/Delhi

September 5, 1995

Mail IS
Deivry & View Urgent
For Your
Information Action

From : Bhaskar Bhattacharji

To : Renato Fornocaldo, Fo. Ind

Subject: Short Term Consultant: K Taori

Copy : Hans-C, Von Sponeck, IND
Bayani Aguirre, FO. IND
Ove Bjerregaard, FO. IND
R. Sudarshan, FO.IND
Neera Burra, FO. IND
Renu Bakshi, FO.IND
Nishu Nirula, FO.IND
Harsh Singh, FO. IND

Enclosures :
taoritor Terms of reference

Parliamentarians' Forum Pilot Initiative

RR has agreed that Dr. Kamal Taori, IAS should undertake a 3-week short-term consultancy under the above initiative beginning 6 September 1995 on an honorary basis but at full Delhi-DSA and with reimbursement of taxi-fares as applicable for transportation to meetings/ calls etc. during office hours (if UN vehicle is not provided). Dr. Taori's Terms of Reference are enclosed. An SSA has already been requested to be drawn up and signed, charging DSS funds. This may kindly be expedited on a priority basis.

It has also been agreed that Ms. Renu Bakshi in the Social Development Unit will be the logistics support officer and focal point for Dr. Taori during the course of his consultancy. She will help arrange his programme/calls/meetings, accompany him and record notes/minutes etc. and liaise with Administration over basic secretarial support (as required) and office accommodation for Dr. Taori, which RR has also agreed should be provided.

Subject to her other responsibilities and time-constraints, Dr. Neera Burra, Chief-designate of the Integrated Rural Development Unit, has kindly agreed to provide additional specialist guidance and advice to Dr. Taori with respect to UN System mandates/operations etc. and to interact with him as necessary to ensure the production of a substantive and practical action plan document within the tight time-scale envisaged.

The above support arrangements make particular sense in the light of the fact that the prospective operationalisation of community-level programmes with UN System support at six sites in the next phase following the drafting of the plan document will need to be owned and managed by the Social Development and Integrated Rural Development units. Very many thanks to all concerned for their kind cooperation and assistance on this initiative.

Best regards.

Dr. Kamal Taori
Dr. Neeru Misra
HDR PF file

Parliamentarian's Forum for Human Development Project

Terms of Reference for Short-term Consultant

Having completed the initial visits to three Members of Parliament constituencies, the Consultant, with the support of senior UN officials aware of the issues and logistic operations and requirements, is expected to produce a blueprint, in relation to the ground realities, principally to identify possible UN System support to potential development possibilities linked to the MPs Local Area Development Schemes in the six chosen project areas. It is understood that the blueprint will include a detailed proposed plan of action for Jabalpur, Coimbatore and Hoogly/Burdwan (areas physically visited by the Consultant), and general proposals for possible follow-up and UN system support to Ratnagiri, Raghubir Nagar (Delhi) and South Dinajpur on the basis of discussions documentary information made available to the Consultant. The blueprint should include:

(1) Identification of a lead activity by a lead UN agency which may commence in direct support of or in parallel to the MP's chosen areas of focus in their Local Area Development Scheme Plan;

(2) Identification of more mid-term (within six months)/long-term (1-2 years) synergistic inputs from one or more other UN systems agencies working together;

(3) A rough estimate of costs for some innovative experimental initiatives linking to other government/NGO/stakeholders on-going programmes in the area.

The process of putting together a practical blueprint in consultation with the MPs and other role-players should involve:

(a) a summarisation of stated expectation on the ground at the project site by the concerned MP along with District administration and beneficiaries;

(b) detailed discussions on the above with relevant UN agencies; including

  (i) those with ongoing programmes in the area and/or who may wish to start programmes; and

  (ii) those who can only provide design/training inputs;

(c) Matching outcomes of (a) and (b) above in a practical time bound stepwise action plan.

It is envisaged that the document would be ready within three working weeks after the commencement of the consultancy from 6 September, 1995. It would then be presented to the Resident Coordinator for further discussion with the Forum Chairperson and MPs in a formal interaction to reach a consensus project document.

New Delhi 29 August 1995

Letter dated 07 September 1995 from Dr. Kamal Taori to Mr. Bhaskar Bhattacharji giving time schedule and action plan.

To: Mr. B. Bhattacharji 5 September 1995
From : Dr. Kamal Taori Ref. :

Kindly refer to my letter dated 31 August 1995

During my visit to Delhi on 28, 29, 30 and 31 August, I had utilised the time for discussing with Mr. David Siaradin, Chief Social Development Unit, World Bank and also with Mr. George Janisehewski, Associate Expert, APCTT. I also had the opportunity to discussing with Mr. S. Chowdhary, Member of Parliament from Katwa. since the declaration of 20 February 1995 issued under the aegis of the Parliamentarian Forum for Human Development, was a new document for me I wanted to have his views with reference to UN systems support.

I have prepared the following schedule for completing my assignment.

(1) Completion of discussion with major UN systems by 10 September 1995.
(2) Preparation of report of Katwa and Jabalpur by 18 September 1995
(3) Completion of other expectations by 28 September.

During my discussion with major institutions like WFP, APCTT, UNICEF, ILO etc. major point emerged that immediate additionality on a major scale, may not to be available with them. But most of them are formulating their project ideas for next year, hence it may be possible to augment additional resources. My emphasis has been on identifying resources with the organizations which need not only be in terms of funds. Various UN Systems have many ongoing programme activities/expertise, dissemination, technologies infrastructure etc. which can also be useful in fully utilizing additional funds which can be made available and as per the project justification. Hence, the discussion lays greatest emphasis on identifying activities/resources which can be started both in the short and long term as per the major priorities of those organizations and also the declaration mentioned above.

Since Katwa has transparency, people's involvement and an excellent local administration, it was suggested by the Hon. MP that in the last stage of the project finalization if workshop by the district administration with concerned Zilla Parishad and NGO could be organized to tap potential of tourism, handloom and rural cottage and small scale based decentralised income generating programmes and it may be a good idea.

Since Katwa and Kalna area has tremendous potential of taking up social, economic, vocational education, infrastructure and empowerment development programmes, through decentralised activities it would be better if a discussion with district administration selected local body and development commissioner small scale, tourism, handicraft could be considered. These are also some of the identified activities for that area.

Report on other discussions would be sent separately.

Letter dated 08 September 1995 from Mr. Hans-C. von Sponeck, Resident Coordinator, UNDP to Inter-Agency members about UN support to MP-Local Area Development Scheme.

RR/O/6/769 8 September 1995

Dear Colleague,:

Inter-Agency Agenda Meeting on Thursday, 14 September, 1995 at 11 a.m. UN Conference Hall

1. There is a full agenda before us between now and the end of the year. I hope that we can all meet on Thursday, 14 September 1995 at 11 a.m. to take decisions on this agenda and also adopt a strategy of implementation in those areas of the HIV/AIDS India programme, the post ICPD agenda and the gender and development programme on which we are conceptually agreed and which we can financially support. The same should soon be the case in the work of the IA group on education. I have followed the work of all these inter-agency groups and feel confident that all have reached a stage at which we can indeed start implementing elements of their respective agenda. I would look to the Chairpersons of the Groups to give us at the 14 September meeting the specifics in this regard.
2. There is a range of other areas which need further discussion:

(i) The next steps in the definition of the Common Framework for the Follow-up to UN Conference; we have made a start with education, we must now decide what next and how we should go about it (Note: The SG's statement to the Beijing Conference, the G-7 Halifax statement, Dr. Nafis Sadik's recent statement) all make it clear that as a system we are expected to produce such a framework. I continue to believe that here in India we can do this without difficulty and that such a framework could be a good alternative to a CSN!

(ii) The establishment of a small and flexible resource facility to be available for UN System initiatives during the next inter-agency meeting a presentation will be made to outline a possible facility and explain why such would be of value for our joint efforts (Note: We have already received some assurance of support including one from IFAD).

(iii) Our third meeting with Minister Scindia may take place before the full 1A meeting on 14 September should this be the case we will have to have a special meeting prior to seeing Minister

Scindia: I suspect, we are likely to meet the Minister after 14 September in which case we can review our approach when we meet on 14 September. Our UNICEF and UNESCO colleagues are working hard to get to us in good time an outline of a possible support programme on education. During a meeting John Kingston (UNESCO), Gordon Alexander (UNICEF) and I had with the DG/UNESCO. Prof. Mayor in June in Paris, he pledged to us that he would activate the Heads of Agencies constituting the "Jomtien Group" to reinforce our efforts in education here in India!

(iv) The UN System support to selected MPs Local Area Development Schemes has reached the stage at which we know the reality on the ground' in the respective constituencies and must now relate concrete UN system contributions to these schemes. For this purpose Dr. Taori, on leave from the UP Government, has been contracted. Our next meeting will give us an opportunity to go over this interesting pilot programme to ensure that we are ready to deliver as soon as Dr. Taori's report is available within the next three weeks. MPs and Dr. Heptullah are anxious that we proceed with our support.

(v) You will recall that we had agreed earlier this year to review possibilities for including a population dimension wherever feasible into our on-going and pipeline projects and programmes. In support of this effort UNFPA has sent two of its CST members from Kathmandu to Delhi. They are presently making arrangements for an inter-agency workshop on population to be held at the end of October (postponed from mid-Sept). I hope that we can all be represented at that Workshop including colleagues from the world Bank as it will introduce to us concrete tools for bringing this important dimension into our programmes.

(vi) We have written separately on the UN 50 Exhibition with a request that we all attempt to make a further contribution to allow this fine inter-agency display to reach a few more locations including Calcutta (19 Sept), Lucknow (5 Oct) and Farukhabad (11 Oct.) The exhibition would, of course, be back in Delhi for a final showing on 24 October, possibly in conjunction with a UN 50 reception about which we must also talk when we meet next.

(vii) Much effort, particularly by UNIFEM and UNICEF has gone into the preparations for Beijing. Follow-up to this UN Conference should occupy us quite a bit not only within the context of the common framework for follow-up to UN Conference mentioned earlier but also from the point of view of discussing other issues. These include our relationship with a wider gender support mechanism, e.g., the IFCB or its successor group the implications of the outcome of Beijing for the work of the inter-agency group on gender and development and our link up with the Parliamentarians Forum on Human Development. You may remember that Dr. Najma Heptulla had already expressed an interest in joining hands with us in a post-Beijing discussion on what next.

(viii) Lastly, a word on our common concerns for lowering our administrative costs. I found the recent meeting with heads of administration which several of you also attended an important reflection of our readiness to achieve economies through various cost reducing measures including the establishment of a common services account. I would urge all of us to support immediate implementation in all areas where this is possible and progressively refine collaboration in sharing our facilities with the objective of bringing down our administrative costs. I am attaching an outline of the areas in which colleagues from the various administrative untis consider savings can be achieved. I have requested OM Fornocaldo to report to me at regular intervals on progress; may be you wish to do the same.

Let me end by saying again that I am very much looking forward to our next IA meeting on 14 September.

With kind regards,

Yours sincerely,

Hans-C. von Sponeck
Resident Coordinator

Mr. Peter Rosenegger, Representative, FAO
Mrs. J. Karavasil, Director, ILO
Mr. Ganti Rao, Director, UNCHS (Habitat-II), Madras
Mr. Christopher Ronald, Director, Regional Office, UNDCP
Dr. Jurgen Bischoff, Director, UN/ESCAP, APCTT
Mr. Peter Godwin, CTA, UNDP/OPS Regional HIV/AIDS Project
Mr. Robert Boydel,, Manager, UNDP/WB Regional Water & Sanitation Group
Dr. John V. Kingston, Director, UNESCO

Dr. Wasim A. Zaman, Country Director, UNFPA
Mr. Rajiv Kapur, Chief of Mission, A.I., UNHCR
Mr. Feodor Starcevic, Director, UNIC
Dr. Jon E. Rohde, Representative, India Country Office, UNICEF
Mr. W.S. Nanayakkara, Country Director, UNIDO
Mrs. Chandni Joshi, Regional Programme Adviser, UNIFEM
Captain Ambrogio Zaffaroni, Staff Officer-in-Charge, UNMOGIP
Dr. Neera Burra, Co-ordinator, UNV Sub-Regional Prog. for South Asia
Mr. Michael W. Ellis, Country Director, WEP
Dr. N.K. Shah, WHO Representative to India.
Dr. Uton M. Rafei, Regional Director, WHO
Dr. Richard O. Wada, Chief, ADB Delhi
Ms. Denise Leonard, Chief, IFC/Delhi
Mr. Richard Hemming, Sr. Resident Representative, IMF/Delhi
Mr. Javad Khalilzadeh-Shirazi, Director, Resident Staff in India, The World Bank/Delhi
Dr. Wasim A. Zaman, Chairperson, IAWG on Population and Development.
Mr. P.J. Brenny, Chairperson, IAWG on HIV/AIDS
Mr. Richard Young, Chairperson, IAWG on Gender and Development
Mr. Ridley Nelson, Chief, Agriculture Unit, World Bank/Delhi
Mr. Adriaan Verspoor, Education Advisor, World Bank/Delhi
Mr. Mansoor Dailami, Principal Economist, World Bank/Delhi
Mr. Anthony Measham, Advisor/PHN (Health), World Bank/Delhi

Non-represented UN Agencies

Ms. Ellen Abrenica, Director, Programme Management Division, ESCAP, Bangkok.
Mr. Hans Blix, Director-General/IAEA/Austria
Mr. A.R. El Hicheri, Director/TCB, ICAO/Montreal, Canada
Mr. Samir Asmar, Director/Asia Division, IFAD/Rome
Mr. Donald J. Kerlin, Director/TCD, IMO/London
Mr. Pekka J. Tarjanne, Secretary-General, ITU/Geneva
Ms. Elizabeth Dowdeswell, Executive-Director, UNCHS/Kenya
Mr. John M. Burley, Chief/TCPD, UNCTAD/Geneva
Mr. Thomas Keller, Asst. Director General, UNESCO/Paris
Mr. M. de Mariay Campos, Director General, UNIDO/Vienna
Ms. Brenda McSweeney, Executive Coordinator, UNV/Geneva
Mr. Thomas E. Leavey, Director-General, UPU/Berne/Switzerland

Mr. J.F. Tremeaud, ASG and Director, Intn'l Training Centre/ILO, Turin/Italy

Mr. S. Radwan, Director/DTCD, ILO/Geneva

Mr. Nissim Tal, Head/UN System Programme, Intn'l Training Centre/ILO, Turin/Italy

Mr. Nigel H. Bradshaw, UNDP/IMF Programme Coordinator, IMF/Washington

Dr. Arap Bogsch, Director-General, WIPO/Geneva

Mr. E. Jatila, Director/TCD, WMO/Geneva

Mr. Kong Fannong, Director/TCPD, DDSMS, UN/New York

Mr. Eduardo Gutierrez, Director, Office of UN System Support & Services, UNDP/NY

Mr. F.R. Haemmerli, Chief/OPD DPCSD, UN/NY

Mr. Derrick Deane, Secretary, CCPOQ, UN/Geneva

Mr. Jean-Jacques Graisse, Director/BER, UNDP/New York

Mr. Alan Doss, Director, UNDP/Geneva

Letter dated 14 September 1995 from Chief, Asian and Pacific Centre for Transfer of Technology (APCTT) to Dr. Kamal Taori.

Dr. Kamal Taori 14 September 1995
Former Chief Executive Officer
Khadi and Village Industries Commission
Gramodaya, Irla Road,
Vile Parle (W)
Bombay - 400 056

Dear Dr. Taori,

We appreciate the initiative taken in visiting our office and the interest evinced by you in our activities. You must have gone through our information brochure to get an idea of Bureau's objectives, role and range of services rendered. As indicated to you, the Bureau was earlier in touch with KVIC and the matter rests with letter no. 339 dated April 28, 1995 received from Mr. N.K. Roy, Dy CEO (Mktg.) of the Commission.

The Bureau, with small enterprises as its target group would be keen to take initiatives towards strengthening of existing technology transfer arrangements for rural industries or join hands with relevant organisations like KVIC to consider new measures. In this regard it may be mentioned that Asian and Pacific Centre for Transfer of Technology (APCTT) a co-promoter of the Bureau, with its regional presence, large affiliations and reach can supplement the efforts in creating the opportunities for experience sharing with other developing countries. Given the whole hearted support of APCTT, the Bureau is suitably placed to promote the indigenous capabilities of enterprises, in the KVI sector especially their technological related achievements. Incidentally we have been approached by a Sanganer based enterprise to promote its technology in recycling of waste paper rags into quality hard board. Steps are afoot to promote this widely. Joint programmes on similar lines could be conceived to bring about two way flow of technology related information in the KVI sector.

You may like to have the matter examined at the KVIC and apprise us of the views should you consider it necessary a meeting could be convened in Bombay or New Delhi to discuss the matter further.

I look forward to hearing for you.

Best regards

Yours sincerely,
Utpal Bajpai, Chief

Letter dated 18 September 1995 from Consultant to Selected UN Systems.

18 September 1995

Dear

Subject: Parliamentarians Forum Pilot Local Areas Initiative with UN System Support

Kindly refer to letter No. IND/PRO/300 (INF-HDRPF) dated 5 September 1995, addressed to you, by the Resident Coordinator.

In the intervening period I have had the opportunity to interact with a few officials of some UN Agencies. Our effort to get time from some other agencies has not been successful. As we continue to try to get some time from senior officials I am writing this letter with the following request for your personal attention.

1. Mr. Hans-C von Sponeck, had requested in his letter that an officer may be designated to kindly coordinate your agency's participation in this initiative and his/her easy accessibility and support to me for the duration of this assignment. This may kindly be expedited.
2. Some of the agencies had also actively participated in the visits to the selected parliamentarians' constituencies. If their views/observations/comments about the type of activities which would be taken up in these areas could also be intimated to me, it will help me greatly in concretising the project proposal in a more effective manner.
3. The nominated officer may also kindly be requested to prepare a short summary of the type of activities your agency has already ongoing in the six selected areas.
4. For your convenience I am again enclosing the copy of the MP's Declaration published in the latest issue of Human Development News.

Kamal Taori

Dr. Jon E. Rohde
Representative
India Country Office
UNICEF

Letter dated 21 September 1995 from Food & Agriculture Organisation of the United Nations to Mr. Hans-C von Sponeck, UN Resident Coordianator, New Delhi.

Ref. UN 3/1.3 21 September 1995

Dear Mr. Von Sponeck

Subject: *Parliamentarians' Forum Pilot Local Area Initiative with UN System Support.*

I refer to your letter No. IND/PRO/300(INF-HDRPF) dated 5 September 1995 and reminder dated 18 September. In line with your suggestions I take pleasure in informing you that Mr. O.P. Dewan Information Officer has been nominated as the overall Coordinator for our organization in this venture.

Today we had a rather positive exchange of thought with Dr. Kamal Taori, UNDP Consultant. It was agreed that FAO would be the coordinator for pilot initiatives in Coimbatore Constituency of Dr. Aram.

It was further agreed that as a first step we would like to send a technical team to Coimbatore for a Consultation with Hon. MP and local authorities to provide follow-up to tentative recommendations of the UNDP consultant. This technical theme will follow suggestions of Mr. Taori and will also contact Dr. Panda, IAS, Secretary (Agriculture) or Tamil Nadu State in order to get his guidance in identifying suitable project ideas.

In informing you of the above, I have to point out that we have no possibility to provide funds in support of the parliamentarians initiative. However, we are ready to cooperate in providing technical assistance within our mandate. We believe identification and formulation of an integrated project of the Coimbatore constituency could be the right step to contribute from our side to this innovative initiative of the UN system.

With best regards,

Yours sincerely

Peter Rosenegger
FAO Representative in India and Bhutan

Mr. Hans-C von Sponeck
UN Resident Coordinator
New Delhi

Letter dated 22 September 1995 by Dr. Kamal Taori, Consultant to selected UNDP officials.

22 September 1995

Dear

Subject: *Parliamentarians' Forum Pilot Local Area Initiative with UN System Support.*

Kindly refere to letter No. IND/PRO/300 (INF HDRPF) dated 5 September 1995 by Resident Coordinator, United Nations and my letter dated 18 September 1995.

I am happy to inform you that FAO Representative in India has offered to be the lead agency for Coimbatore District and have already nominated Mr. Dewan to be the overall coordination on behalf of FAO. Same way UNICEF has nominated Mr. Rath to be the coordinator. WFP Country Director has also already nominated Mr. J. Fleurens to be the coordinator for Jabalpur which will be then lead district.

I am addressing this letter with the following request:

1. If your agency has still not nominated the officer it may kindly be done immediately. This will help in my interacting with your organisation.
2. WFP has sent a note about their perceptions of the programme and the areas which they would like to be attended. I have made some observations and am enclosing a copy of the same with the request that your organisation may like to suggest some more issues so that they may be included if necessary in my blueprint report.

I am again enclosing a copy of letter dated 18 September 1995. Shall be grateful if you could please communicate your valued views.

With regards,

Yours sincerely,

Dr. Kamal Taori, IAS
Consultant

Mail dated 12 October 1995 from Mr. Bhaskar Bhattacharji to selected UN representatives for meeting on 13 October 1995

12 October 1995

October 12, 1995 11:56 am Mail IS--
From : Bhaskar Bhattacharji
To : Hans-C von Sponeck, Ind
Bayani Aguirre, FO.IND
Ove Bjerregaard, FO.IND
R. Sudarshan, FO. IND
S.D. Badrinath, FO. IND
Neera Burra, FO. IND
Renu Bakshi, FO. IND
Vivek Rae, FO. IND
Tilak R. Maakan, FO. IND

Subject: Parl. Forum SHD Init:Taori Rept
Copy : Nishu Nirula, FO.IND

This is to reconfirm that our Consultant, Dr. Kamal Taori, will present for discussion his draft Blueprint for Action under the Parliamentarians' Forum Pilot SHD initiative to the UNDP internal group (+Mr. Ellis, WFP and Dr. Neeru Misra, UNDP Project Coordinator at the Forum) at 11 AM in the Committee Room on 13 October. After a 15 minute presentation by Dr. Taori, Constructive discussion for another hour or so should help us reach agreement on the final document for presentation first to the Inter-Agency group soonest possible and then equally speedily to the Parliamentarians' Forum for implementation.

All addressees are invited to attend. The meeting may run till 1 PM we are hoping to let all of you have advance copies of the Executive Summary of the draft report this afternoon (for evening reading).

Many thanks and kind regards.

HDR 95 file

Gist of discussions with Mrs. Bimla Bissal of World Bank

We had to explain the entire scheme of Parliamentarian Forum, their Declaration and need for convergence. She after giving patient hearing was kind enough to mention the limitations of the bank since Department of Economic Affairs would have to be involved. However, she mentioned about standing project grant and some assistance if criteria of other grants could be fulfilled.

She also suggested that if a project proposal could be made by giving a concept paper to social development unit may be funding into longer run could be available. She mentioned to us various ongoing programmes but diversion may be difficult.

It seems the social development unit will have to be involved in a more articulated way for long term advantage. For short term as per the criteria of World Bank proposals may have to be sent.

Programmes within UNDP and their Synergisation

Programmes of UNDP

Enroute Sustainable Development
Jute
Leather
Hand made paper
Volunteers for development
Women Thrust areas
APTEC
Technology
HRD

SALIENT FEATURES OF THE ASSIGNMENT

Important points for action in Assignment principally it is to identify possible UN System support to potential development possibilities linkway to the MP Local Area Development Scheme in the six chosen project areas. The blueprint will include a detailed proposed plan of action for Jabalpur, Coimbatore and Katwa and general proposal for possible follow-up and UN System support to other constituencies.

The blueprint should include:

1. Identification of a lead activity by a lead UN agency which may commence in direct support of or in parallel to the MPs chosen areas of focus in their local area development scheme plan;
2. Identification of more mid-term within six/long term 1/2 years synergistic inputs from one or more other UN System agencies working together.
3. A rough estimate of costs for some innovative experimental initiatives linking to other govt/NGO/stakeholders on-going programmes in the area.

The process of putting together a practical blueprint in consultation with the MPs and other role-players should involve; a summarisation of stated expectations on the ground at the project site by the concerned MP along with District administration and beneficiaries; detailed discussions on the above with relevant UN agencies, including those with on-going programmes in the area and, or who may wish to start programmes, and those who can only provide design/training inputs matching outcomes in a practical time-bound, stepwise, proposed action plan.

The above terms of Reference for short term consultant call for a very elaborate exercise. Though it is a very tough work it is possible with coordinated and well worked strategy to come out with a implementable plan of action provided there is clarity and vision allround all the important stake-holders.

SOME INTERESTING READING MATERIAL

During this honorary assignment I had the opportunity of going through various literature apart from interacting with diverse and seemingly conflictory groups. The literature mentioned below had given me a totally new picture not only by looking at my own experience of diverse fields, as will be clear from my enclosed bio-data, but at the end it exposed me to various current and under currents affecting the development scenario of our time. I am grateful to those who thought of this assignment for me.

1. *The Indian Journal of Public Administration,* October-December 1994 issue edited by Shri T.N. Chaturvedi.
   Power has been defined in different ways by political philosophers, sociologists and administrative officers in different ways, but there is common recognition of the fact that power, in one form or the other, is the mainstay of all human organisations. All ideologies, in fact, do nothing more than spell out justifications of reordering concentration of power at particular level(s) and the manner in which it has to be discharged to bring about change of social, political and economic nature.
2. *Khadi Gramodyog, Journal of Rural Economy,* No. 2 November 1993 issue edited by Shri Kamal Taori.

   A. In the present day times, when the condition in respect of capital funds is worsening, work culture is deteriorating and only the organised are trying to corner the benefits, it has become imperative socially to pay attention on this.

   B. There is a necessity of re-examining various factors including those which bind India together. It has been earnest efforts to locate those pockets, activities and groups of people who have been propagating the cause of sustainable development, through environmental friendly rural oriented activities of industries, services and business sectors. After all it came to be realised that India is not a creation of 20th Century alone. It has inextricable historical linkages and many historians have acclaimed its age-old traditions and culturally rich way of life, tolerance and openness to differ. It is in this process of examining, analysing, thinking and interacting, without any iota of doubt that it was realised that Khadi and village Industries related institutions have a lot to contribute in hope generating, particularly with reference to the problems of unemployment, power work culture and development models for replication. When practicsed in good spirit, it would show some sustainable processes bringing cheers to desperate souls.

3. *Khadi Gramodyog Journal of Rural Economy,* No. 6 March 1992 issue edited by Shri Kamal Taori.
   The industrialisation has opened up possibility of mass production and also generated mass demand for the paper. This also presupposes aggressive marketing strategy by big manufacturers of paper who managed to create the demand. One of the reasons why handmade paper industry is sick can be attributed to its incapacity to market its product properly and to analyse its strengths and weaknesses.
4. Organising Unorganised Rural Labour for Social Justice Strategy and Methodology.
   The Ministry of Labour and Rehabilitation (Department of Labour) in collaboration with the National Labour Institute, New Delhi, had organised a four-day National Seminar from the 5th to the 8th January, 1984, on Rural Unorganised Labour, at Vishva Yuvak Kendra, New Delhi. The Seminar was directed to an in-depth study of the problems of various categories and sub-categories of unorganised rural labour to conceptualise and identify the various objectives and constraints of such organisations, and to lay down a strategy and methodology for organising them into trade unions, cooperatives, associations and such other forms as may be considered feasible in their best interest. The Seminar was attended by academicians, research scholars, representatives of trade unions, voluntary agencies, social action groups, International Labour organisation, Planning Commission, representatives of Central and State Governments and honorary rural organisers appointed in few States etc.
5. *Economic and Political Weekly,* January 14, 1995 issue
   New World order and Indian intellectuals, Disempowerment of bureaucracy: A Class analysis. Genes and the Moral Majority.
6. *Small Scale Sector and Big Business,* February, 1984 issue edited by S.K. Goyal, K. S. Chalapati Rao, Nagesh Kumar.
   Criteria for selection of Items for Reservation (73); Expanding List of Reserved Items (74); De-reservation of Already Reserved Items (75); Partial De-Reservation (77); Products Meant for Captive Consumption and by-products (91); Preferred Industries (92); Reserved Items and Existing Large Scale Producers (93); Identification of Reserved Items manufactured by Large Scale

Sector (102); Non-applicability of Licensing for Reserved Items (110); Marketing of Small Scale Sector Products (115).

7. *Case Study Method in Management Development,* edited by Roy Winterburn.

   It has been assumed that many cases will need to be developed from book and journal resources: to assist this, other than the references to cases and the case method, there are sections on public administration (to help update the 1981 bibliography); on training in general; and on women, this last set is included in that it is one of the disadvantaged groups in developing countries to which the commonwealth secretariat is devoting much concern and attention.

8. *Economic and Political Weekly,* July 30, 1994.

   Class and surplus value: A re-examination of concepts.

9. *Economic and Political Weekly,* July 23, 1994.

   The balance sheet of 25 years of bank nationalisation undoubtedly provides a telling lesson: the changes in the financial system, however revolutionary, are not very effective when the economic environment is inherently unbalanced and unequal, both regionally and functionally, and when structural changes in the real economy are not geared to correcting those imbalances and inequalities in an effective manner. Even so, what has been achieved under the public sector dispensation in commercial banking in particular and in the financial system generally, even in the midst of structural disabilities of the Indian economy, is commendable. While this progress has brought in its train manifold problems inefficiency, weak staff and financial structures, low profitability, large non-performing assets, bureaucratic interferences, etc. in their operations, the financial infrastructure created across the country over the years provides the necessary foundation so important for the more rapid and diversified development of the Indian economy.

10. *Third Concept,* March 1991.

    Mirage of Full Employment, Cultural Aspect of Planned Development.

11. *Economic and Political Weekly,* April 2, 1994

    Self-government of any kind must have not only a clearly demarcated field of activities, but also the instruments with which to govern in this field. Consequently, an essential power the states must endow the panchayats to recruit and control their own staff. At the same time, unless traditional notions like permanent employment, security, service cadres and reserved posts are reconsidered, panchayats will be unable to innovate instrumentalities suited to their purpose.

12. *The Economist,* April 16th 1994.
Poor relations. Are third-world commodity producers condemned to eternal poverty?
13. *Economic and Political Weekly,* April 2, 1994.
While gobalisation liberalisation, deregularisation and privatisation are the focus of the New Economic Policy at the macro level, it is important to get a clear understanding of both the threats and the opportunities emerging out of these processes at the micro level for individuals, families and local communities.
14. *Economic and Political Weekly,* April 2, 1994
Science and Ethics Decision-Making. Case of Big Dams, K. Subramaniam.
15. *India Today,* April, 30 1994
Business Feature, Voluntary Retirement. Keyed to the Future "Golden handshakes can work. As success in Gujarat shows, all it needs is a good mixture of entrepreneurial spirit, infrastructural support and counselling".
16. *India Today,* April 30, 1994
The Dividend of Openness, Experiments with Untruth.
17. *India Today,* April, 30, 1994.
Reined in "The Supreme Court clamps down on the Chief Election Commissioner for his remarks on the functioning of the judiciary, restricting his initiatives on the model code.
18. *Business World,* February 1994.
International News, Changing Gear "Growing dissatisfaction with "shock therapy "reforms has forced the Russian Government to slacken the pace.
19. *Business World,* 22 February, 1994
The Professor as consultant "More and more B-school teachers are taking up consultancy work on a part-time basis.
20. *Business World,* 9-22 February 1994.
Technology, Back to Nature "Several gene banks, which will help preserve medicinal plants, have come up in the country.
21. *Sunday,* 10-16 April 1994.
An Anthropological Survey of India project shatters some entrenched myths.
22. *Economic and Political Weekly* issue dated 26.3.1994.
Agricultural Growth in West Bengal in the 1980s, A disaggregation by Districts and Crops" by Anamitra Saha and Madhura Swaminathan and "Distribution of Landholdings in Rural India 1953-54 to 1981-89. Implications for Land Reforms by H.R

Sharma.

23. *Economic and Political Weekly* issued 26 March 1994.
"Fiscal Correction and Human Resource Development. Expenditure at Central and State Levels" by S.P. Gupta and A.K. Sarkar. The writers say following:
"This paper attempts to examine whether human resource development has been adversely affected by the macro-economic and sectoral policy reforms undertaken by the Government of India since 1991. It analyses the human resource development expenditure of the central and state governments since 1988. The analysis may help in judging whether the economic costs of adjustment are fast getting transposed into heavy social costs."

24. *Economic and Political Weekly* issued dated 26.3.1994.
"Change and Turbulence in Indian Society" by MS Gore. The writer says as follows:
"This is a collection of 10 papers by MN Srinivas written at various times over a period of 26 years, 1962-1988. The publication is welcome because it brings together the writings of a senior and internationally acclaimed scholar which would otherwise not be available in most college libraries. The Oxford University Press had earlier published two other collections of Srinivas's paper focused on two specific areas--the dominant caste and Sanskritisation. This one is focused on the current of development and change--and the consequent turbulence--in Indian society.

25. *Sunday* issue dated 10-16 April 1994.
"Socialism cannot be restructured" contained interview of Economist Lord Meghnad Desai on the country's economic reforms. In interview Desai said following:
"The pro-poor faction believe that by putting hurdles in the path of the reforms they will help the poor--this is a fallacy. The pace of reforms has to be accelerated to help the poor. In my opinion the political leadership has failed to create a coalition of the groups that will benefit from the reforms.

26. *The Economist* issue dated April 2nd 1994.
"Uncle Sam's helping hand". Sematech was meant to revitalise American chip making. Did this model for a new technology policy deliver the goods?

27. *The Economist* issue dated April 2nd 1994.
"Italian small business: change in the heartland" and "family values"

28. *Kisan World* Issue of March 1994.
"On the Road to Prosperity" by Dr. N. Mahalingma. The writer says:
"India has the talent and enterprise to make the country a major

economic power provided the deal weight of red tape and regulation is removed", observed Mr. Goh Chok Tong, Prime Minister of Singapore, while addressing the Economic Ministers of the Association of South East Asian Nations (ASEAN).

29. *The Economist* issue dated March 5th 1994.

    "India in a hurry". The writer says in this article following:

    "India is solid, but has yet fully to unleash its entrepreneurial potential; China is more exciting but also more dangerous. Both are trying to change. At the Communist Party plenum last November, China announced a programme to create a properly functioning central Bank, foster an independent banking system, develop commercial low and sort out the tax system. These changes cannot be made quickly, or easily: there is currently a row between Beijing and the provinces over a proposed new value-added tax; confusion over a new capital-gains tax is depressing China's fledgling markets; and the commission trying to draw up a law to regulate financial markets is struggling with a seventh draft. Meanwhile, however, India is trying to throw away its solidity without being able to match China's vigour.

    India's impatience is understandable: it has been frustrating to watch its great rival pull ahead. But if inflation and government finances get out of control, the country could lose its reputation for steadiness. Asia's success stories argue that macroeconomic stability is a necessary condition for long term prosperity. The tortoise did not win by pretending to be a hare."

30. *The Economist* issue dated January 21st 1995.

    "After Kobe". The writer says:-

    "This is one of many cases, such as global warming, where the most useful thing that man can do for now is merely to add to his understanding. But the saving of lives does not always have to wait upon perfect knowledge. The earth's crust and climate are bogglingly complex systems, still little understood. Yet there is good reason to believe that the reduction of ozone-eating chemicals now under way will soon start to save lives. And even after this wretched week for kobe there are people alive who in an earlier age would surely have been killed by so great an earthquake. Therein lies some consolation, and an affirmation of the power of technology rather than its weakness.

31. *Time International* issue 12 July, 1993.

    (a) Where Have all the Leaders Gone". By James Walsh. The writer says:

        I Cannot think of a period where there have been so few

great leaders.

(b) "The Paper Wall" By Kumiko Makihara. The writer says: Japan's regulatory web is under attack--and just by foreigners.

32. An Asian Perspective on the Human Development Report 1993." By C.P. Chandrashekhar. The writer says:-

In the post-war history of the world, the 1980s are remarkable for crowding into a single decade a set of profound and parallel transitions. These include: the end of the cold war and the consequent decline of militarism; the collapse of centralized socialist regimes based on command economy structures and the restoration of political democracy, conventionally understood, in most of those countries; an almost universal trend towards more market-based development strategies in countries that had for decades adopted relatively insular and highly dirigent regimes; the transition to democracy in many developing countries, some of which had long histories of military or authoritarian rule; and, finally, experiments with the institutions of civil society, involving the decentralisation of political and economic authority and the emergence of relatively diverse forms of people's organisations that serve as agents of development and instruments of countervailing power.

While the fall-out of these transitions has not been necessary or uniformly positive from the point of view of human welfare, they can all be read as having contributed to one positive tendency, viz., a growing role for the people in influencing the processes that shape their lives. As voters, activists, workers, entrepreneurs and communities, people now appear to have the opportunity to be more closely involved in economic, political, social and cultural processes and directly or indirectly widen their access to centres of decision-making and power.

33. "Human Development: from Concept to Action, A 10-point Agenda" by Inge Kaul and Saraswati Menon. A report of Human Development Report Office, Occasional Papers published by UNDP. The ten agenda given in report are as follows:

One--Making the Human Development Concern country-specific.

Two--Preparing a human development statistics.

Three--Improving human development statistics.

Four--Setting human development goals and targets.

Five--Costing the attainment of human development targets.

Six--Identifying possible policy options.

Seven--Mobilizing financial resources and opportunities.

Eight--Formulating a country strategy for human development

Nine--Agreeing on a global compact on human development

Ten--Encouraging public demand for human development.

A Note on Implementation

34. "Popular participation, NGO/World Bank Joint Statement and Proposal for Action".

A. Motives for Promoting Participation

1. The committee NGOs argued that participation is much more than a means to successful projects. They stressed that people taking control of their lives is the fundamental goal of development. They argued that popular participation in development decision-making allows people to become actors in their own development, shaping it to be continuous with their history, culture, and sense of identity. They stressed that "people power" is a major underutilized force for global progress. They also said that public participation in decision-making is a right, and that support for democracy should feature prominently in the conditionality of official aid.
2. The Bank Members of the Committee noted that the World Bank has no mandate to promote participation as an end in itself or as political goal. The Bank's charter forbids its staff from engaging in a member country's politics. The Bank's mandate is to support economic growth, the reduction of poverty, and environmental protection. Yet experience shows that popular participation is important to the success and sustainability of many of the projects and programs in which the Bank is involved.
3. Governments often bring yet another set of motives to efforts to promote popular participation. Nearly all governments want to reduce popular discontent, and democratic governments are formally responsible to their citizens. Some governments may actively promote popular participation as one way to circumvent opposing power structures and mobilize grassroots support for themselves and their policies. Decentralized governmental structures tend to be more accessible to popular participation than a centralised system.

35. An interim report on "Expert Committee on Integrated Rural Development Programme" prepared by Rural Planning and Credit Department, Central Office, Reserve Bank of India, Bombay. an extract of the report is given hereunder:

"The Integrated Rural Development Programme (IRDP) is a direct instrument for attaching India's rural poverty, which is both extensive and endemic. The normal growth process appears to by pass the rural poor and hence IRDP is designed to provide them with access to assets, skills, support services and institutional arrangements, with the basic objective of enabling them to cross the poverty line through additional employment and income generation."

36. Report of International South North Linking for Development Conference held in Bulawayo, Zimbabwe, November 28-30, 1990.
"In its growing outrage at present practices, the South is reiterating the principle that responsibility for the development of the South lies in the South and in the hands of the people of the South."
"Development partnerships not responsive to the principles of human dignity and respect, can only be described as insensitive, domineering and colonial."

37. "Effectiveness of KVIC as an organisation in various terms in servicing, Khadi and Village Industries. By Dr. Kamal Taori Report to ILO ARTE (1994)
    1. Organisation developed.
    2. Infrastructure created.
    3. Rebate grants, rebate subsidies and loans have been utilised.
    4. How migration from village to cities has been controlled or regulated.
    5. How the Industry has been supported resulting in its survival growth and competitiveness, compatability development. These include training, Human Resources development, Science & Technology.
    7. Organisations of the beneficiary so that they can fight for their rights.
    8. (a) With increasing emphasis on environmental aspects of industrialisations, have these industries become more relevant and acceptable.
       (b) Utilisation of Bank finance and other local resources.
       (c) It is proposed that a general review of Khadi and Village Industries Commission on the above points with reference to the data base be done to understand the defectiveness over a period of time.

38. "Action Plan for Promoting Village Industries'' By Amri Patel and Praful Pandya.
Action Plan for Village Industries:
The report of International Labour Organisation (1990) has concluded that the employment in agricultural sector decline from 73% to 59% due to the impact of mechanisation.

39. "Privatisation or Liberalisation--Strategic Options for LDCs" By S. Saroja.
Focusing on liberalisation as Policy prescription to bring about acro economic equilibrium in LDCs, the author cautions against blanket adherence thereto in view of varying economic environment and needs (particularly of efficiency and accountability) among LDCs, and suggests adoption of a balanced approach based on proper analysis of available policy options keeping in view the long term interests.
40. Project TBCHs--An Alternative for U.P. NTC Mills" By Kamal Taori, K.C. Misra and Kancha Kumar.
The problem of sickness, specially in the field of textiles, has assumed very serious proportions. There are no simple solutions to the problem. Project TBCH (Textile Back to Charkha and Handlooms) which has been discussed here, if implemented may go a long way to enhance the viability of decentralised industries if proper coordination is established.
41. "Realism and Vision in International Development" *Journal of the Society for International Development,* 1981:1.
42. "National Oil Seeds and Vegetable Oils Development Board" Brief Review of Novod Schemes Implemented during 1986-87 to 1992-93
43. Newsweek Slice! Cut! Ouch! The Job Crisis: Dangers and Benefits of Downsizing, Issued February 6, 1995.
44. *Economic and Political Weekly,* Issued August 13, 1994. Maharashtra: Politics of Culture.
45. "Talking About Teaching" Howard Wolf in Conversation with Muriel Wasi, Issue Span September 1993.
46. Strategies for Competitive Advantage" Issue January 11-16, 1993. (Programme Material by ASCI Hyderabad.)
47. Promoting Exports the Work of the Export Market Development Division of the Commonwealth Fund for Technical Co-operation, Commonwealth Secretariat.
48. His Holiness Maharishi Mahesh Yogi--A Glimpse of the New Technology for the Development of Full Creative Potential, Issue of 1974.
49. DECTA The Developing Countries Trade Agency London" Report on the Competitive Position of the Indian Ready-Made Garments Industry, vis-a-vis its Competitors in the UK.
50. *The Times of India,* Bombay, September, 6, 1993.
51. *Financial Express,* Bombay, September, 7, 1993.
"Management" Making of a global manager by Vidya Hariharan.

52. *The Economic Times,* 3 September, 1993.
"Profile/K.C. Krishanadas on Nilgiris" M. Cheniappan, a man who has become a legend in his lifetime".
53. *Non Violent Revolution,* August 1993.
Editor: Dr. G. Ramachandran.
"Unity in Diversity" has been the immemorial message of India culture. It has been the key-note of all schools of Indian philosophy. Our immortal prophets have echoed and re-echoed this message. Budha, Sankara, Ramakrishna, Tagore and Gandhi upheld this glorious truth. The warp and woof of Indian life have demonstrated it through the centuries. Hindu philosophy spoke of the many rivers flowing into one ocean. The Indus, the Ganges and the Brahmaputra rise from the same mountain. Flowing over different terrain they all enter the Indian ocean. The great religions of the world are like these great rivers. They rise from the Himalayas of the Divine and enter the ocean of God's Grace. This truth, like every other, can and has been distorted. Diversity has often shattered unity in human history.
54. *Financial Express,* Bombay, September 13, 1993.
"Subsidy As Incentive" By H.P. Ranina.
The dictionary meaning of "subsidy" is a grant of money from a Government to a private enterprise considered as beneficial to the public".
55. *Economic and Political Weekly,* July 31, 1993.
"Liberalisation Debate: Some Careless Mistakes" By Amitava Bose. This brief note discusses some instances of careless economic reasoning which have marked the otherwise very welcome debate among economists on economic liberalisation.
56. *Can Bureaucracy Meet the Challenge of Liberalisation?* By B.G. Deshmukh, I.A.S., (Retd.)
"Forum of Free Enterprise"
57. *The Times of India*
"Attitudes and Skills" By Vincent D'Silva.
58. "Arusted Ethic" By V. Venkatesan.
59. *The Economic Times,* 24 September, 1993.
"Et Esquire" Extract/PK Saragi on how role analysis in two divisions of Indian Oil helped improve the work environment.
Greasing the cogs of a corporate wheel.
Role set members were brought together to discuss issues like communication, personal growth, and group dynamics.
There were two approaches to role analysis: repeat of the action research effort and analysis of new roles at other locations.

60. *The Sunday Observer,* Bombay, Dec. 29-Jan 1992.
"India one for the Road"
61. *Economic and Political Weekly,* October 3, 1992.
"Continuing Relevance of Socialism" By Rajeev Bhargava
62. *Financial Express,* Bombay, August 31, 1993.
"Thinking in terms of institutions"
63. *The Times of India,* Bombay, August 30, 1993.
"From popper to the boardroom" By S.A. Sapre, Director, Institute for the study of work, discusses the pros and cons of Karl Poper's Concept of Piecemeal Social Engineering as a method of restructuring organisations.
64. *Financial Express,* Bombay, September 14, 1993.
"Power of Communication" By M.D. Mukhi.
65. "Dynamism--A Sword in the Manager's sheath" By R. Meenakshi.
66. *Financial Express,* Bombay, December 10, 1993.
"Steps to improve organisational effectiveness" By Sunil K. Dhawan.
67. *The Economic Times,* December 17, 1993.
"Making the most of mindscapes".
68. *The Times of India,* Bombay, October 30, 1993.
"Ascent"
Reaching out effectively. Effective communication requires planning and skill in execution argues Sushik Bahl.
69. *The Economic Times,* October 1, 1993.
"Et Esquire"
Adding that third dimension. All new recruits have to go through a programme called "Feel at Home" which includes a meeting with the MD.
70. *The Economic Times,* Bombay, October, 2, 1993.
"Sci-Tech"
Vestige of Indian Renaissance. The spirit for which Saha stood is withering away and the dark shadow of counter-renaissance looms large.
71. *The Times of India,* Bombay, October 16, 1993.
"Career objectives and academic courses.
Young people should clearly examine whether they would like to have a national career or an International one, opines by P.N. Singh.
72. *The Economic Times,* Bombay January 3, 1994.
"Managing by wire"
An intelligent company integrates "what's going on out there" with "how we do things around here, "opines Stephen H. Haeckel and

Richard L. Nolan.

73. *The Times of India,* Bombay, December 27, 1993.
"Ascent"
Corporate transparency.
74. *The Economic Times,* December 31, 1993.
"Announcing the horizontal alternative".
Downsizing does not change the fundamental way work gets done. To do that takes a different organisational model.
75. *The Times of India,* Bombay, December 22, 1993.
"Gearing up for the competition"
In order to safeguard ourselves, we tend to blame the environment for our mediocre performance, opines Ranbir Sarkar.
76. Gujarat Health Study.
"Lung disease hits textile workers".
77. *The Times of India,* Bombay, December 25, 1993.
"Ascent"
Coping with changing standards.
78. *Jagriti,* December 1, 1991. By Kamal Taori.
"Organisers Training for Employment through Rural Industries Cluster".
79. *India Today,* October 15, 1991.
"How the World sees India" By Raj Chengappa.
80. *Economic and Political Weekly,* October 2, 1993.
"Amartya Sen's Unequal World" by G.A. Cohen.
In Section I of this article the author describes the leading idea-capability--which Amartya sen has brought to the discourse on problems of equality and its absence in his book *Inequality Reexamined.* He then takes up one of the book's sub-themes, the connection or lack of it between freedom and control. In the final section he defends Sen against some scepticism about the practical relevance of his work expressed in this journal a few months ago.
81. *The Asian Age,* February 22, 1995.
"India can be the choicest flavour of the decade" Thinking Aloud
82. Stockholm Environment Institute, December 4, 1994.
"Guidance for growing group of councils".
83. *The Economic Times,* Bombay, June 6, 1995.
"La Creme de la Creme"
The most basic task of corporate leaders is to unleash the human spirit, which makes creativity, initiative and entrepreneurship possible, say Christopher Bartlett and Samantra Ghoshal. Beyond systems to people.
84. *The Times of India,* Bombay, June 22, 1995.

"Ascent" The implementation of an objective and purposeful performance appraisal procedure fulfils the purpose of optimising the crucial human element output, avers Raju Vir.

85. *The Independent,* Bombay, March 27, 1992.
"Rural employment is a distance goal."
86. *The Times of India,* Bombay, January 1, 1994.
"Radicalised and Globalised". Hypotheses on Indian Society, By Arvind Das.
87. *The Hindu,* January 16, 1991.
"Scientific temper down the ages".
88. *Economic and Political Weekly,* November 11, 1989.
"From the Ivory Tower"
Science, Technology and Self-Reliance, by Arun Ghosh. The life story of Pandurang Khankhoje, whose researches yielded the revolution in wheat production in Mexico where he was director of agriculture but who when he returned to India after independence never got the slightest nod general approach to the application of science and technology for our development.
89. *Business India,* August 19-29, 1993.
"Overtaking the competition".
Total Quality Management, Just-in-Time production and computerised data management will not be enough for Indian firms to attain world class productivity and quality.
90. *Business India,* August, 16-29, 1993.
"Forced priorities" Foreign banks have scrambled to fulfil their priority sector lending targets to avoid attracting adverse attention. The priority sector is perceived as a shady credit risk.
91. *Business India,* August 16-29, 1993.
"Labour" Focus on flexibility. Managements are now demanding total flexibility, multiskilling and more participative methods of management.
92. *Business India,* August 16-29, 1993.
"Ideas in Economic Development: The Model and the Metapher".
93. *Newsweek,* August 30, 1993.
"Endangered Family" For many African-Americans, marriage and childbearing do not go together. After decades of denial and blame, a new candour is emerging as blacks struggle to save their families. A black child has only one chance in five of growing up with two parents.
94. *Newsweek,* August 30, 1993.
"In Paris, Small Artisans Survive".
95. *Newsweek,* August 30, 1993.

"Looking Out for Their Own Skin"
Haiti: Don't cry for the 'repugnant' rich.

96. *Mahatma Gandhi and Peaceful World Order,* by Dr. Kamal Taori,
97. *Beekeeping in India-Role of KVIC,* By Dr. Kamal Taori.
98. *Five Powers for Today,* By Dr. Kamal Taori.
99. *Unemployment and Poverty Issues Relating to Rural Industry Expansion,* by Dr. Kamal Taori.
100. *Social Objective of Economic, Legislation, Generation of Employment and Income, Alleviation of Poverty and Enhancement of Quality of Life,* by Dr. Kamal Taori.
101. *Sustainable Development-Real Issues,* by Dr. Kamal Taori.
102. *Religion Work,* by Dr. Kamal Taori.
103. *Rural Industries Galvanising Services (RIGS),* by Dr. Kamal Taori.
104. Some Extracts from J.C. Kumarappa's Book on Economy of Permance, by Dr. Kamal Taori.
105. *Application of Science and Technology for Integrated Agricultural and Rural Development,* by V.R. Gaikwad.
106. *When 'Minor' Becomes "Major" Some problems of Ground Water Management,* by B.B. Vohra.
107. *"Working for Reform (WFR),* by Dr. Kamal Taori.
108. *Debt State situation in Marketing* by Dr. Kamal Taori.
109. Wardha District Plan on Gandhian Lines" by Govt. Technical High School Centre, Wardha for Planning Commission, Government of India, April 1982.
110. Unemployment and poverty issues relating to rural industry expansion, by Dr. Kamal Taori.
111. "Food Processing Industry in the Small and Unorganised Sector: Public Policy Analysis for Effectiveness" by Dr. Kamal Taori.
112. "Two sides of the same paper"-"Eco-friendly stationary is the buzzword in corporate circles these days by Rucha Chitrodia published in the *Economic Times* dated 9-15 June, 1995.
113. "RBI panel moots radical changes in IRDP" published in *The Economic Times,* Bombay dated 23 November 1994.
114. *Need to Free Village Industries,* by Dr. Kamal Taori.
115. *Agri Business* by Dr. Kamal Taori.
116. Self supporting integrated Rural Development Through Rural Industrialisation, by Dr. Kamal Taori.
117. *Institutions of Wardha,* by Dr. Kamal Taori.
118. "Rural Development and Privatisation" by Dr. Kamal Taori.
119. *Asian Seminar on Rural Development--The Indian Experience* Edited by M.L. Dantwala, Ranjit Gupta, Keith C.D'Souza published by Oxford & IBH Publishing Co. Pvt. Ltd., Delhi.

120. "Gram Yojana" by Dr. Kamal Taori, The author says:-
"Anna saheb Hazare has taken about 300 villages in Maharashtra for replication of Relegan Sidhi. Though this model is highly successful and acclaimed a time has come to add Rural Industries-Technology-Entrepreneurship-Marketing/Bankability components in this project. These are the most difficult areas and require very coordinated approach.
121. A paper titled "Workshop on Rural Industrialisation and Employment Generation for Members of Parliament (February 3-6, 1992).
122. "Areas for Diversification for Strategic Competitive Advantage" by Dr. Kamal Taori.
"The Inclined of Quality" by Frank S. Leonard and W. Earl Sasser published in *Harvard Business Review* of September-October 1982 issue. The writer says:-
"No Longer just an afterthought, the management of product quality determines market success.
123. Strategy is a pattern of Purposes/Goals/Objectives which Determines what an Organisation is and what it ought to be"
124. "Men and Institutions" by Ananda reprinted by *Bhavan Journal* Vol. 36; No. 15 to 20; March 15, 1990 to May 31, 1990. The writer says:-
"In examining the interaction of men and institutions in society, "Ananda" deals with:-
1. The movement towards universal society in the great era of communication;
2. The importance of voluntary organisations and the ills to which they are exposed;
3. The irrelevance of the Darwinian conception of evolution as one of thc 'survival of the fittest'.
4. The winds of change in Russia and the communist countries of Eastern Europe;
5. The correctives that capitalist societies have found necessary;
6. The mushrooming of new institutions and the cracking up of old institutions in India; and
7. The role of leaders of men and leaders of institutions."
125. "Changes in the system-Around us" by Dr. Kamal Taori (IAS Training Course, 6-10 January 1992, Tata Institute of Social Sciences, Bombay).
126. "Is India a tiger which has caged itself with its economic and other policies?" by Dr. Kamal Taori.
127. "Hypothesis--people are greedy and hence to be more and more

laws to curb their greed" by Dr. Kamal Taori.

128. "Privatisation: what went wrong" published in *Asian Business* of August 1990 issue.
129. "Local Initiatives for sustainable Development" a summary of conference organised by International North South conference in Berlin on 14-17 October, 1992.
130. *Government and Business* by A Dasgupta and NK Sengupta published by Vikas Publishing House.
131. Empowering Women Workers by Nandini Azad published by Working Women's Forum, Madras.
132. *Pride and Style in Selling, Ideas, Services and Products* by Walter Vierira published India Book House Pvt. Ltd. Bombay.
133. *The Silva Mind Control Methods* by Jose Silva and Philip Miele.
134. *India's Maladies and Remedies* by Dr. M.S. Srinivasan Published by First Public Protection Trust, Madras.
135. *Social Order in India* by S.K. Ghosh published by Ashish Publishing House, New Delhi.
136. *The Indian Mafia* by S.K. Ghosh Published by Ashish Publishing House, New Delhi.
137. *How to Look Younger* by Eric Taylor published by Sudha Publications Pvt. Ltd.
138. *AIMA Diploma in Management-study Material-Financial Management* published by All India Management Association, New Delhi.
139. *AIMA Diploma in Management-study Material-Financial Management-I,* Booklet-III published by All India Management Association, New Delhi.
140. *Cartman*-Vol. 1 of March 1994 (Special Issue). A Journal of the Action Research and Technology for Man, Animal & Nature.
141. *AIMA Diploma in Management-study Material-Business Environment* published by All India Management Association, New Delhi.
142. Report of the Committee for Six Year Plan and Organisational Structure for Khadi and Village Industries by KVIC, Bombay.
143. *"Neurophysiology of Enlightenment"* by Dr. Ropbert Keith Wallace-paper presented on 26th International Congress of Physiological Sciences at New Delhi in October 1974.
144. *Kurukshetra* of March 1990. A Journal of Department of Rural Development, Government of India, Delhi.
145. "Cottage Industries, Handicrafts and Non-Farm Employment" a progress report by International Labour Office, Geneva, March 1984.

146. "Khadi & Gramodyog of April 1994" published by Khadi and Village Industries Commission, Bombay.
147. *Modern Science and Vedic Science,* issue of April 1987 published by Maharishi International University, Fairfield.
148. *Modern Science and Vedic Science,* issue of December 1987 published by Maharishi International University, Fairfield.
149. *Modern Science and Vedic Science,* issue of January 1987 published by Maharishi International University, Fairfield.
150. *The World Conspiracy* by Nicola M. Nicolov Published by Nicola M. Nicolov, PO Box 784, Portland 97207.
151. *Nature's Ecofriendly Economical Miracle* by Dr. Sanwarmal Sedmal.
152. "Trusteeship, An Alternative Ideology" by M.L. Dantwala published by Indian Association of Social Science Institutions, New Delhi.
153. *"Poverty in Rural Asia"* edited by Azizur Rahman Khan and Eddy Lee. Published by Asian Regional Team for Employment Promotion for International Labour Organisation.
154. *Human Resource Planning.* The Asian Experience edited by Rashid Amjad. Published by Asian Regional Team for Employment Promotion for International Labour Organisation.
155. *Public Policy and Policy Analysis in India* edited by RS Ganapathy, SR Ganesh, Rushikesh M. Maru, Samuel Paul and Ram Mohan Rao Published by Sage Publication, New Delhi.
156. *The Indian Heritage,* by V. Raghavan Published by The Indian Institute of World Culture.
157. *The Governing of Men,* by Austin Ranney published by Holts Rinehart and Winston, Inc. New York.
158. *Limited Options, Women Workers in Rural India,* Edited by A.V. Josi Published ILO.
159. *India's Contribution to World Thought and Culture,* Editors Lokesh Chandra, Swarajya Prakash Gupta, Devendra Swarup, Sitaram Goel Published by Vivekanand Rock Memorial Committee, Madras.
160. *The Sweet Gold* by N. Hanumaiah and KD Kamble of Directorate of Palm Gur Industries published by Khadi & Village Industries Commission, Bombay.
161. Hunger 1994 Transforming the Politics of Hunger" Fourth Annual Report on the state of World Hunger.
162. A Project report on "Rural Women and Khadi Spinning". A study based on the socio-economic status and problems of women spinners in Eastern Uttar Pradesh prepared by M. Showeb, Gandhian Institute of Studies, Ranghat, Varanasi.
163. Report of the Task Force on Handicrafts for the VIII Five Year

Plan by Office of the Development Commissioner (Handicrafts), Ministry of Textiles, Government of India, New Delhi.

164. *The India Magazine,* Issue of December 1986.
165. "Projects under All India Coordinated Programme Rural Artisanal Leather Industries"-Phase-II, supported by Department of Science and Technology, New Delhi organised by Centre for Tech. & Development, New Delhi in April 1991.
166. *Kurukshetra* issue of August-September 1986. A journal of Ministry of Rural Development, Government of India, New Delhi.
167. *Fibre Industry,* published by Khadi & Village Industries Commission, Bobay.
168. *Science and Technology in KVI Sector* published by Directorate of Publicity, Khadi & Village Industries Commission, Bombay.
169. *Profiles of Improved Technologies for Cottage Industries, I-Pottery* published by Asian Regional Team for Employment Promotion.
170. *Profiles of Improved Technologies for Cottage Industries, II-Cane and Bamboo* published by Asian Regional Team for Employment promotion.
171. *Upgrading of Technology in Rural Industries in India*--A review of experience by Devendra B Gupta Published by Asian Regional Team for Employment Promotion.
172. *Poverty, Unemployment and Rural Development,* edited by Baidyanath Misra, Published by Ashish Publishing House, New Delhi.
173. Partnership in Practice by Department of Environment, U.K.
174. "World Development Report 1991. The Challenges of the Development" published by World Bank, Oxford University Press.
175. Environment & Development in Africa" selected case studies by Jonathan M. Blackwell, Roger N. Goodwille and Richard Webb published by EDI Development Policy Case Series No. 6
176. Manual for IRDP and Allied Programmes of TRYSEM and DWCRA published by Ministry of Rural Development, Government of India, New Delhi.
177. *Khadi & Village Industries: Policy, Issues and Perspectives* published by Planning Commission, Government of India, New Delhi in February 1989.
178. A *Worker's Cooperative Organisation,* published by International Labour Organisation.
179. Report of the Committee on Control and Subsidies, May 1979 by Director, Economic Research & Bank Finance.
180. *Self-Employment Programmes: Retrospect and Prospect* by A.V.K. Sarma, Published by SEDME, Vol. XVII.

and Implementation Strategies" January 10th to 15th, 1990 held at Pune, India which was joint initiative of the Federal Republic of Germany, BMZ, Bonn, GTZ, Eschborn, BORDA, Bremen and Republic of India, Ministry of Energy, DNES, New Delhi, UNDARP, Pune.

219. *Manpower Planning in ASIAN Countries,* Pub: Regional Institute of Higher Education and Development, Singapore.
220. Measures for Rural Employment Generation (Report of APO Symposium, 1989) Pub: Asian Productivity Organisation, Tokyo.
221. *Labour Markets and Human Resource Planning in Asia:* edited by M. Muqtada and A. Hildeman Pub: UNDP and ARTEP
222. *Rural Industrialisation and Employment in Asia* edited by Rizwanul Islam, Pub: ILO-ARTEP.
223. *Social Exclusion: Rhetoric Reality Responses* edited by Gerry Rodgers, Charles Gore and Jose B. Fiqueiredo Pub: ILO, Geneva.
224. Rural Industrialisation, A Report of International Workshop Hyderabad (India) 21-25 June 1993 Pub: Afro-Asian Rural Reconstruction Organisation, New Delhi.
225. The Financing of Exports from Developing Countries Pub: International Trade Centre, UNCTAD-GATT.
226. Proceedings of the First Meeting of the Asian Employment Planners (Bangkok, Thailand, 26-29 November 1985) Pub: ILO/ARTEP.
227. Upgrading of Technology in Rural Industries in India: A Review of Experience by Devendra B. Gupta Pub: ILO/ARTEP
228. *Guide to the Evaluation of Trade Promotion Programmes,* Published by International Trade Centre, UNCTAD-GATT.
229. *Cost Recovery in Public Health Services in Sub-Saharan Africa* by Brian Nolan & Vincent Turbat, Pub: World Bank.
230. *Agricultural Research in an Era of Adjustment Policies, Institutions, and Progress* edited by Steven R. Tabor, Pub: The World Bank.
231. Human Development Report 1993 Pub: UNDP
232. Human Development Report 1991 Pub: UNDP
233. *Managing Inflation in Socialist Economies in Transition,* edited by Simon Commander Pub: World Bank.
234. *Peace Initiatives,* Vol. 1 No. 1 July-August 1995, Published by the International Centre for Peace Initiatives
235. *Development Seeds of Change, Village through global order,* 1987:1 Pub: The society for International Development.
236. *Economic Growth and Private Initiative: The Republic of Korea's Experience,* Pub: UNDP in September 1989.
237. *"Profiles of improved Technologies for Cottage Industries" I--*

Pottery (from Bangladesh), Pub: ILO/ARTEP.

238. *Profile of Improved Technologies for Cottage Industries. II--Cane and Bamboo (from Bangladesh),* Pub: ILO/ARTEP
239. *Global Finance 1996,* Pub: Global Finance, New York
240. *"Industrial Distribution"* Issue September 1995 Pub: Cahners Publication.
241. A study of women's participation in Programme implemented by Employers' Organisation in South Asia: Promotional Action to facilitate Greater involvement of women in mainstream economic activities and development by Dr. Coomi Singh. Pub: ILO.
242. "Women in Management: An Annotated Bibliography with emphasis on Commonwealth sources", Pub: Commonwealth Secretariat.
243. *Education for All Role of Panchayat,* Pub: State Institute of Panchayats, West Bengal.
244. Cooperative Identify and Revised Principles of Cooperation by Dr. R.C. Dwivedi (Paper presented by Dr. Dwivedi at NCUI-Vamnicom policy makers' Seminar on Cooperation, 24-25/8/95 at Vaikunth Mehta National Institute of Cooperative Management, Pune.
245. Report of study Group 9, Seminar-Workshop for the Indian Administrative Service, International Approaches to Rural Development and Poverty Alleviation 8 April-24 May 1991.
246. Nutrition and Productivity in India (A preliminary study) by A.P. Paul. Pub: ILO.
247. *Holistic Health--An Approach.* Pub: ASSEFA (Association for Sarva Seva Earms).
248. *Community Centered Approach to Rural Development Association for Sarva Seva Farms* by Chris Wilde, Pub: Foster Plan International, New Delhi.
249. Hunger 1994 Transforming the Politics of Hunger (Fourth Annual Report on the State of World Hunger, Pub: Bread for the World Institute.
250. *Environment and Development in Africa* by Jonathan M. Blackwell, Roger N. Goodwillie, Richard Webb, Pub: World Bank.
251. *Employment and Mobility:* A Study among workers of Low Income Household in Bombay city by Sarthi Acharya and A.V. Jose. Pub: ARTEP/ILO
252. *Partnerships in Practice,* Pub: Department of the Environment, Great Britain.
253. A report on "Workshop on Participatory Development & Organisation of Communities" prepared by R.K. Rath, Indira Roy, Raji Nair and Richard H. Young.

254. *A Handicraft Cooperative Management,* Pub: ILO, Geneva
255. ASSEFA Silver Jubilee 1969-94.
256. Accelerating Socio-Economic Rural Development prepared by Bhartiya Vidya Bhavan's S.P. Jain Institute of Management and Research, Bombay.
257. A project report on Village Pottery proposed at Madanapalli, Rishi Valley, Chittoor, Distt. (AP) or Shilpa Raman, Craft Village, Madapur (Near Hyderabad) prepared by Shri R. Prabhakar Rao, State Director, KVIC, Hyderabad.
258. *The Order Path* by Hernando de soto, Pub: Harper & Row
259. Adjusting to Reality Beyond "State versus Market" in *Economic Development* by Robert Klitgaard, Pub: International Center for Economic Growth Publication.
260. *Dynamism in the Informal Sector in a Fast Growing Economic:* The Case of Bangkok" by Henny B. Romijn Published by Asian Regional Team for Employment Promotion and International Labour Organisation.
261. "Upgrading of Technology in Rural Industries in India: A Review of Experience" by Devendra B. Gupta published by Asian Regional Team for Employment Promotion and International Labour Organisation.
262. "Growth of Rural Industries in Post-Reforms China: Patterns, Determinants and Consequences" by Rizwanul Islam published by Asian Regional Team for Employment Promotion and International Labour Organisation.
263. Micro Interventions for Poverty Alleviation: Experiences of Some Asian Countries" by Salehuddin Ahmed published by Asian Regional Team for Employment Promotion and International Labour Organisation and United Nations Development Programme.
264. "Report on Industrial Dispersal, National Committee on the Development of Backward Areas" published by Planning Commission, Government of India in October, 1980.
265. *Taiwan:* A Case Study in Rapid Economic Growth" by K.T. Li Published by Forum of Free Enterprise, Bombay.
266. *Management Challenges for the 90s* by Rahul Bajaj published by Forum of Free Enterprise, Bombay.
267. *Public Action to Remedy Hunger* by Amartya Sen published by Forum of Free Enterprise, Bombay.
268. *How to Respond to Petroleum Crisis in India* by Ajit D. Kamlani, S.S. Rekhi and Ranjan Sanghi published by Forum of Free Enterprises, Bombay.
269. *Economic Development and Deregulation-The Role of Industry*

by M.S. Patwardhan published by Forum of Free Enterprise, Bombay.

270. *Is There a Middle Way?* by Dr. Fredie A. Mehta published by Forum of Free Enterprises, Bombay.
271. *New Imperatives of Human Security* by Mahbub Ul Haq published by Rajiv Gandhi Institute for Contemporary Studies.
272. "Urban Policy and Economic Development--An Agenda for the 1990s", A World Bank policy paper published by World Bank.
273. *The Lessons of History* Arnold Toynbee.
274. *Report of the Task Force on Handicrafts for the VIII Five Year Plan,* published by Office of the Development Commissioner (Handicrafts). Ministry of Textiles, Government of India, New Delhi.
275. *Economic and Political Weekly* Vol. XXIX No. 5 of 29.01.94 published by Sameeksha Trust Publication.
276. A paper entitled "Structural Adjustment Programmes: Impact on Small and Medium Scale Enterprise" prepared by Jean-Claude Kessous. UNIDO Consultant for Round Table Discussion on the Restructuring of Small-and Medium-Scale Enterprises with Special Focus on African/Asian Co-operation held from 29 September to 2 October 1992 at New Delhi.
277. Adjustment, Employment and Equity in India" by S. Guhan and K. Nagraj, Professors at Madras Institute of Development Studies published by International Labour Organisation.
278. *The Frontiers of Management* by P.F. Drucker published by Truman Talley Books, New York.
279. APCTT Annual Report-1994 published by Asian and Pacific Centre for Transfer of Technology.
280. *District Planning : Lessons from India,* published by Food and Agriculture Organisation of the United Nations.
281. *Time International,* No. 36 issue dated September 7, 1992.
282. *Jobs for Millions Some Issues* by Dr. Kamal Nayan Kabra published by Directorate of Advertising and Visual Publicity, Ministry of Information and Broadcasting, Government of India.
283. *Kurukshetra* (A Journal of Department of Rural Development) Vol. XXXVIII No. 6 of March 1990.
284. *Kurukshetra* (A Journal of Department of Rural Development) Vol. XXXVIII No. 9 of June 1990.
285. Paper of "International Seminar on Linkage of Self Help Groups with Rural Financial Institutions" held on 19-22 December 1995.
286. *Most Farmers in India are Women,* published by FAO.
287. Paper prepared by Maithreyi Krishnaraj for the ILO Regional

Workshop "Self-Employment Schemes for Rural Women" in New Delhi from 19th to 21st September 1990.

288. *Yojana,* Volume 28, Number 14 & 15 dated 15 August 1984 published by Director, Publication Division, New Delhi.
289. *Development Co-operation--India 1990* published by United Nations Development Programme in December 1991.
290. Rural Industrialisation--Man for Future, Vikas Publication.
291. Green & Gramin--A Story of Handmade Paper, Regency Publication.
292. Marketing of Unorganised Sector, Regency Publication.
293. Entreprenuership in the decentralised sector, Regency Publication.

PROFILE OF UNITED NATIONS EDUCATIONAL, SCIENTIFIC AND CULTURAL ORGANIZATION

Name of Country: India
Name of Aid Agency: Address in India

A. Global Assistance

(i) Aims and Scope

The United Nations Educational, Scientific and Cultural Organization (UNESCO) was found on 4 November, 1946 and at present its membership stood at 183. Its specific mandate is that of building a world of peace and prosperity for all, through the educational, scientific and cultural relations of the peoples of the world and founded upon the intellectual and moral solidarity of mankind.

The task is arduous and involves a wide variety of actions to promote and to assist countries in fostering literacy, democratizing education, training teachers, promoting human rights and peace, safeguarding cultural identity, fostering intercultural dialogue and cross-cultural understanding, preserving the world's natural and cultural treasures, conserving the collective memory of mankind, fostering free flow of ideas strengthening communications capabilities, setting up ocean observation systems, alerting populations about tidal waves and earthquakes, encouraging sustainable development and sound environmental practices, setting international standards, providing access to information, sharing knowledge and advising decision-makers.

(ii) Programme Size

UNESCO's resource base is its regular budget-based on contributions from its Member-States, voted once in two years. The budget is meagre-about $227 million a year, compared to the immensity of the tasks. Therefore, UNESCO's refines and adapts its "course of action" every two years and sets priorities that match resources.

B. Assistance to India

(i) Substantive Focus

UNESCO's involvement in India is concentrated in five main areas- 1, Education, 2. Science and Technology, 3. Culture, 4. Communication, information and informatics and 5. Social Sciences. In Education, there is a commitment to eradicate adult illiteracy and to provide basic education for all, especially by expanding education access to girls and women in rural areas and other special underprivileged group. In science, priority to environmental concerns and to applying environmental sciences to the management of natural resources; also important are the upgrading of university education and the promotion of research and training in basic engineering science.

Culture has emphasis on the cultural dimensions of development and on the protection of the cultural and natural heritage.

In communication, emphasis is on strengthening the free flow of ideas by word and image, and improving communication and information capabilities.

In social science, stress is laid on institutional development, improved training and research through networking and mobilizing youth talents in the service of social development.

(ii) Geographical Focus

UNESCO activities are not confined to any particular geographical area rather it is spread all over India. Priorities are given to the least development states.

(iii) Trends in Volume

More funds are being allocated to the Education Sector namely, District Primary Education Programme (DPEP) and innovative Educational Alternatives to Formal Education, Distance Education and Open Schooling. The E-9 Summit saw distance education as an alternative modality in the context of Education for All.

In the Science Programme, Local productivity of Laboratory Teaching Equipment, University-Industry Cooperation in Science and Technology, multi-media course material for University Physics and Science for villages are worth mentioning.

PROFILE OF UNITED NATIONS CHILDREN'S FUND

Name of Country: India
Name of Aid Agency: Address in India

A. Global Assistance

Aims and Scope

UNICEF supports programme initiatives by government and NGOs aimed at improving the physical quality of life of communities, especially children and women. UNICEF cooperation, is therefore, directed to accomplish the following:

- -- Capacity building for improved planning and implementation of programmes benefiting women and children.
- -- Community empowerment aimed at increased awareness of child rights, enlisting participation in maintenance/management of systems/services, reducing gap between service providers and receivers and promoting family/community based initiatives for accelerated development of women and children.
- -- Deliberate programming for convergence of services through integrated delivery systems and inter-departmental coordination.
- -- Area-specific programming for provision of basic services to communities and urban slums.
- -- Strengthening existing delivery systems including Education, Health, Water and environmental sanitation programmes through reorientation of approach, appropriate training of functionaries and selective support to infrastructural facilities.
- -- Special interventions focussed on especially disadvantaged groups such as child labour and children in especially difficult circumstances as well as prevention of childhood disability.
- -- Strengthening information, education and communication components of programme implementation to enhance participation of communities, panchayats and local bodies, media, religious as well as political institutions in aspects of programme implementation.

B. Assistance to India:

Substantive Focus:

UNICEF assistance to India focusses on the following aspects:

-- Sustaining universal immunization coverage of infants against diphtheria, pertussis (whooping cough), tetanus, polio, childhood tuberculosis and measles.

-- Elimination of neonatal tetanus.

-- Reduction of measles mortality and morbidity.

-- Universal iodization of salt.

-- Elimination of poliomyelitis as a step towards polio eradication.

-- Control of diarrhoeal diseases by enhancing the usage of Oral Rehydration Therapy to 80 per cent and ensuring access and use of ORS.

-- Reduction of deaths due to pneumonia by its early recognition and treatment under the ARI control component of CSSM Programme.

-- Improved access to antenatal care of pregnant women and prevention of maternal mortality by decreasing delays in care to women with complicated pregnancies as well as by improving access to First Referral Units for early emergency care.

-- Elimination of Vit. A deficiency through support for prohylactic Vitamin A to young children and increasing consumption of Vitamin A rich foods.

-- Control of Protein Energy Malnutrition and reduction in severe and moderate malnutrition by 20 per cent in children below 5 years through an increased focus on preventing malnutrition in younger children.

-- Reduction in low birth weight babies.

-- Reduction in iron deficiency anaemia in girls and women, especially pregnant women.

-- Discourage use of breast-milk substitutes and enable a system for establishing Baby Friendly Hospitals in all institutions delivering more than 1000 babies in a year.

-- Promoting growth monitoring in ICDS and Health services.

-- Promotion of early childhood education activities.

-- Universal primary education aimed at 100 per cent enrolment, and reduction of drop-outs as well as gender gap in primary school education.

-- Eradication of guineaworm disease.

-- Provision of safe drinking water to all communities and improved access to safe means of sanitary disposal.

-- Reduction of gender-based disparities in access to, availability and utilization of basic services.

-- Community mobilization in urban slums and rural areas, especially using panchayat system and through orientation of the newly elected panchayat and Nagarpalika members to play an increasing role in social development.

Programme Size

UNICEF's funds come from voluntary contributions from governments, NGOs private sectors and individuals as well as the sale proceeds of its Greeting Cards operations. Allocations to different countries is determined by factors such as GNP per capita, infant mortality, size of population of children under 5 years of age, literacy levels, etc. Total annual programme expenditure by UNICEF globally is between $800m and $900m.

Geographical Focus

Most components of the UNICEF Country Programme are implemented on all-India basis. Phasing of implementation, however, is such that in respect of certain programmes all states/districts may not be covered during the programme cycle 1991-1995. Moreover, focus of certain interventions are state-specific, e.g. Bihar Education Project, being confined to that state, guineaworm eradication to Rajasthan and Madhya Pradesh, child labour to Tamil Nadu and Uttar Pradesh, household food security project to Orissa etc.

Trends in Aid Volume

The committed assistance for the country programme as a whole is of the order of $90m annually. However, assistance delivered from 1991 to 1994 is $235m. This is due to low absorption capacity of projects during the first-two years and inadequate donor funding for components to be implemented with supplementary resources.

C. Directors of Assistance

UNICEF assistance to the country programme is not likely to undergo major revision in terms of scope and content during 1996 and 1997 which will be used as bridging years between GOI's Eighth and Ninth Five Year Plans. Need for any reorientation approach will be considered as part of the full scale country programme for the period 1998 to 2002 synchronizing with government's Ninth Five Year Plan. This will be based on the outcome of analysis of the situation of women and children in India and in specific geographical areas, status of access/ availability of demand for services and feasibility states on viable alternatives. Convergence of social sector programmes in the context of emerging decentralization as a result of the 73rd and 74th constitutional amendments, Convention on Rights of the Child and the World Declaration on the survival, protection and Development of children with the National Plans of Action and State Programmes of Action on Children will continue to be guiding documents for the UNICEF support to programmes in India.

D. Future Directions

UNICEF's next programme of Cooperation for 1998 to 2002 will tie up with the Government of India's Ninth Development Plan to be launched in April 1997. The process for preparing the Situation Analysis of Women and Children in India is being set in motion. The Situation Analysis will form the basis for evolving strategies governing the future programme that will be developed jointly with various ministries and departments of the Government of India. As bridge to the new Country Programme, a two-year programme of cooperation for the years 1996-1997 is now being prepared jointly with the Government of India. UNICEF programmes will continue to focus on primary education, health of women and children, nutrition and environment with a special focus on safe water supply and safe means of excreta disposal. The Convention on the Rights of the Child, World Declaration and Plan of Action will continue to guide the UNICEF programmes in India. The recent decentralization that has been set in motion through the 73rd and 74th constitutional amendments in India will further bring about certain modifications in the development assistance as already envisioned jointly by our government counterparts.

INDEX